AUDUBON NATURE YEARBOOK 1991

1991
AUDUBON NATURE

MOSS-DRAPED BIGLEAF MAPLE IN OREGON'S COASTAL RANGE, BY GARY BRAASCH

YEARBOOK

LES LINE, EDITOR

Meredith® Press, New York

COVER PHOTO: COUGAR BY JEFF FOOTT/BRUCE COLEMAN INC.

For Meredith® Press:

Director: Elizabeth P. Rice
Editorial Project Manager: Barbara Machtiger
Editorial Assistant: Valerie Martone
Production Manager: Bill Rose

Produced by Soderstrom Publishing Group Inc.
Book design by Nai Chang
Typography by Rochester Monotype Co.

Meredith® Press and the producer extend admiration and thanks to
the entire *AUDUBON* staff—past and present—for their roles in the
creation of the distinguished articles upon which these yearbooks are
based. For additional contributions this year, special thanks go to these
AUDUBON staff members:

Editor: Les Line
Executive Assistant: Karen Witte
Production Editor: Mary McCarthy
Picture Associate: Scott Hanrahan

Distributed by Meredith Corporation, Des Moines, Iowa

ISSN 0891–981X
ISBN 0–696–11052–0

Printed in the United States of America

10 9 8 7 6 5 4 3 2 1

CONTENTS

THE CONSERVATIONISTS IV

OF PLANTS V AND MAN

SPECIAL VI PLACES

P R E F A C E

There is a powerful and provocative article among the selections I have made for this fifth edition of the *Audubon Nature Yearbook*—our annual compilation of the best writing, photography, and art from past issues of *Audubon* magazine. It is "Game Laws Weren't Writ for Fat Cats," which originally appeared in Ted Williams' "Incite" column. And no, I didn't mispell *insight,* although there is a lot of that, too, in Williams' regular contributions to our pages. Check for synonyms in your thesaurus and you'll understand: words like *enliven, vivify, fuel, ignite, propel, exhort, goad, persuade, prod.* That's a good description of what Ted does on matters of concern—and controversy—to all conservationists, whether nature watchers or hunters (the terms, of course, are not mutually exclusive). That's why he inspires—incites—more letters to this editor than any other writer.

You could say that Ted Williams, like another gentleman of the same name, is a heavy hitter. The topics he tackles for *Audubon* are predestined to arouse passion on all sides. Fact is, ballplayer Edward French Williams and our Theodore Samuel Williams have a lot in common. Both have strong ties to Massachusetts. Both are authors. Both are ardent fishermen. Both are known to the world at large as Ted. And there the confusion begins. The folks at Orvis once mailed journalist Ted a shockingly expensive flyrod and reel to test on New Brunswick's legendary salmon river, the Miramichi. He tried to return it, telling Orvis he wasn't the "real" Ted Williams, but they insisted he keep it. Slugger Ted once was praised by his Bahamas bonefishing guide for his angling stories in *Gray's Sporting Journal.* "I'm not the writer," he explained. "I'm the baseball player." The guide was perplexed. "Oh, I don't follow baseball."

Ted Williams, a.k.a. the Splendid Splinter, is a member of the Baseball Hall of Fame. And a couple of years back, I wrote that, "If there should be a similar shrine for conservation writers, Ted Williams, a.k.a. various epithets hurled by those who have caught one of his hard liners in *Audubon,* undoubtedly will be bronzed therein." It seems I was prescient: Ted recently received the highest honor of the Outdoor Writers Association of America, the Jade of Chiefs Award for Distinguished Service to Conservation. Moreover, his "Fat Cats" article reprinted in this yearbook won the Izaak Walton League of America prize for writing on the subject of outdoor ethics.

The matter at hand here is hunting ethics. Or more specifically, the apparent lack thereof of a shameless minority of hunters who believe that being rich, important, or politically connected entitles them to cheat. The matter is also the vital importance of game laws and efforts to handcuff the beleaguered agents of the U.S. Fish and Wildlife Service. Or rather, as an organization called the International Shooting and Hunting Alliance (ISHA) sees it, to stop them from discriminating against VIP hunters through "overzealous enforcement of game and gun laws."

This is not, I want to emphasize, an anti-hunting screed. To put it simply, game laws are meant for every hunter to obey, and that creed is more important today than ever. America's wildlife is under more pressure—from habitat loss, from environmental blight, from poaching—than at any time since the dreadful market-hunting days early in this century. And as one federal wildlife agent told Williams, "We really don't have a lot of time left. What we're trying to do, however successful we are, is not enough. And it never will be enough until the American people jump in and support us so it's not a fight all the time to save things for them and their children."

All the noise-making by organizations like ISHA and the Wildlife Legislative Fund about alleged misdeeds by "anti-hunting and overzealous" federal game agents, however, did lead the director of the U.S. Fish and Wildlife Service to appoint a Law Enforcement Advisory Commission. Its report, issued about the same time Ted Williams was being enshrined in OWAA's Circle of Chiefs, must have sorely frustrated the Fat Cats and their defenders.

A "complaint voiced by several groups and individuals was that Service law enforcement policies focus on 'busting big shots,'" the report said. "The commission examined this issue carefully. Although some wealthy and influential individuals were involved in some cases, it was not apparent that they were 'targeted.' Hunting is becoming more expensive. This is especially true of international trophy hunting. It is also true, however, in instances where leases must be purchased, exclusive clubs must be joined, or guides must be paid. Many individuals who can afford such hunts are generally more affluent and may therefore be more influential and politically oriented. The fact that some of these people violate wildlife laws has more to do with the hunting economics, environment, and activity in which they are involved than who they are." The Commission also noted that much of the criticism of Fish and Wildlife Service agents was anecdotal and impossible to verify.

There are other controversial articles in this gathering of the best from *Audubon*. With a debate raging over reintroduction of wolves to Yellowstone National Park, it is timely to ask whether wild wolves can be trusted around humans. The top authority on our preeminent predator, David Mech, provides the answer in "Who's Afraid of the Big Bad Wolf?" And as George Laycock points out in "Cougars in Conflict," few people in western states have neutral opinions about the great cat. "Stock growers insist that steer-killing cougars are nudging them toward bankruptcy," he writes. "Pet owners grieve for lion-killed cats and dogs. Parents fear for their children." And animal preservationists in California have rushed to defend the mountain lion against sport hunters.

The nutria, a 20-pound rodent imported to Louisiana from Argentina in the 1930s to be raised for its fine fur, is not a threat to humans (keep your fingers away from its huge teeth!), but this alien with a voracious appetite for aquatic plants has devastated Gulf Coast marshlands. In "Orange-Tooth Is Here to Stay," Donald Dale Jackson tells the bizarre tale of the nutria's arrival, its mysterious escape and population boom, and its role in a classic scam.

The story of another South American mammal, the spectacled bear of Andean mountain forests, is by contrast one of desperation. As Peter Steinhart writes in "Bear of the Clouds," "It is the most arboreal of bears and feeds on fruits and bromeliads high in the branches of trees. It even sleeps in trees." But its habitat has become fragmented by logging and farming, illegal hunting pressure is intense, and there are fears that the continent's only bear may perish.

Steinhart also contributes "Empty the Skies," a sobering account of the disappearance from California of vast flights of wintering ducks and geese. "Over most of the state, the great flocks of waterfowl are gone," he writes. "They have gone because the wetlands are gone." For of 5 million acres of California wetlands in 1850, only 400,000 acres remain. Sobering too is David Wilcove's essay, "In Memory of Martha and Her Kind." Martha was the last passenger pigeon, and her passing in the Cincinnati Zoo in 1914 closed the book on what was once the most abundant bird on Earth.

For a young Franklin Delano Roosevelt, the hobby of collecting birds' eggs and nests gave an excuse to stray from his Hyde Park home and an overprotective mother. But ornithology became a serious avocation for the future president, as the acclaimed Roosevelt biographer Geoffrey Ward tells us in "FDR: Birdwatcher." Given a shotgun on his twelfth birthday, within two years Roosevelt had collected and identified more than 300 species native to New York's Dutchess County.

History also sings in "Untrammeled by Man," T.H. Watkins' account of the making of the Wilderness Act of 1964. Like the Civil Rights Act and the Voting Rights Act, also signed by President Lyndon Johnson, "the Wilderness Act was nothing short of revolutionary," Watkins writes, "an attempt to enshrine in law a principle designed to change the way we live on Earth."

Blueberry muffins are as American as apple pie, and each summer some 50 million pounds of blueberries are harvested in eastern Maine. In "Taming the Wild Blueberry," Frank Graham Jr. takes us to the rocky "barrens" created by a glacier's retreat 12,700 years ago. There we learn that growing blueberries is no longer left to nature's whims, and that the rapid growth of the industry may bring profound changes to the landscape, the blueberry plant itself, and the life of the people who come in August to rake the fields.

We close this collection with a trek the length of the Rio Grande by author David Quammen and photographer Jim Bones. It is a journey that begins on the tundra of the Continental Divide in Colorado and ends at the sandy beaches of Padre Island on the coast of Texas, a journey along the course of "a long river with a long history and a vast, confused inventory of contemporary problems." Still, as Quammen's words and Bones' pictures attest, it can be a special place.

Les Line

Les Line, Editor, *Audubon* Magazine

MOSTLY MAMMALS

COUGARS IN CONFLICT

TEXT BY GEORGE LAYCOCK • PAINTING BY SHANNON STIRNWEIS

When the phone rings on Joe Oliver's desk, he often has a twinge of anxiety. Has someone spotted another of California's cougars in a carefully tended subdivision, lost a poodle to a marauding lion, or, worse yet, called to report the mauling of a child?

Oliver, friendly, efficient, and impeccably dressed, is chief of Animal Services for Orange County. He supervises a crew of fifty or so animal control officers who take lion reports seriously. Experience tells them there really may be a wild, free-roaming mountain lion out there in some citizen's suburban backyard. And, in an area where the big cats have made national news in recent years for attacks on children, a mountain-lion sighting can push pope, president, or the Los Angeles Dodgers off the front page.

In a recent eighteen-month period Oliver's office logged fifty-one reports of lion sightings. Oliver does not seek out mountain lions; he has them thrust upon him. "Basically, we're a rabies control group," he says. But he dispatches officers to save people, pets, and property from coyotes, bobcats, rattlesnakes, and assorted other beasts. "When it comes to mountain lions, we're experts by virtue of the fact that we picked up the phone."

Within minutes of a lion report, one of his animal control officers is rushing to the scene in a pickup truck. There, he may be greeted by heavily armed police and officers from the California Department of Fish and Game, all of them probably preceded by television crews hungrily scanning the landscape for the slightest glimpse of a cougar of any sex, size, or point of origin.

Controversy swirls around the cougar today perhaps more intensely than ever before. In California, and elsewhere, few people have neutral opinions about the great cat. Hunters complain that these tawny, eighty- to two-hundred-pound cats destroy deer herds. Stock growers insist that steer-killing cougars are nudging them toward bankruptcy. Pet owners grieve for lion-killed cats and dogs. Parents fear for their children. And, while preservationists rush in to defend the lion against all threats, real or imagined, harried public officials attempt to reason with everyone on how best to handle encounters with this six-foot-long cat.

Mountain lions are endowed with the strength to kill animals considerably heavier than themselves. A ninety-pound lioness can kill an elk weighing hundreds of pounds, then drag it several hundred yards before covering it with brush. Many years ago a powerfully built, six-foot-tall Texas rancher found that he could not budge the body of a six-hundred-pound steer he found dead. When he returned with a team of horses, fresh tracks told him plainly that a cougar had dragged the animal away.

This is astounding in view of the cat's size and structure. In California, a biology professor placed a box of bones on the table before me. The box was twelve inches wide, seventeen inches long, and four inches deep. "This is the complete skeleton, skull and all, of an adult mountain lion," the professor said. "That's all there is. The animal is all muscle and sinew."

The strength of the big cat's heavy jaws goes unmeasured, but the cougar can kill a deer with a single bite through the skull or neck or, in the case of larger animals, by breaking the victim's neck as it brings it down.

This sounds easy, but life is no snap for the predator. The slightest error could break one of the lion's bones, damage teeth, cave in ribs, or drive a stick through an eye, possibly bringing death from starvation.

Given all its equipment, the cougar is still not the fighter or hazard to human life that some people claim. One professional lion hunter, who can no longer count all the lions he took in his quarter-century as a state hunter, told me, "I've been in thick cover with lions, I've been in trees with lions, and the worst thing that happened to me was I bumped my head on a limb."

The mountain lion specializes in stealth. Two of us came, one afternoon, upon the four-inch-long footprints of an adult mountain lion that had recently walked a sandy trail along a California mountainside. With the aid of a small receiver and hand-held directional antenna, we not only identified the radio-collared female but even pinpointed her position some seventy-five feet away in a patch of chaparral. We watched for half an hour, and she did not move. We never saw a glimpse of her. Were we being watched ourselves? Almost certainly. And the knowledge that we were being studied by a predator of such strength heightened our sense of wilderness.

The prospect of suffering harm by tooth or claw brings with it a special brand of fear that may reach all the way back to the plains of Serengeti. The cougar, like the grizzly bear, fascinates us because it lets us know what it is like to be the prey.

North America's mountain lions, with few exceptions, are now limited primarily to the wilder parts of several western states, southwestern Canada, and Mexico. They once lived all across the continent and were viewed by earlier settlers as enemies to be eliminated. Massachusetts was paying bounties on cougars in 1764. Pennsylvania's years of panther killing ended with the death of the state's last cougar in 1891.

Even earlier, by the 1600s, Jesuit priests in lower California were offering the natives one bull for every mountain lion killed. The state of California began paying twenty-dollar bounties on mountain lions in 1907, and in 1919 began employing hunters with dogs to drive the cats into trees and shoot them. One of these hunters, the famed Jay Bruce, was credited with capturing nearly seven hundred cougars. Bounty hunting of California mountain lions continued until 1963. Six years later California joined other western states granting the lion protection as a big-game animal.

In 1972 California, considerably enlightened and no longer wanting to see its native big cats eliminated, enacted a moratorium on lion hunting to give the animal a chance to recover. For fifteen years the lion was protected. Then in 1987 a limited hunt was again slated, amidst much acrimonious public debate. But before the season was opened the lion hunt was blocked by a California superior court decision calling for a further study of the cougar's status by the State Fish and Game Commission.

During the years of the moratorium nobody could prove that the lions were increasing, but some indicators suggested they were. Confirmed incidents of lion depredation on livestock showed a sharp increase. From five incidents in 1971 the figure climbed to fifteen in 1975, forty-one in 1980, and 138 in 1985.

Reports of lion encounters became increasingly common. Although lion deaths on highways were practically unheard of in other western states, an average of four lions per year were killed on California roads between 1972 and 1981. A party of quail hunters complained that a mountain lion killed their dog while they were hunting. Elsewhere, a lion dashed into an occupied residence through an open door, then leaped out a window only to be treed by dogs in the backyard. On a U.S. Forest Service campground, mountain lions killed eight dogs. One couple reported meeting a lion on a Santa Cruz sidewalk at dusk.

These were still rare events, widely spaced over time and distance. The truth is that few people ever see a wild, free-running mountain lion. But stories of such encounters are welcomed and repeated by those individuals and groups stumping for liberalization of laws that protect the big cats.

Among the most determined and best organized of these groups are the stockmen. Rancher complaints about lions are nothing new. But, with accounts of stock depredations by lions increasing dramatically, ranchers insist that the state's system of permits limiting them to killing specific trouble-causing cougars was not enough to keep lion numbers down. Outside a hearing room in Sacramento, where the California Fish and Game Commission heard testimony on reviving the lion hunt, I talked with a ruddy-faced, square-jawed rancher who has lived most of his sixty-eight years on the Santa Barbara ranch where he runs two hundred head of cows. In recent years, with depredation permits, he killed five lions for taking calves. He estimates that he loses six or seven head of cattle annually to lions.

Inside the hearing room another rancher told the Fish and Game Commission that the hunting season should be reopened because the lions are killing cattle. He computed his losses to lions the previous year at more than $12,000, and with a touch of bitterness said, "I'm going out of the business. That's what I'm doing." Preservationists in the audience applauded.

Lion complaints are not limited to California ranchers, but ranchers in southwestern states apparently have more problems with lions than do stockmen to the north. Some ranchers admire and defend the cougar, but this attitude is rare in, for example, New Mexico. In Santa Fe, Wain Evans, assistant director of the state's Game and Fish Department, claims that ranchers in his state have a "lion phobia." Evans, a native of New Mexico, adds, "These cowboys can't stand for anyone to tell them they can't kill anything they want to kill on their ranches. They tend to say their lion troubles are society's fault, that we're all supposed to go out and help them tame that wilderness."

Lions do kill sheep, Evans adds, but he thinks they would kill fewer if the flocks were more carefully tended. On the other hand, Evans questions whether many cattle ranchers suffer serious losses to mountain lions. Most ranchers report no lion problems. From 1973 to 1982 New Mexico each year issued depredation permits to an average of about eleven ranchers, less than one percent of the state's total number of ranchers.

The New Mexico lion situation came to a head in 1983 when the "cowboys" tried, and failed, to return lions to varmint status by changing the law that protects the cats as game animals. Hoping to quiet the issue, the legislature passed a resolution directing the New Mexico Department of Game and Fish to report on the status of the mountain lion.

"The strength of the big cat's heavy jaws goes unmeasured, but the cougar can kill a deer with a single bite through the skull or neck or, in the case of larger animals, by breaking the victim's neck as it brings it down."

However, the report raised a furor. In recent years, it concluded, the number of cougars killed in New Mexico "appears to have reached an all-time high and, once again, cougar numbers are apparently declining." The report warned that the potential collapse of the state's cougar population could "not be entirely discounted."

"This was not what the cowboys wanted to hear," says Evans. "They claim that they know the answers better than the trained biologists do—to almost anything. They said there were much, much larger populations than our data showed. But even if there were twenty times as many lions as our data show, cougar numbers would still be insignificant."

Another who doubts that the mountain lion is a serious threat to cattle is Pete Hughes, a powerfully built outdoorsman who gets around the mountains on a large, snow-white mule. Hughes has an abiding respect for mountain lions. Before his recent retirement he spent twenty-four years as a state hunter, traveling the rugged New Mex-

ico mountains, responding to ranchers' lion complaints. "Lion numbers are down," he says. He blames the state's winter hunting season, when lions can be pursued by hounds through deep snow. Hughes views with regret and perhaps a touch of contempt the ways of the modern lion hunter. He sees no fairness in the methods of weekend guides out of Albuquerque who cruise logging roads in heated pickup trucks and use dogs wearing radio-equipped collars to lead them to treed lions. Says Hughes:

"Then the guide goes to the phone and calls his hunter, who maybe lives in Boston. While the guy is flying out here, the dogs hold the lion in the tree waiting. It's plum easy. I've had lost dogs that held a lion in a tree for more than twenty-four hours. The lions are just not gonna last."

Some have insisted that more lions must be killed to make the world safer for people, but biologists question this argument. If lion hunting is essential to keep down the number of attacks on people, they ask, why

14

haven't there been attacks in Glacier National Park, where they have 1.5 million visitors a year and no hunting, or in Olympic National Park, which is a cougar stronghold, with more than 2 million human visitors a year and no hunting? And why are there so many lion attacks in British Columbia, where hunting has been in effect for decades?

In British Columbia the possibility of a close encounter with a cougar is a long-standing fact of life. Carnivore research specialist Frank Tompa has listed more than two dozen such attacks since 1914, most of them on Vancouver Island. Four of these have resulted in fatalities. In 1940 a mountain lion killed a boy. In 1949 a young male lion stalked, attacked, and killed a seven-year-old girl. In 1971 an old male lion in poor condition killed a twelve-year-old girl. The most recent fatality was in 1976. Tompa sees no evidence of trends or changing conditions in his figures. Why are there more attacks in some areas than in others? "It's just that different lion populations have learned different ways," says Maurice G. Hornocker, Idaho's noted mountain lion authority.

Arguments on whether to kill more lions indiscriminately soon come down to how many lions there are and what the population trends are. But there has never been a really reliable system for counting these elusive large cats. In the early 1970s California's best estimate was that the state had 2,400 mountain lions. More recently the Department of Fish and Game, measuring occupied lion range and using its best lion-density figures, calculated that California may now have 5,100 mountain lions. The department calls this figure "very conservative."

Meanwhile, some officials wonder if the increased reports of close encounters between people and lions really reflect higher lion populations. Clouding the issue is the possibility that people, made more lion-conscious by the flood of publicity, are quicker to report lions—or yellow Labrador retrievers and other lion look-alikes—than previously. Also, if lions are reducing deer herds to dangerous levels, as hunters often insist, the lions may indeed be shifting their hunting to the suburbs, where pets provide a ready substitute. If this is true, and again nobody knows, there is a possibility that lions do present a growing threat to humans.

Perhaps, deep down, we welcome the excitement that comes with the presence of a large predator and, consequently, tend to exaggerate the potential of an encounter. Stanley P. Young, an early biographer of the cougar and a federal biologist for some forty years until his retirement in 1959, wrote: "The almost universal fear of the puma is based mainly on its mysterious ways, size, and power to do harm, not on its aggressiveness, for as a rule it is notoriously timid in relation to man."

But the exceptions command our attention. Some mountain lions, just as some people, are not timid and submissive. They may be conditioned to the presence of people, or they may be taken by surprise while guarding food or young. Whatever the cause, cougar attacks on people, although rare, are always possible.

Stories about mountain lions attacking people are really nothing new. Across North and South America, where the cougar is native, these tales have been told for hundreds of years. Many had their roots not in fact but in the frontiersman's feelings about the mountain lion. Settlers rarely saw the cats but knew they were out there, feared them as a threat to human life, detested them as killers of domestic stock, and methodically destroyed them. In the western mountains, the big cat became choice raw material for campfire storytellers. James Ohio Pattie, a restless, Kentucky-born, beaver-trapping mountain-man, told of awakening one dark night to find a "painter" stretched out on a log within six feet of him, ready to spring. "I raised my gun gently to my face and shot it in the head." It scarcely matters that Pattie was known to respect the truth too little. Such yarns fed the legend. The cougar's reputation grew, and in some circles it continues to grow.

While naturalists labeled such encounters rare, or even unknown, here and there was an old record that had the doleful ring of truth. A quarter of a century before the American Revolution, according to his tombstone and some sketchy records, a citizen of Chester County, Pennsylvania, was attacked and killed by a cougar along the edge of a woods. This tragedy occurred half a mile from the quiet country cemetery where he was laid to rest and his grave marked by a stone on which was chiseled, *"Here lye the body of Philip Tanner who departed this life May 6 1751 aged 58 years."* The engraver carved the rough image of a cougar on the headstone.

In his *Mammals of North America,* Victor H. Cahalane wrote in 1947, "Very few cases of undoubted attack on humans are recorded." He then tells of a fatal attack by a lion on a fourteen-year-old Washington boy in 1924. The year before that, a California lion, apparently crazed by rabies, attacked three young people. Two of them later died

15

of the disease, perhaps the only known cases of rabies transmission to humans from a cougar.

One famous mountain-lion attack on a human occurred late in the morning of January 20, 1974, at Arroyo Seco in New Mexico. Eight-year-old Kenneth Nolan was playing with his stepbrother among the rabbit bush and piñon trees, unaware that a mountain lion was watching them.

This lion, using vegetation to screen its approach, stalked the boys for several hundred yards, exploded from the bushes, and killed Kenneth Nolan. It was later killed by the boy's father and a neighbor. The cat was thin but, aside from weighing only forty-seven pounds, healthy. Its age was judged to be less than two years, suggesting that it was not yet living on a well-established hunting ground of its own. Says Hornocker, "Most mountain-lion attacks on people have been by dumb, inexperienced youngsters. They have also been predominately on children."

In more recent times mountain lions have brought nationwide publicity to the Ronald W. Caspers Wilderness Park, which sprawls over 7,600 acres in Joe Oliver's territory south of Los Angeles.

The park lies adjacent to National Audubon Society's secluded, 3,900-acre Starr Ranch Sanctuary, which is closed to the public. Starr Ranch, in addition to being in mountain-lion country, has deer, coyotes, and, according to sanctuary manager Jeffrey Froke, a bird list of more than 160 species. Among the birds are thirteen species of nesting raptors, including black-shouldered kites and what is probably the last pair of nesting golden eagles in Orange County.

These scenic foothills of the Santa Ana Mountains are dominated by towering ridges that fall away in steep grassy slopes and in chaparral-covered fields to ribbons of sycamore and California live oak that mark the course of little streams. It is the kind of magnetic wild setting that draws people away from the densely populated cities of southern California. Caspers Wilderness Park is also adjacent to the sprawling wilderness mountains of the Cleveland National Forest's Trabuco District.

On a Saturday in October 1986, Doug Schulthess of Cypress, California, his wife, and two small children drove out to Caspers Wilderness Park for an afternoon of hiking and exploring. They stopped along the trail, and while his wife held their two-year-old daughter in her arms, Schulthess snapped a picture for the family album. The developed picture caused a sensation. It clearly showed the close-up face of an adult mountain lion staring at the family from the edge of a thicket only a leap or two away.

This sighting attracted special public attention because it followed a serious lion attack nearby. Earlier in the year five-year-old Laura Small had been dragged down and mauled by a mountain lion in the same park. By the time she was rescued she had suffered a fractured skull, partial paralysis, a serious eye injury, and numerous lacerations on her face. This attack is the basis of a multimillion-dollar lawsuit against assorted defendants, including National Audubon Society. The victim's parents claim that those named in the suit knowingly harbored a dangerous animal and failed to warn people of the hazards.

A second attack occurred the day after Doug Schulthess took his famous photograph. Not far from the same spot, Timothy Mellon of Huntington Beach took his family on an outing into Caspers Wilderness Park. His son, six-year-old Justin, was running ahead with other children but stopped to tie his shoe. Animal behaviorists have long noted that a small child in a vulnerable position seems to trigger a predatory response in large cats.

The children's screaming brought a knife-wielding Timothy Mellon to his son's rescue. The lion released its grip on the boy's head and escaped into the brush. Justin was treated in the hospital for multiple lacerations of the head, chest, and back.

Orange County officials promptly closed the park to visitors, and it remained closed for two months. In the wake of these attacks at least one politician, testing the waters of public opinion, called for removal of all the lions. But a surprising force of people came forward testifying in defense of cougars and wilderness.

There have been other lion attacks on people over the years. But until recently no one had brought details of these encounters together in one place. In 1986 Janis E. Schmidt, a student at the University of California in Davis, completed a search of old records that turned up reports of lion attacks on people in the Western Hemisphere from 1750 to 1986. The list includes sixty-six attacks, twenty-three of them fatal. It may be incomplete, and in some instances the facts are sketchy.

Extension wildlife specialist E. Lee Fitzhugh, of the University of California in Davis, supervised Schmidt's work. "Of the thirty-three attacks in the United States," he says, "twenty-five were in, or west of, the Rocky Mountains. Eight occurred in California and involved eleven people. Seven of

JUST THE FACTS

Common names: Cougar, puma, mountain lion, panther; less commonly, painter, catamount.

Scientific name: *Felis concolor* (literally, "cat of one color").

Description: Males, up to nine feet long including tail; females, about a foot shorter; weight, from 80 pounds for a small female to 200 pounds for a big male; two color phases, one tawny to reddish and the other grayish to bluish.

Range: The Americas, from British Columbia south to Patagonia; in the United States, limited mainly to the western mountain and desert regions, southern Texas, and southern Florida.

Numbers: The U.S. population may number around 16,000; in southern Florida, perhaps no more than 30 survive, the only known cougars east of the Mississippi.

Behavior: Generally solitary; preys primarily upon deer, including elk in parts of its range, but will also take beavers and hares; large kills are usually fed upon for several days; one to six young are born from late winter to early spring; lifespan may exceed fifteen years.

Historical perspective: Once common throughout the United States; by 1900, reduced to its present range by intensive hunting and predator-control programs; only Texas still allows unrestrained killing of cougars; the eastern (probably extinct), Florida, and Costa Rican subspecies are protected by the federal Endangered Species Act.

cougar confrontations in the West have spurred efforts to loosen lion protection.

these people died as a result of the attacks."

California's on-going debates led to bitter divisions over how best to deal with the state's mountain lions. Hunters and stockmen favored professionally managed hunting seasons, while others demanded full protection. This cougar controversy grew increasingly vitriolic, until the animal rights fraternity gained strength enough to put the issue to a vote of the people. As a result, in June 1990, 52 percent of the state's voters approved a new law forbidding mountain lion hunting for the next thirty years.

In addition, this new law directs that each year $30 million of various state funds be taken from other projects—including endangered species work—and spent instead to improve habitat for mountain lions and deer. Hunters and stock growers report, meanwhile, that mountain lions are already abundant.

One professional California wildlife manager labels this "crummy legislation." But jubilant animal rights militants are now inspired to "save" other wild animals. Biologists see much of this effort as misguided and insist that the important matter is welfare of the species, not simply saving every individual with little regard to the impact on other wildlife or habitat.

Because of the increased sightings, some observers speculate that California mountain lions may be inhabiting marginal habitats where formerly they were rare. "The mountain lion is a highly adaptable animal," says Hornocker. "It can make adjustments to the presence of people. It can readily learn to live on pet cats and dogs."

Apparently, a mountain lion killed a five-year-old boy in a rural area of western Montana in September, 1989. The child was riding his tricycle near a wooded area some thirty yards from his home.

Although people may encounter lions more frequently than they once did, Hornocker sees no signs that the cats are changing their behavior toward humans. Mountain lions, he explains, have always lived closer to us than we realized.

But attitudes toward mountain lions are changing. Increasingly, people accept their presence as part of the scene, and few would any longer want them eliminated.

"The lion is a large predatory animal that can be dangerous," Hornocker says, "and it has to be viewed that way. But this doesn't mean that we should do away with all mountain lions any more than we would try to kill all the mice in a valley because one got into the camp oatmeal."

WHO'S AFRAID OF THE BIG BAD WOLF?

TEXT BY L. DAVID MECH

"MOONLIT TRACKS—WOLVES" © 1990 R.S. PARKER

A twig snapped, and I knew the wolves were returning. Straddling the carcass of the moose that fifteen of them had just pulled down, I peered through the snowy birch and fir trees to see two of the creatures rushing straight toward me. I was twenty-two years old back then and had a quick decision to make: Should I reach for my movie camera or my revolver? (A film of those two big beautiful animals bearing down on me would be incredible, but why had the Park Service insisted I carry a gun?) I pulled the revolver.

Instantly I realized my mistake. Just the movement of my hand was enough to show the wolves that it was a human being who had usurped their kill, and they vanished.

Meanwhile, above me, Don Murray spiraled around in the little ski plane from which we had watched the whole pack swarm over this four-hundred-pound moose calf and, despite valiant charges by the cow, bring its struggling body down. When I invited the

18

bush pilot to join me in inspecting the remains, he politely declined. "A pilot belongs in the air," he proclaimed solemnly. "I'll watch from above."

Later, Murray told me that he had seen most of the wolves run off when I was still 150 yards from the kill. And we had both watched the last couple of wolves reluctantly leave when I was within about a hundred feet. Murray then saw all of the animals assemble 250 yards away while I was examining their kill. Eventually the two rambunctious wolves decided to race back toward the carcass, no doubt forgetting I was still there.

I don't know how many times in the thirty years since that scene on Michigan's Isle Royale I have regretted pulling the gun instead of pointing the movie camera. Over and over again during my career as a wolf biologist I have found that rather than worrying about whether wolves would attack me, I worried about how I could get closer to them.

Nevertheless, a large segment of the public still believes that wolves are dangerous to humans. The issue of possible wolf predation on humans has arisen several times during the current public debate over whether to reestablish wolves in Yellowstone National Park. For example, in a 1989 booklet called "Wolf Reintroduction in the Yellowstone National Park: A Historical Perspective," author T. R. Mader lists several alleged threats and attacks by wolves under the heading "Misconception 10—wolves pose no threat to man himself."

Though it's certainly true that a number of aggressive encounters between wolves and humans have been documented, few if any have led to serious injury, and they often involve extenuating circumstances. So what is the actual situation? Can wild wolves be trusted around humans or not? To answer that question, we must explore well-documented reports of wolf–human encounters.

One of the earliest and best accounts of a wolf attack was reported in a 1985 issue of *Arctic*, published by the University of Calgary Press. In the winter of 1915 a team of scientists with sled dogs was camped near the northwestern coast of Canada's Northwest Territories. When an adult female wolf, thought to be in heat, attacked the lead sled dog, the men rushed out of their tents half-dressed. The wolf then attacked two of them. One man shooed it off "with the flapping front" of his wool shirt. The other, ethnologist Diamond Jenness, threw a boulder at it. When the wolf tried to bite Jenness' leg, he grabbed the animal by the back of the neck, and "it screwed its head round and fastened its teeth in my arm," Jenness said.

"I tried to choke it with the left hand—unsuccessfully—but after a moment it let go and moved away a little, when the Dr. immediately shot it."

Of interest here are the presence of the dogs, the turmoil, the fact that one man so easily shooed off the wolf and another actually grabbed it. It's not surprising that the wolf "screwed its head round" and bit Jenness, for most wild carnivores will try to bite when grasped by the back of the neck, in order to escape. That the wolf came so close to Jenness that he had to grab it in self-defense is most significant. It is likely that the wolf was highly frightened and confused. And when feeling trapped, wolves may respond automatically with a quick, short bite. Twice I have been so bitten by tame wolves and once by a wild one.

Another interesting wolf–human interaction also involved a dog. One December day in 1970 Sanford Sandberg, a logger from Skibo, Minnesota, brought his dog to his cutting in Superior National Forest. Sandberg and a partner were cutting logs when a deer bounded within a few yards with two wolves almost on top of it. The deer stopped, the loggers waved their arms, and the wolves ran off.

While the loggers discussed the incident, a wolf rushed back and began fighting with the dog at Sandberg's feet, its tail banging against the man's leg. The wolf soon gave up and ran off, and Sandberg picked up his frightened dog.

Suddenly, the second wolf came dashing back, leaping up at the dog, catching its lower canine on Sandberg's red-and-black-checkered wool jacket, and tearing a six-inch rip in it. For an instant Sandberg looked right into the mouth of the wolf before the animal dropped down and ran off. Sandberg never claimed he had been attacked. He said, "I'm sure the wolf was after my dog."

On a snowy January day in 1982, nineteen-year-old Ron Poyirier was out snowshoe-hare hunting in a thick cedar swamp north of Duluth. He caught a glimpse of movement just ahead, when a wolf came from nowhere and knocked him down. He rolled on the ground with the wolf and grabbed it by the throat to hold it away. It kicked and clawed him but did not bite. Poyirier's .22 rifle was still in his hand but not pointed toward the wolf. Nevertheless, the youth fired a shot, and the wolf disappeared. Poyirier suffered a one-and-a-half-inch scratch on his right thigh from one of the wolf's claws. The most reasonable explanation for this incident is that the youth was wearing hunting clothes laced with buck scent. The wolf may have

Wolf authority Dr. Dave Mech (pronounced "MEECH") here discusses claims that wolves are dangerous to man.

Artwork in this story courtesy of the artists and Mill Pond Press, Inc., Venice, Florida 34292.

been chasing a deer—which could have been the movement Poyirier glimpsed—and confused the youth's scent with that of the deer.

No such circumstances surrounded the wolf–human interaction on Ellesmere Island in the High Arctic when a pack of six wolves closely checked out a team of scientists. As reported in a 1978 issue of the *Journal of Mammalogy,* the scientists saw the wolves approach and threw clods of tundra at them to ward them off. But the wolves kept coming. One jumped up and grazed the cheek of botanist Mary Dawson, leaving saliva on but not injuring her. In that region wolves have not been hunted or persecuted and are generally neutral toward humans, showing neither fear nor aggression. What the wolf pack was up to when they approached Dawson's team defies explanation.

Somewhat more explainable, but still highly unusual, was a report in a 1985 *Journal of Mammalogy* in which three zoologists were harassed by at least three wolves about nine miles southeast of Churchill, Manitoba. On June 29, 1984, the three men had just stopped to rest when they spied a wolf charging them from ten yards away. One man yelled and stamped his feet. The wolf stopped about twenty feet away and retreated just as a second wolf charged and came to within ten feet of Peter A. Scott. Scott sounded a "bear horn" used for scaring away polar bears. "Wolf B responded by blinking once, twitching its ears, and completing its third lunge in a slight divergence off course." It landed about a yard from Scott, trotted off at a right angle, and paused ten feet away.

The zoologists climbed trees and watched the wolves trot back and forth in an arc fifteen to thirty-five yards long for four hours. The men finally retreated two miles to their vehicle after not seeing a wolf for fifteen minutes. Later they found a den and evidence of pups in the general area.

Other, less detailed reports of wolf attacks on humans include the following: In August 1987 a young girl camping in Algonquin Park, Ontario, was bitten by a wolf when she shined a light at the creature; in British Columbia, a forester was treed by wolves, and a woman was reportedly injured trying to beat off a wolf.

What is notable in all these reports, besides the highly unusual wolf behavior, is the fact that no one was seriously injured. If a wolf or pack were really to attack a person like they attack prey, the result would be instant and deadly. I have seen wolves attack several prey animals, and there is nothing hesitant about the attack. No one could ever

grab a wolf by the neck or throat if it lunged the way it does at prey. Wolves can crack open the heavy upper leg bones of musk oxen and sever a cow's tail at the base with a single bite. To kill moose and other large prey, they must tear through several inches of hair and very thick hides. Indeed, captive wolves, wolf–dog hybrids, and, for that matter, even dogs who have been mismanaged have killed or seriously injured people in very short attacks.

The wolf attacks related above seem to represent either threats, defensive reactions, or some other kind of nonpredatory interaction. In addition, when appraising alleged wolf attacks, one must always consider the possibility that the attack was made by a tame wolf. Such an explanation immediately comes to mind for the Algonquin Park incident. Many people who own pet wolves that they acquire as pups need to get rid of them as the wolves mature. Because Algonquin Park is so well known for wolves, it would be a likely area for such a release.

Of course if a wolf is stricken with rabies, as sometimes happens in North America in latitudes above 60 degrees north, it is a different story. Rick Chapman, a graduate student of mine, was attacked by a rabid wolf at the Arctic National Wildlife Refuge in Alaska. He had spent months studying a wolf den there and was working on his doctorate. Chapman was watching the den when he noticed a strange wolf approach the pack and fight them. The next day the same wolf came near Chapman at his tent. After rattling pots and pans to scare it off, he finally had to resort to bopping the wolf over the head with a hiking boot. The wolf left and returned again only to meet the same fate. On the wolf's third attempt, Chapman knew something was wrong with the animal, and he shot it. The wolf turned out to be rabid, as did several of the wolves it had fought with at the den.

That incident is reminiscent of a record in the *Journal of Mammalogy* in 1947. A wolf attacked a trainman who was riding on a little railroad "speeder" through the bush in Canada. The man hit the wolf with implements several times, and was later assisted by a train crew that happened by. Finally the wolf was killed. Although the wolf was never checked for rabies, rabies would certainly be a good explanation for the animal's bizarre behavior.

Rabies may also explain numerous newspaper accounts of wolf attacks on humans in Mideastern countries, where the disease has been a regular problem throughout history. On the other hand, colleagues of mine in

India and the Soviet Union have told me of accounts of attacks on humans by nonrabid wolves that they believe are true. The reports from India usually involve youngsters from rural villages who are attacked while relieving themselves in fields in the morning. They are often carried away and later found dead.

This "child lifting" is popularly attributed to wolves, and twenty to thirty reports a year have reached me, giving the names, ages, and villages involved. The problem is that the incidents have not yet been properly investigated by competent biologists. In an article in the *Times of India,* a local leopard hunter disputed the official view that wolves were attacking children and claimed the attacks were made by leopards. Not an unreasonable explanation considering that leopards are known to kill people. But until foreign reports are thoroughly checked, judgment on them must be suspended.

Even if found to be true, we must not conclude too much from the Eurasian reports. There is too much evidence that North American wolves are not dangerous to humans. Some 19 million visitor days with no wolf

attacks have been recorded in Minnesota's Superior National Forest alone. In addition, the national parks of Canada and Alaska could boast many millions more safe visitor days, as could Canada's provincial parks.

Furthermore, there have been incidents of humans interacting positively with wolves in the High Arctic (above 70 degrees north latitude), where wolves are not persecuted by humans. For example, ornithologist David Parmelee once grabbed a wolf pup and carried it back to his tent. The mother wolf followed at his heels and slept outside his tent until he released the pup.

Frank Miller, a Canadian Wildlife Service caribou biologist, reported in a 1978 issue of *Musk-ox* (University of Saskatchewan) that G. A. Calderwood surprised two wolves near the U.S.–Canadian Arctic weather station, Mould Bay. "The wolves rose to their feet but did not flee. When Calderwood knelt on the ground to put film in his camera, one of the wolves approached, licked [his] face, uttered a gurgling sound, then turned and trotted off with the other wolf."

While this may sound incredible, my own

experience leads me to believe it. During four summers I have spent my vacations in the High Arctic studying a pack of wolves who were just about as friendly. I have had seven adults surround me as I lay watching their den, a yearling steal my fake fur hat when it blew off me, and pups and their mother howl within a yard or two of me as I took notes. In another case a four-week-old pup toddled up to me while I filmed its mother a few feet away and yanked on my bootlace until it untied the bow!

The most dramatic demonstration of how tolerant of me the pack is occurred when they killed a musk-ox calf in front of me and a companion. As they tore apart the carcass, I crawled toward them on hands and knees to take notes on what they were eating. The subordinates (younger wolves) allowed me to within about thirty-five feet before leaving, but the alphas (elders) continued to feed undisturbed while I sat twenty feet away.

The tolerance shown by this wolf pack has allowed me to gain tremendous insights into wolf social behavior that could not have been obtained in any other way.

During all of my interactions with this pack, the wolves accepted and never threatened any of us. In fact, a photographer, unbeknownst to me, actually invaded the den itself when the pups were two to three weeks old. I am not certain how the adults behaved, but I know they did not attack him. On the other hand, for the rest of that summer the mother of the pups was much less tolerant of me than she had been during the previous two years. For the next denning season she abandoned the den and bore her pups many miles away. The point here, however, is that despite what the wolf must have considered an extreme intrusion, she did not attack.

Of course, individual wolves and packs are highly variable. Some might attack under conditions in which others might not, and the potential for a wild wolf to injure a human during an attack is great. Thus one can never say never when discussing the possibility of wolf attacks on humans. Nevertheless, the weight of evidence indicates that humans have little to fear from healthy wild wolves. Certainly the remote possibility of wolf attacks should in no way inhibit sound wolf reestablishment.

ORANGE-TOOTH IS HERE TO STAY

TEXT BY DONALD DALE JACKSON

The airboat skidded over a floating mat of reeds and bounced into a small pool. Four gray-brown animals that looked like a cross between a beaver and a rat slid off a platform of dead grass and churned nose-high through the water like toy PT boats. Reaching the reed carpet, they scurried off in a run that was part scoot, part waddle, and part humpbacked hop. One stood and flashed a quick, irritated glance that displayed a set of long orange teeth.

"This is the day to see nutrias," Greg Linscombe said cheerily. "They're out sunning on their nest platforms." A biologist with Louisiana's Department of Wildlife and Fisheries, Linscombe is America's foremost expert on the strange South American immigrant we were tracking through this slab-flat marsh a few miles from the Gulf of Mexico.

Suddenly he slowed the boat and reached over the side, where a nutria flank protruded above the surface although its head was underwater. "He thinks he's hiding," Linscombe said. The biologist seized it by its long, ratlike tail and set it down in the boat. The nutria looked remarkably placid, befitting its reputation for docility despite teeth that can gnaw off a human thumb. On close inspection it looked more like the large, fifteen- to twenty-pound rodent it is, with its small eyes and ears and stiff white whiskers. But this was a rodent with some peculiar equipment, including dexterous, monkey-like forepaws and webbed, ducklike hind feet. Linscombe released its tail, and the exhibit dove overboard.

Within fifty feet of where we were cruising I could see a dozen more of them—swimming and belly-flopping off their mound-like platforms and scampering through the winter-low grass. "This is the ideal habitat for nutrias," Linscombe said. "They can walk on what they eat. We calculated the population here at about eighteen an acre a few years ago."

Today it looked even more congested. We headed down a canal-like boulevard of dark water filled with water hyacinth and other marsh plants. Nutrias of all sizes, solo and in

C. C. LOCKWOOD

bands of up to five or six, peeled off their basking stations as we came near. We appeared to be on the Main Street of Nutria City. Their color ranged from reddish-brown to dirty gray to rich dark brown. A few dimwits tried the head-in-the-mud ploy, but most dove as we neared, their hind feet vanishing crisply through the surface like the feet of an Olympic swimmer making a turn. I tried counting, but gave up when I passed one hundred.

"The little ones are like popcorn for alligators," Linscombe said, but the gators were hunkered down today; too cold. The only real predator in view, besides us, was a hawk scanning the horizon from the roof of a two-foot-high muskrat house. Just above the nutria mainline a great blue heron bustled aloft and slowly unfurled into its long, languid flight profile.

Like the nutria itself, the story of nutrias in the United States is a bizarre, one-of-a-kind

The nutria veered off its assigned course early and often, and became a kind of scuffling, four-legged symbol of human folly.

23

A model from Rosenberg & Lenhart, New York furriers, shows a dyed nutria coat.

ROBERT RATTNER

phenomenon. It's not just that as a Latino alien the nutria is an exotic, like the starling and the Norway rat, but it's what has befallen the animal since it arrived here to stay in the 1930s. Originally it was imported live from Argentina to be raised for its fine fur, as in several European countries. But in the United States the nutria veered off its assigned course early and often, and in the end it became a kind of scuffling, four-legged symbol of human folly.

The pioneer Louisiana nutrias got out of their pens and into the marsh under circumstances that remain mysterious even now, a half-century later, raising questions about the intent of their sponsor, the noted naturalist–conservationist–Tabasco tycoon E. A. (Mr. Ned) McIlhenny. Though extensively trapped in Louisiana (and to a lesser degree in a dozen other states) nutria never really caught on with American fur manufacturers or buyers. It caught on instead as the come-on in a skin game in which honey-tongued promoters huckstered "breeding pairs" to gullible buyers at prices that were truly exotic. When the would-be fur ranchers finally despaired of turning a profit, they often liberated their charges, while other nutrias dug or swam their way out of captivity—and into more trouble.

The problem was the nutria's reproductive prowess—early parenthood, two-and-one-half litters a year, and four or five in a litter—coupled with a vegetarian appetite totally devoid of fussiness: They never met a plant they didn't like. In their preferred habitat, the coastal marshes, they gobble the grasses that help prevent erosion by holding the marsh together. They nibble rice and sugar-cane and dig burrows in rice levees. In good farmland, like Oregon's Willamette Valley, they nosh corn and wheat, oats and alfalfa, and anything else they can reach. In every state with a remnant population save Louisiana the nutria eventually became that most forlorn of creatures, a "pest species"; in Louisiana its reputation, harnessed to its cash value, skittered up and down with the shifting state of the European fur market.

In an age of heightened animal awareness, the poor nutria—kidnapped, praised, and coveted, then abandoned and detested—is about as friendless as a critter can be. On the totem pole of mammal lovability it's crouched at the bottom, its eyes darting about warily. "If it were more important economically, or if it were a truly big-league pest, we'd know more about it than we do," Linscombe says. But alas for scientific curiosity, hardly anyone is disposed to study a minor-league varmint.

Decades of such disdain have left us with a skimpy dossier of nutria natural history facts sprinkled with just enough intriguing tidbits to give us a yen for more. For starters there's the name. "Nutria" is actually a misnomer—it's Spanish for otter. Europeans favor its Indian name, "coypu," which means "water-sweeper," but—well, maybe the word sounds better on European tongues; would you want to raise coypu? Cajuns call it "nutra-rat," which sounds like a rodent caught in the basement of an organic food store.

Besides its dirty-orange teeth and its aptitude for procreation (females often mate again right after giving birth), the nutria's most distinctive feature is the female's mammary glands, which are on her back. While this might be awkward in some species, in nutrias it is thought to facilitate suckling while afloat. Nutrias divide their time between water and land, and they make their nests, either platforms or burrows, where land and water intersect. Valves on their ears and nose close when they're submerged.

A nutria is born ready and willing—the coat's in place, the eyes open, and the half-pound newborn can swim and forage for itself from the opening bell. Such precocity is clearly handy in a habitat full of foes—alligators are the main menace, but raptors, snakes, turtles, and other predators also snatch little ones. When a nutria detects trouble, it's most likely to do so with its ears; both its eyesight and sense of smell are below par.

The animal's social life is largely a blank to biologists, though nutrias seem to congregate in large groups and there is evidence of a hierarchy led by a single male and several females. Primarily nocturnal feeders with a minimal zest for travel, they usually live out their allotted span (two to three years) in a home range less than a mile long.

They like to sunbathe when it's not too hot and groom themselves with some care, sometimes scratching with their hind feet like a dog. Their cry is a "wahhhh" that sounds eerily like that of a human baby. "You hear it in the late afternoon or early morning when they're moving around," says Lonnie Legé, manager of the National Audubon Society's Paul J. Rainey Sanctuary in the Louisiana marsh.

One persistent puzzle about nutria behavior is how much cold they can take. Linscombe and others have noticed that they seem to suffer acutely after a few days of sub-freezing weather, and biologists have reported ninety percent die-offs in cold-country wild populations in a severe winter. Yet farm-bred nutrias, paradoxically, have thrived in precincts as frosty as Poland, where millions are currently raised for fur and meat, and Canada, where one breeder reported a litter born on a day when the thermometer read 63 below.

Ned McIlhenny, squire of his family's salt- and Tabasco-producing principality near New Iberia, Louisiana, had only the most rudimentary knowledge of the animal when he imported thirteen orange-toothed specimens from Argentina and penned them inside a twenty-five-acre compound on his grounds in early 1938. "Mr. Ned loved to experiment, the man was interested in everything," says eighty-one-year-old Ted Bonin, an associate of McIlhenny's. Mr. Ned's interest was apparently piqued by the offer of an Argentinean nutria breeder to introduce the animals to Louisiana.

McIlhenny was a visionary conservationist who almost single-handedly created Louisiana's glorious network of wildlife refuges, but he was no yokel when it came to the bottom line. "He always wanted to get ahead of you," an elderly trapper recalls. Surviving acquaintances disagree on whether Mr. Ned wanted to breed nutrias in captivity, thus retaining any profit from their hides for himself, or intended to release them into the wild, so they could become a new fur resource for the state (with Mr. Ned getting a share of the take from those caught on his land). It sounds like B of the above in a 1938 letter he wrote to a U.S. Department of Agriculture official, which refers to his recent purchase of "a number of nutria I hope to introduce into our muskrat marshes."

His original intent became relevant only later, following The Great Nutria Escape of 1940. It was then that some 150 of them somehow got out of the McIlhenny pens— in a storm, the official story goes, though some still maintain they were deliberately set loose. A few years later, having found their new habitat rewarding and multiplying with their customary abandon, nutrias in Louisiana numbered in the hundreds of thousands. They were a boon to all, especially the Cajun trappers who put food on the table with what they got for their pelts. But by the time another decade had passed, the millions of descendants of Mr. Ned's thirteen original colonists were chomping marsh grass and infiltrating farmers' fields with such cheeky ardor that their classification was changed from protected furbearer to outlaw, with a twenty-five-cent bounty on them.

Few critters have undergone the pendulum swing in reputation—from savior to pariah, blessing to plague—that nutrias in Louisiana have endured. Before 1955, as

COURTESY OF E. A. McILHENNY ENTERPRISES INC.

TABASCO tycoon E. A. (Mr. Ned) McIlhenny imported the first live nutrias from Argentina in early 1938. Two years later, several dozen nutrias escaped from his pens into Louisiana marshes, their numbers quickly multiplying into the millions.

Louisiana writer Cherry N. O. Lynch put it, "the nutria was a noble experiment to broaden the trapping industry. Afterward, the story said they were brought here to be ranched, escaped and [became] a freak of nature." Mr. Ned seemed to lose interest in nutrias even before the great getaway and their

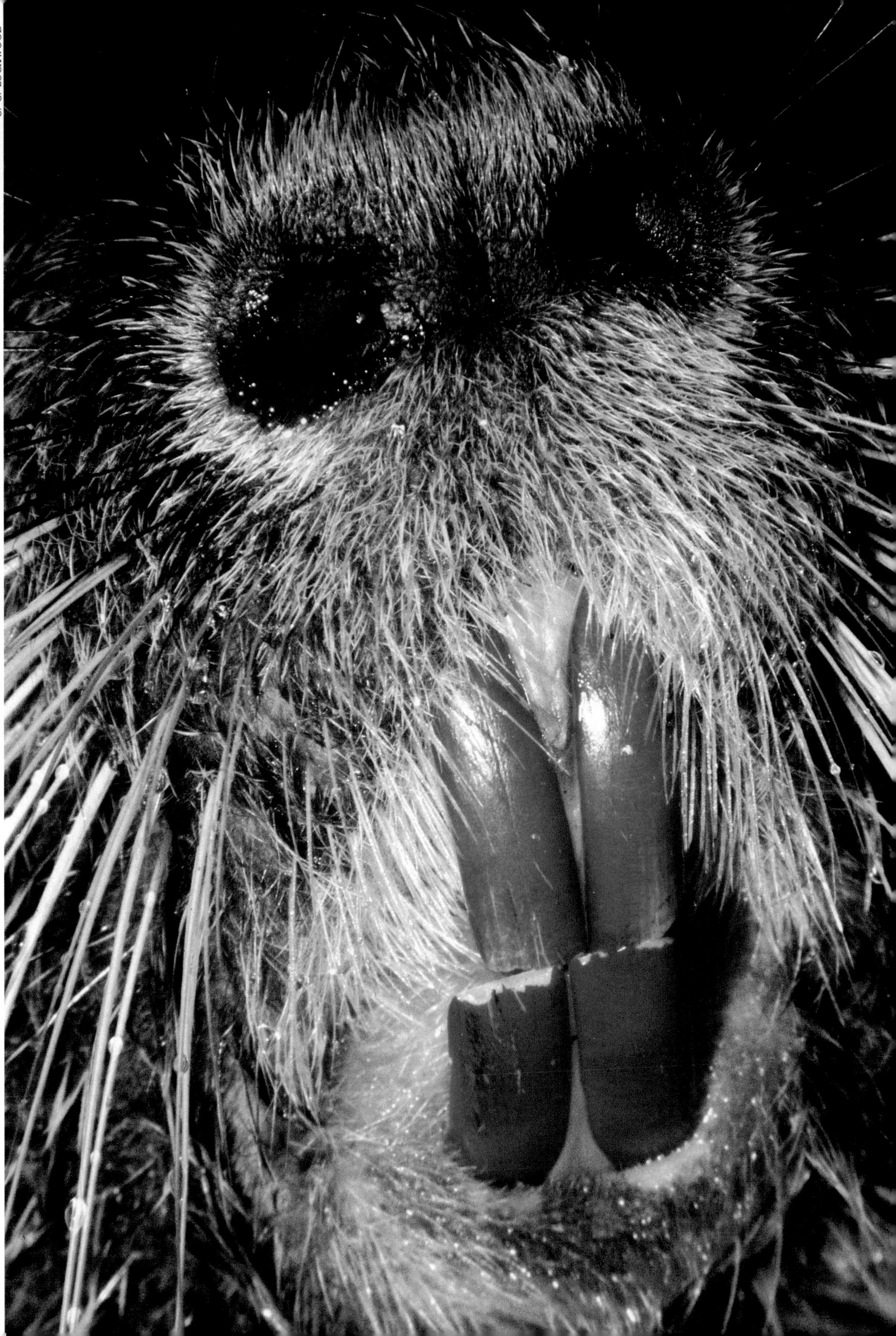

C. C. LOCKWOOD

subsequent descent into infamy. When a magazine editor proposed an article on his nutrias in 1939, he pooh-poohed the idea and suggested a piece on egrets instead.

The nutria population explosion, which some believe reached as high as 20 million in the 1960s, is reflected in Louisiana trapping statistics. From 436 trapped in 1943–44, the number boomed to 160,000 in 1953–54 and 1.3 million in 1963–64. Trappers say they're such dolts that it's no trick to catch one. "They are the dumbest animal I've ever seen," says Lonnie Legé, who grew up trapping with his father. "You could put a trap in the middle of a table and they'd go right into it. You never bait a nutria trap. It's like they're saying, 'Please take me.'"

Ted O'Neil was chief of the wildlife department's fur division in the 1950s and 1960s. "I never thought this goofy animal could do what it did," he said. "That really got me. They spread out and ate so much marsh vegetation they turned the coast into a mud puddle for a time. Then Hurricane Audrey came along in 1957 and pushed them into the cane- and ricefields." But when the European market for nutria perked up in the mid-sixties, Louisiana nutrias were struck from the outlaw list and restored to quasi-respectability.

"We tried to promote them for the American fur market, too," O'Neil said, "so we could get rid of them and make them worth something. But it never took here." He shook his head and pulled on his cigar. "The good fur dressers were in Europe. Shipping charges. Too many middlemen. We were selling a takeout order from the swamp."

In a move smacking of desperation, state wildlife officials even commissioned an experiment with nutria meat, cooking it in various guises (nutria gumbo, nutria chop suey, nutria meat loaf) and reporting success with volunteer tasters. But when Louisiana's Governor Jimmie Davis dropped in on a barbecue designed to promote nutria for nutrition, Cherry Lynch wrote, he "took a hasty bite and then retreated to a steak house." Though nutria meat is eaten in Europe and South America, it has never penetrated American menus, except possibly under an assumed name.

The native beasts that would seem most vulnerable to competition from nutrias are muskrats, which share both habitat and some food sources with the alien. Muskrat numbers plunged as nutrias exploded in bayou country, and the intruder eventually displaced the muskrat as the state's top fur producer, but Greg Linscombe doubts that it was cause and effect. "I believe the musk-

PHILIP GOULD

rat decline was as much due to man-caused changes in coastal Louisiana as to nutrias," he says. "I don't think nutria drive muskrat out. When conditions are good they coexist with no problems."

Louisiana nutrias finally peaked and began to decline in the 1970s. "That often happens with exotics; they boom and then they find their level," says Linscombe. Weather extremes—hurricanes, droughts, freezes—along with trapping, changes in marsh hab-

Previous page: Teeth of the docile-appearing nutria can gnaw off a human thumb. Above: Louisiana Wildlife and Fisheries biologists mark a section of nutria-ravaged wetland for study. The immigrant devours grasses that hold coastal marshes together.

itat, and escalating alligator numbers are among the reasons given for the turnaround. Linscombe, who thinks about nutrias more than anyone else in North America, isn't certain whether the varmint has been an overall plus or minus for his state. "If we could make them pay, it would help us fight erosion by giving marsh landowners a financial incentive for preserving their land," he says. "But we'd probably be better off if they'd never shown up here."

Lonnie Legé has a different perspective: "The creature Cajuns once called 'le rat Ned' has destroyed habitat, but it's also helped sustain a way of life for Cajuns that might have gone belly-up otherwise."

In the same years that old orangetooth's reputation was roller-coastering in Louisiana, the animal was being touted by money-grubbing hustlers elsewhere in the United States as a surefire ticket to gracious living. The promoters operated at state fairs and home shows and through mailers, offering "breeding pairs"—which in the nutria's case means any two of opposite sexes—for up to $2,500 to folks with a little land and a dream. "Would you have the vision to recognize opportunity if it laid its fur-lined paws on your shoulder?" a flier for an Oregon outfit called Purebred Registered Nutria of America challenged. The "mink of tomor-

row," the ad claimed, would soon put its owners on a first-name basis with their bankers.

Dozens of similar companies sprang up, primarily on the West Coast, with names like Purebred Nutria Associates and Cabana-Nutria Breeders Association. Some promised to buy back individual pelts from their members for as much as thirty dollars each at a time when the market price was less than ten dollars. For a certain kind of American—rural or semi-rural, familiar with animals, perhaps close to retirement and looking for a nest egg—the prospect of "gold nuggets in fur," as another ad identified the object of all this attention, was irresistible. At the crest of the nutria-mania wave in the early 1960s, there were as many as a thousand nutria ranchers in Oregon alone, and perhaps five times that many nationwide. One of them was Orville Cofman of Lancaster, Ohio.

"We bought a pair for $1,200 at the Pumpkin Show in Circleville, Ohio, in 1958," Cofman recalls. "The man was from the Cabana-Nutria Breeders. It sounded like a good thing. They promised us they would multiply, and they surely did that—we had 190 in two years.

"For the first couple of years it was pretty good. They paid us thirty dollars a pelt, like they said they would. Then they started paying less and less, the fur graders got real par-

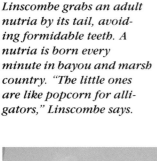

Louisiana biologist Greg Linscombe grabs an adult nutria by its tail, avoiding formidable teeth. A nutria is born every minute in bayou and marsh country. "The little ones are like popcorn for alligators," Linscombe says.

ticular about the coats and said they weren't pure. And they charged us a fee to register every newborn. Pretty soon it was costing more to keep them than what we were getting for them. I stayed with it until 1973. It was no paying proposition, that's for sure. I sold my last hundred to a man in New Jersey who was using them in some kind of research."

The directors of the company that euchred Cofman and thousands of other buyers out of an estimated $3 million were convicted of mail fraud in Los Angeles in 1961. They were given suspended five-year prison sentences and fined $1,000 each, less than their price for a breeding pair.

The prices that fur dealers offered for nutria pelts never approached the hucksters' inflated promises. Breeding nutrias, as Cofman learned, cost more than they were worth. The National Better Business Bureau and fur industry periodicals issued warnings that pointed out that the only way breeders could profit was by selling to other, more gullible breeders. The nutria business was circular, with no product except more nutrias. Those who had felt opportunity's fur-lined paws eventually gave up. Many disgustedly turned their animals loose.

Nutrias seemed stubbornly resistant to every attempt we made to cash in on them. The misguided schemes had started as far back as the 1940s, when detachments of nutrias were released in several southern states in the belief that they would destroy vegetation that clogged lakes and ponds. They did, but they neglected to stop there, moving on to nearby gardens and cornfields. Brought in as waterplant croppers at a Texas duck hunting club, they chewed gunstocks and sank duck blinds by gnawing away at their supports.

The result of the various introductions, paroles, and breakouts was that by 1967 nutrias had been reported at one time or another in forty states, but had inspired affection in none. Their career in Utah illustrates the pattern in cold-belt states. A junior-grade Mr. Ned first imported a few in 1939. They were traded back and forth, some were released, nature followed its inexorable course, and seventy-five pulled a major bustout in 1941. They prospered in the marshes around Great Salt Lake for a while and then blew it by raiding cash crops. The state declared them an outlaw in 1957. Today they're gone.

They persevered longer and got into more

trouble in less wintry venues. Texas farmers complained about their depredations on ricefields and other croplands. In Oregon they wiped out a quarter of one farmer's sugar beets in the 1960s, chomped four acres of another's peach seedlings, girdled trees, and made themselves an all-around nuisance, especially in the Willamette Valley. Lee Kuhn, a retired ecology professor from Oregon State University, thinks severe winters may have whittled their numbers in Oregon. Trappers in recent years have taken them in twelve states, mainly in the South, but also in Oregon, Washington, Oklahoma, and Maryland.

It's clear now that old orangetooth is here to stay, and Louisiana at least will be living with him for the duration, thanks to Mr. Ned. In the bayou and marsh country there's a nutria born every minute. Greg Linscombe worries about making the best of this bounty, perhaps with a marketing campaign aimed at Oriental fur buyers, but he is not giddy with confidence. "Nutria are out there," he allows, "and they're going to be, and people will either trap them or not." If they don't, we're likely to hear more sullying of the nutria's reputation.

It's possible, of course, that Americans and nutrias will reach an accommodation and embark on a new era of peace and harmony, a new start. And if you believe that, I've got a breeding pair I want to show you.

Top photo: In the aerial photograph, a test plot in Atchafalaya Bay—fenced to exclude nutria—shows marsh regeneration. The surrounding water would be grassy marshland if not overgrazed by nutria. Above: A nutria at its den entrance.

BOTH: C. C. LOCKWOOD

BEAR OF THE CLOUDS

TEXT BY PETER STEINHART • PAINTING BY JOHN DAWSON

Creature of the Andes, the spectacled bear is little known even on its own continent. Squeezed into small, isolated populations by forest destruction, the bear has small chance of surviving.

There are bears shambling over the American equator. Not the huge, shaggy, hibernating bears of the wintry North, but South America's only species of bruin, the spectacled bear. It is a skinnier creature with a stubbier, more doglike face. Cream-colored markings on its muzzle and around its eyes give it its popular name. Closely related to the North American black bear, it is the most arboreal of bears and feeds on fruits and epiphytic bromeliads high in the branches of trees. It even sleeps in trees.

It is a creature of the cloud forests that grow a mile up either side of the Andes from Peru to Venezuela. The cloud forest is a spectacularly rainy place, dense and tangled, perpetually wet, drizzling, and wrapped in mists. Tree trunks are lost in the grip of strangler figs, and branches are covered with epiphytic vines, grasses, bromeliads, and orchids. There may be more than a thousand different plant species in a square kilometer, and perhaps two-thirds of them take root in the branches of trees. The forest floor is deep in shadow, dense with dripping leaf and stalk.

Mixed flocks of tanagers, in dazzling emerald greens, brilliant blues, and extravagant yellows, flit from tree to tree. There are solemn trogons sitting in the shadows, noisy toucans rattling overhead, stunning blue morpho butterflies in the clearings, monkeys in the treetops. At night the air is full of the drip of rain, the squawk and whistle and burp of frogs, the ragged flutter of bats. The forest floor glows ice blue in places from luminescent bacteria. Earthworms with luminescent segments look like trains passing in the night.

Living in this forest requires watchfulness and appraisal. Biologist Bernie Peyton, who began studying the bears in the late 1970s, observes that forest food sources are widely dispersed and, in the absence of seasonal variations in sunlight and day length, appear erratically. A fig tree, for example, may fruit twice in one year, then take three more years to fruit again. Moreover, figs don't occur in groves as trees do in temperate zones. So tropical animals can't concentrate at a food source; they are, like the trees, widely dispersed in the forest. Peyton observes, "Bears will patrol. I've seen bears walk through the woods and put their feet on the trunk of a tree and sniff. They'll check out twenty or thirty trees that way. Eventually, they'll come to a tree with rotted fruits on the ground."

At the same time, a bear must be cautious. At lower levels on the western slope, jaguars may prey upon them. This predation probably keeps bears out of the lowlands along the coasts of Colombia and Ecuador. Humans hunt them too. Whenever Peyton has seen a wild bear, it has usually seen or heard him first and run up a hill to a rock or a stump that affords a view. "It will sit down and wave its paws toward its face while turning its head," he says. "Local people think they're bringing air to their faces to concentrate scents."

Because it lives in this obscure world, the spectacled is the least known of bears. Americans express surprise that there are bears in South America. Our natural histories tend to ignore South American species. Even on its own continent the bear is little known. On the streets of Quito, an Ecuadorian doctor told me she had never heard of bears in her country. The forest is too tangled, too dark, too misted, too lacking in vistas to offer even a researcher a chance to follow bears closely. The bears are too wary and elusive. No researcher has put a radio collar on a spectacled bear, for the hilly terrain swallows radio signals. In four years of field study Bernie Peyton, now a University of California graduate student, saw wild bears only eight times.

The spectacled bear's presence has not always been so little noted. In Inca times Andean bears were regarded as a link between the earth and the gods. The gods dwelt on mountaintops. The bears roamed the forest but from time to time moved up out of the dark tangle of tree and vine into the *páramo,* the treeless land above the forest. To the Indian the bear seemed to move from the moral obscurity of the forest to the dazzle of the open, to shamble between evil and good and, along the way, to talk with the gods. Even today, in parts of Peru, Indians believe

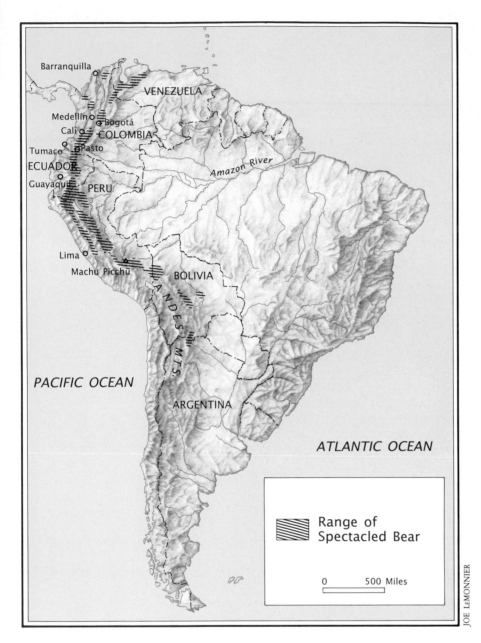

Barranquilla
VENEZUELA
Medellín
Cali
Bogotá
COLOMBIA
Tumaco
Pasto
ECUADOR
Guayaquil
PERU
Amazon River
Lima
Machu Picchu
BOLIVIA
ANDES MTS.
PACIFIC OCEAN
ARGENTINA
ATLANTIC OCEAN

Range of
Spectacled Bear

0   500 Miles

JOE LeMONNIER

tual order. And the new myths now mix with the old ones in Indian communities. Peasant farmers crush *puya,* a bromeliad that bears eat in the *páramo*, and rub it on the chest of a newborn male child to make him strong. They covet bear fat as a cure for bruises and a remedy for frostbite. Modern-day peasants feed bear scats to their cattle to make them stronger. Peyton says that during his field studies, "my bear scats were constantly being stolen." Indians frequently offered to accompany Peyton into the *páramo* when he went out to look for bears because it gave them a chance to address rituals to the mountain gods. They wrapped vicuña fat, bear claws, and coca leaves in bundles and, while whispering prayers, tossed the bundles into a fire. When Peyton asked them about the ritual, they told him they used the claws "because the bear can communicate to the gods. The bear lives near the gods. The bear is tremendously powerful."

For most Latin Americans, the bear inhabits neither the spiritual nor the real landscape. If you take a satellite view of the Andes, you can see why. A thousand years ago the valleys of the Andes, from Lima in Peru to Barranquilla in Colombia, were densely forested. Today they are practically treeless. A flight from Quito to Guayaquil shows that the forest from the Andean crest to the Pacific coast has vanished. Colombia has lost half the forest it had in 1966, 62 million acres, an area the size of the state of Oregon. In the Cauca River Valley, from Cali to Medellín, there is simply no forest to be seen. In place of its vast diversity and complexity are the plain, treeless rectangles of single-minded agriculture.

Few places are so badly out of sync with nature. The forests once acted like a sponge, soaking up water, purifying it, and releasing it slowly. Because the forests are gone, erosion is severe. Dams that were expected to provide electricity for decades have silted up in five years. Landslides often close main roads for months at a time. Without forest, even though this is one of the world's wettest places, there are water shortages. At Ricaurte, a campesino village in southwestern Colombia, people tap water from small streams coming off the hillside and avoid the main river, the Guiza, which is polluted. In dry months they may carry water from nearly a mile away, even though the broad Guiza flows underneath their windows and porches.

As South American nations fall deeper into debt, they mine the forests for hardwoods and minerals to gain foreign exchange, using up the resources and re-

that the souls of bad people are consigned by the mountain gods to eternal drudgeries, such as rolling large blocks of ice around mountaintops. Modern-day Indians sometimes dress in bear costumes, climb the mountains at midnight, chop up blocks of ice, and bring them down in the belief that they are liberating the souls of *condenados* so that they can go on to heaven. Without that intervention, they say, the *condenados* must go on working forever, or be killed by the blows of a spectacled bear.

Europeans brought a different view of the bear. As white-skinned colonists arrived, new myths, in which bears kidnapped and impregnated women, spread over the Andes. Bears became symbols of human machismo, emblems of human desire rather than spiri-

planting nothing. In ten years virtually all the valuable forest lumber in Colombia's Magdalena Valley was removed. *Prioria* trees, more valuable than mahogany, have been exhausted in some regions. *Dialyanthera,* a valuable species around Tumaco in the southwest, is almost gone. The forest is the future of South America. And it is in trouble.

So is the bear. All over the Andes the forest has been so cut apart by settlement that bears are being crowded into islands of habitat. Even the national parks are not safe harbors for bears. In Peru's Machu Picchu Historical Sanctuary, for example, more than half the land is farmed. Only twenty-five square miles of the reserve offer bear habitat. In 1982 Bernie Peyton found bear sign in only half of that.

Where bears survive, hunting pressure is intense. In all Andean nations it is illegal to shoot spectacled bears, but the law is not enforced. Farmers shoot the bears when they raid their cornfields. Sport hunters post handbills offering rich rewards to campesinos who will lead them to a bear. Having talked to Indians and hunters who saw bears in the past but no longer see them today, Peyton believes that the population has declined to a third of what it was thirty years ago. He worries that, as the bear is squeezed into small, isolated populations, it will lose its genetic integrity and perish.

There are bears at La Planada, a privately run nature reserve on the western slope of the Colombian Andes, 7,000 feet above sea level and not far from the Ecuadorian border. It has five captive-reared bears that are being eased into their natural habitat. No one knows how many wild bears are hidden in the 2 million acres of undisturbed forest that spill out to the southwest of the reserve. That forest is inhabited only by Awa Quaquer Indians, who maintain their traditions of hunting and gathering and practice a shifting agriculture. They live widely dispersed in huts on stilts, perhaps near a small patch of maize. Many have never seen a road or a village. Says Jorgé Orejuela, director of the La Planada reserve, "The Indians have been hunting for a long time here without exhausting the resource. They are masters of the use of tropical rainforest. They know how to work the slopes and do it sustainably. They use over one hundred different kinds of trees. No one else has discovered how to live sustainably in that ecosystem."

La Planada is cloud forest, almost perpetually wreathed in mist, dense and green and tangled under gloomy skies. Orejuela came to the area in 1981, when La Planada was a farm. He concluded that its 3,900 acres might have as many as thirty species of birds found nowhere else, a number that gives it, he says, "the highest concentration of endemic bird species in the world." The richness of La Planada proved manifold. Over 350 species of orchids—half the number found in all of Mexico—have been found in the vicinity. Orejuela expects further collection to push the number beyond five hundred. More than sixty species of frogs have been found on the reserve. "We know for sure that there is no other place with as high a diversity of frogs," says Orejuela.

By 1986 Orejuela had become director of ecology projects for *Fundación para Educación Superior,* a Colombian nonprofit organization devoted to education and conservation that had, with World Wildlife Fund help, purchased La Planada. Bears had not been observed in the reserve, but Orejuela accepted three captive bears that had been taken as cubs and bottle-fed by hunters who had shot their mothers. He built a concrete, bunkerlike cage for them in the secondary forest of the reserve and began digging a deep moat to enclose fourteen acres on which the bears might later be given liberty. Ultimately, he hopes they or their offspring will populate the vast surrounding forest.

On an August morning the moat was complete, and the first three bears were released. They charged through the forest, knocking down bushes, tearing branches from trees, climbing with abandon, plundering bromeliads twenty feet off the ground. Every few moments they stopped to sniff a flower, to examine a twig, to look long and hard at things, to learn the particular attributes of snake or frog or orchid. They pulled down slender trees, bent them to the ground, and jumped up and down on them to break them and examine their crowns. Wherever they went there was a fierce rustle of leaves and cracking of branches. When they melted into the center of the island, where the forest was deep, the noise of breaking branches and tearing leaves was loud and joyful.

They did not look much like messengers to the gods. They seemed too playful, too curious, too interested in the world around them. Watching them, Orejuela could not help but ponder their future.

The cloud forest that is their home is much diminished by centuries of growing human populations and expanding agriculture. Campesinos have deforested the interior valleys and are now spilling down the western slopes toward the Pacific and down the eastern slopes into the Amazon Basin. They are already at the edge of La Planada. Orejuela stands at the highest point on the reserve, looking southwest over ridges of dark, dense forest, with no field or shanty in sight. He turns around and looks down 2,000 feet into the broad valley of the Guiza River, where canefields back up the slopes like a flood tide. Cattle are pastured on the ridges above the canefields.

The campesinos harvest wood to heat their homes and to cook sugar into hard brown blocks called *panella,* its only marketable form. They also cut wood to sell to the hundred or so brick kilns in the neighborhood. The bricks go to Cali and Bogotá to feed the construction industry, Colombia's largest industry and the means by which the government seeks to combat unemployment.

Eighty percent of the wood cut in Colombia today is used for fuel. The cost of firewood has increased fivefold in the past four years. The government has yet to establish fuel-wood plantations. All along the road between Ricaurte and Pasto, on porches and in yards, are piles and bundles of firewood that will make their way to the kilns. The need for fuel is taking a toll on the forest. Up the hillsides leading to the reserve are rectangular scars where the forest has been cut. They look like patches shaved on the back of a dog. On each clearing are small tin-roofed ramadas, under which the firewood is curing.

The future that is climbing these hillsides is a bleak one. Clearing is followed by farming and grazing. But in this forest nearly all the biomass is in the treetops. When the trees go, so does the mass of nutrients stored high off the ground. Without the trees, heavy rainfall leaches soil nutrients. Plant corn or sugarcane and the soil is exhausted in a few seasons. "In the forest this life-style is not sustainable," says Orejuela. When the soil won't support crops, cattle are turned onto it, but it will support the cattle for only three or four years, and then it is no good even for grazing. "The colono will last four to five years," says Orejuela, "and then he will have to move on and become a colono again. He will destroy the land." And the bear will vanish.

In North America the solution would be to create a park or wildlife refuge. But in Latin America national parks have no political constituency and are frequently violated. Colombia's La Macarena National Park was established with more than 3 million acres, but now has only 1.5 million. In Ecuador the government built a road along Cayambe-Coca Ecological Reserve to service an oil pipeline from Amazonian oilfields to consumers in the Andean valleys. The colonos swarmed in along that road. In 1987, only ten of Colombia's thirty-three national parks even had staff, and only five or six had management plans. To declare the forest around La Planada a park would not save it.

"We felt the way conservation was seen was not the answer," says Orejuela. "You have to address the cause: The campesinos in attempting to survive are destroying the resource base. But the campesino is here and has a right to be." Rather than just draw the line and tell the campesinos to stay out, Orejuela seeks to delve into the forest and find the things that will allow the campesino to live a satisfying life without endless expansion. "We felt we had to look for ways to improve the socioeconomic development of the neighbors, to slowly provide for a tree-based culture, to convince people to plant trees, to sell the idea that the forest is providing a number of services: good water, good air. We need to integrate conservation and development."

Orejuela hopes to find in the forest's diversity the kinds of plants that will break the narrowness and dead-endedness of the colonization pattern. For example, there are trees farmers could plant that would hold the soil in place and provide fuel for their sugarcane and cooking needs and fodder for their cattle and pigs. There are wild relatives of domesticated crops that could have enormous commercial value. These plants could help deliver Latin American peasants from dependence on crops, such as sugar and coffee, that are subject to worldwide price fluctuations. Orejuela hopes to take what he learns into new schools that teach sustainable husbandry of native trees to increase fuel, forage, and food, instead of quick profits from coffee, corn, and sugarcane followed by flight to the city.

To keep the campesinos out of the forest that surrounds La Planada while he looks for sustainable ways of life, Orejuela hopes to have the forest declared part of a United Nations biosphere reserve. He hoped to have the entire area surrounding La Planada declared an Indian reserve. The 540 square miles on the Ecuadorian side of the border are Indian reserve. North of the border, reserves have been set aside in patches but not enough to promise protection to all the 2,700 square miles of forest inhabited by Awa Quaquers in Colombia.

So how will Orejuela accomplish all this? Latin American governments can't be counted on to address these problems. The continent has too short a history of conservation. Colombia's oldest natural resource agency is the Cauca Valley Commission, established in 1962 to develop the Cauca River. When such agencies were established, Latin American nations were blind to the speed and consequences of deforestation. The missions of these agencies have not been changed legislatively. Other needs are so pressing that national politicians are unlikely to act in behalf of conservation. Colombia has watched the market for two of its major export products, coffee and sugar, collapse. Guerrilla activity demands increasing expenditures of money, leaving little for education, health, and agriculture. On top of that, 60 percent of the country's income must go simply to service foreign debt. The government is tempted to get into quick development schemes, such as coal concessions, oil drilling, and timber exploitation, that will provide immediate but not long-term gains.

The politician's view is an urban view. Seventy percent of Colombians live in cities, where they have little inkling of what goes on in the countryside. There is so little consciousness of natural heritage that Latin American countries don't have neotropical bird guides and natural histories available in Spanish. In the bookstores the bird guides and animal books describe European species and are printed in Spain.

Orejuela believes the work of conservation will have to be borne by nongovernment organizations. In a land that has little history of citizen involvement in political matters, that is a revolutionary idea. A surprising number of citizen's groups have sprung into being. In 1987 representatives of five hundred nongovernment organizations met in Colombia to discuss the relationship between environment and development. But only a few of the organizations are even nominally environmental groups, and most of them devote their efforts to environmental education and do little lobbying. Funding is also a difficult matter for these groups, since there are no tax deductions for charitable giving in Latin American nations and so no tradition of philanthropy.

Still, if the logic of politics devours the forest there are nevertheless values snoozing in the campesino outlook that might help to reverse the trend. On a hill above the town of Ricaurte is the finca of Francisco Citelly. Citelly is a businessman in Pasto. His father owned this land and sold it. Citelly bought it back and now as a hobby grows bright red anthuriums, Colombia's national flower. He sells them locally and has plans to export them to Germany. He also experiments with orchids, with palms that might provide fiber for baskets or hats, and with fruit trees that might offer a novel drink for export to the United States. Trained in agronomy at the University of Georgia, Citelly sees the immense resources that are available in the forest of his native land. He grows achiote, a fruit that provides a bright red coloring for chicken dishes; combs the forest for gualpe, which supplies fiber for baskets and crafts; and raises bijao, the leaves of which are used to thatch houses and to wrap virtually everything in the Colombian marketplace.

We in the North tend to think of the forest in terms of its animals and birds, as if the life-forms in it were chiefly important as a catalog of personalities and characters and its purpose were to be an encyclopedic guide to human conduct. In the tropics one looks instead at the immense variety of plants. One thinks of the foods, the fibers, the woods, the novel chemicals of the leaf, the root, and the stem.

Latin Americans love this diversity of design and use. All over Ricaurte are porches with bright potted flowers growing on them, or with big green houseplants groping toward the hammocks in the shadows. In the markets of Andean cities such as Quito and Pasto, women serve a dozen different kinds of juices from forest fruits such as guava, maracuya, lulo, mora, zapote, guama, fresa, mango, naranjilla, and tomate. It is a different way of seeing, and North Americans have a hard time understanding it. We want open country, sweep, power, a sense of dominion. The forest people want a sense of richness and variety. It is this same love of diversity that moves the spectacled bear through the forest.

To watch the bears in La Planada is to see that the bear's problems are the continent's problems. The same fate awaits bear, campesino, and Indian. In that legend of bear delivering man from eternal torment on bleak mountaintops there may be truth. The real hope of having bears is that where bears survive, people can live.

If people are to find in the forest an alternative to the dead-end of deforestation, they will probably do so only by accepting the forest's complexity and by learning how to live with the forest and with themselves. And that, after all, is exactly what the bear is doing in the mists of the Andes.

DOOMED CANARIES
OF TADOUSSAC

TEXT BY JON R. LUOMA

*Opposite page: Biologist
Pierre Béland with the
skull of a beluga whale,
which some call "canary
of the sea."*

Early in the morning, from my bed in a room at the Hotel Tadoussac, I knew there was fog outside; fog again, fog still. An hour before, just at daybreak, I'd stepped groggily to the latticed dormer window and found, for the first time in days, that I could see beyond the wet sweep of hotel lawn and its little white tables and sodden umbrellas to the rain-slicked road to the harbor, beyond it to the marina, and even beyond that, to the fog-shrouded headlands of the St. Lawrence. The fog at last was lifting.

False start. Now, only an hour later, I could hear again the dirgeful *aaaiiiiyouuuuuuu* of the horn at the lighthouse on the green waters of the St. Lawrence and the fainter, counterpoint *waaaaa* of another, somewhere.

During the first two days of pea soup, I'd walked the hills of the little Quebec village with umbrella in hand, nursed coffee at the marina café, stared out the café's tall windows at the fog-socked fleet of pleasure cruisers. The passing hours were scored by the murmur of Quebecois French and the interplay of the horns. By the third day of fog, the wet village had lost any charm for me. In fact, it had become gloomy, and so had the unrelenting horns.

I was in Tadoussac to visit Pierre Béland, a biologist who studies the beluga whale, and to see what could be seen of the remnant population of St. Lawrence River belugas, a few hundred creatures that have come to be called the most polluted mammals on Earth. Their range is less than one hundred miles long, but the St. Lawrence is about twenty miles wide here; with its tides and moderately saline water, it is more properly an immense estuary than a river. I quickly understood why studying this population of whales could be such slow work. In winter the weather is often brutal, the estuary rimmed with ice. In summer, fog envelops the area for days at a time, and the small group of scientists working out of a ramshackle house above the harbor in Tadoussac can only wait it out.

Happily, we'd already seen belugas, and we would again. Béland had picked me up at the Quebec City airport in his aged Volvo, with his daughters—Martine, eleven, and Eliane, five—in the back seat. We had wound our way for three hours through the hills and mountains on the St. Lawrence's lightly populated northern shore until we came to the mouth of the Saguenay River, where the

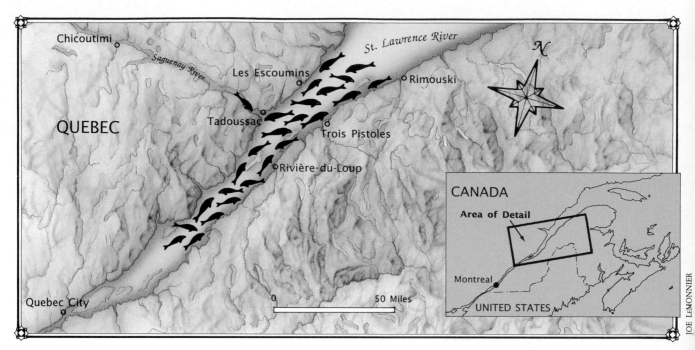

Beluga whales gather in the St. Lawrence River near Tadoussac because of an upwelling of nutrient-rich water.

highway ends and a car ferry begins. Across the mouth lay Tadoussac, bathed in the amber sunlight of a summer evening.

It was Martine, mindful of her father's promise of a present for sighting the first whale, who shouted, *"Papa, baleines!"* To me she declared, gravely and precisely in English, "There are whales out there." Sure enough, as we pulled over to wait for the ferry, a half-dozen whales were at the mouth of the Saguenay no more than a few hundred feet before us. Two were slate-gray, the others Ivory-soap white, their backs arcing briefly in and out of the water.

And, on the afternoon of that miserable day I awakened to the horns, the fog eventually dissipated enough that we set off with a crowd of tourists for the St. Lawrence, in the hotel's whale-watching ship, the restored schooner *Marie Clarisse.* It isn't the preferred method of surveying belugas, but the fog was still too thick for the little rubber-pontooned Zodiak, or indeed for anything without instruments. Béland had carefully lowered my expectations. We would doubtless see whales, he said, but probably not belugas.

He was wrong. Perhaps twenty minutes out, Martine, again, shouted "Belugas, papa!" and bobbing through the mist were two small groups of the white whales, perhaps six animals in all, thrusting their heads out of the water like men swimming the breast stroke. Unlike other whales, belugas can turn their heads. And these were doing just that—swimming closer, stopping to observe us, porpoising closer and pausing again before diving out of sight a few dozen feet from the ship.

Béland speculated that the belugas had approached us out of sheer curiosity: Their superb echolocating sonar had reported a wood-hulled boat in the steel-filled St. Lawrence. "We think that's why they'll come so close to our Zodiak, because of the rubber," he said. On occasion, a beluga has eased its head over one of the Zodiak's pontoons to regard the scientists aboard.

We spent the day after our schooner trip on the Zodiak, searching in vain for more belugas. But in the evening, as we ferried across the St. Lawrence from Les Escoumins to Trois Pistoles, we crossed paths, spectacularly, with about one-third of the St. Lawrence beluga population, more than a hundred whales. They bobbed and dived for miles around us like sheep scattered at deep-blue pasture.

It is no accident that the whales teem in the waters around Tadoussac. Through a sort of geological twist of fate, the St. Lawrence across from the village is a prime environment for sea creatures. A nautical chart shows why. Upstream, the St. Lawrence is about eighty feet deep. But roughly across from Tadoussac the floor falls abruptly to about a thousand feet, forming a trough that runs into the Gulf of St. Lawrence. The plunge of sea, in combination with the tide's ebb and flow and varying water temperatures, creates powerful upwellings of cold, salty, silty, nutrient-rich water. At the same time, the Saguenay pours the fresh, icy flows of northern Quebec into the estuary at a rate of 50,000 gallons per second. With all this water action, the St. Lawrence just off the river mouth is a swirl of rips, standing waves, and whirlpools.

For marine mammals, it is paradise. The nutrients also feed a rich community of small organisms, from phytoplankton to krill to fish. The invertebrates and small fish feed the water-filtering minkes, finbacks, and an occasional blue whale; the larger fish feed thousands of harp seals during the spring birthing season—and the belugas.

Belugas are among the smallest whales. Gray as youngsters and pure white as adults, they are downright puny beside their distant cousins the blue whales, which sometimes appear this far up the St. Lawrence in summer. A blue whale can grow to 100 feet and weigh 140 tons. A full-grown beluga is about fifteen feet long from its domed head to the end of its flukes, and it weighs a mere ton-and-a-half. Belugas are also dwarfed by the finbacks, which were exhaling in great whoofs beside the *Marie Clarisse* that foggy day. Despite their recent popularity in zoos and aquariums, belugas have been surprisingly little studied in the wild, probably in part because much of their habitat lies in Arctic waters open for only about two months each year.

According to researcher Robert Michaud, who often works with Béland, the St. Lawrence is the best place to study beluga behavior in the wild, because it is possible to observe the whales most of the year. Michaud and others have in the past few years identified and attached names or numbers to about sixty whales. That's no easy task with an all-white or all-gray creature, but Michaud's research teams pick out visual cues: One whale has a slightly twisted spine and is thus named Scolio (as in the spinal deformity

scoliosis); another, whose back bears a propeller mark that looks like a napkin draped over an arm, is Walter the Waiter.

Moreover, the researchers have observed a beluga birth. A tight-packed ring of, apparently, adult females carefully excluded two gray juveniles that swam nearby; then a female suddenly surfaced with a wrinkled baby beluga on its back. The newborn slipped off repeatedly, only to be brought back to the surface by one of the adults.

Worldwide, belugas are less endangered than other cetaceans. Populations in Hudson Bay and off Alaska run into the tens of thousands. But the St. Lawrence belugas have not been biologically connected with their relatives in the Far North since before the last glaciation, and their story is disturbingly different.

Once the St. Lawrence belugas numbered as many as 5,000. Early this century they could be seen upstream, in increasingly fresh water, as far as Quebec City. Then they were hunted nearly out of existence for their oil, hide, and meat. Fishermen also thought of belugas—which have teeth and eat fish—as enemies. They shot them with rifles and, in the 1930s, even bombed them from airplanes in a government whale-control program. Today Béland and his colleagues can identify one older beluga by the wound in its back.

Whaling for belugas dropped off sharply in the 1960s. Some locals still shot at belugas out of concern for fish or simply to pass the time, but the hunting pressure was light. In 1979, thanks largely to the vigorous efforts of scientist Leone Pippard, the St. Lawrence be-

Children from a St. Lawrence village gather near carcasses of belugas killed by local whalers in the late 1930s.

lugas were fully protected. Yet the population didn't rebound. The relatively few conservationists concerned about the white whales of the St. Lawrence long suspected that the creatures were in some sort of undefined trouble. Béland has been helping to define it.

Pierre Béland didn't set out to study belugas. Trained as a population biologist, he did his PhD research on the population dynamics of the winkle, a type of snail, and his post-doctoral work on "several not-very-important things" in New Caledonia and Australia. Through much of the 1970s he worked as a sort of paleontologist–ecologist, reconstructing the ecosystems of the dinosaurs for Canada's National Museum of Natural Sciences in Ottawa. "I started as an ecologist with the dinosaurs," he says, "assuming that if the rules of ecology apply now they must have applied then."

That led to a lengthy project involving Devonian fishes, which led, in turn, to a position as a research ecologist with the Canadian Department of Fisheries and Oceans. In 1982 Béland was asked to set up and direct a new St. Lawrence fisheries ecology lab at a branch of the University of Quebec in the town of Rimouski.

Studying fish was Béland's charter. Studying whales was not. And that's precisely what he told Daniel Martineau, a government veterinarian who sought out Béland shortly after he opened shop in Rimouski. Martineau said he had seen the white whales often while sailing in the St. Lawrence and yearned to know more about them, perhaps why so few remained. There was no funding, and hence no authorization, for whale studies, Béland said.

But Béland knew about the whales too. As a boy, he'd spent summers with his family along the shore at Rivière-du-Loup. "When I was a kid, we saw belugas all the time," he said. "And it was obvious that there weren't as many anymore. Like Daniel Martineau, I began to wonder why."

In September 1982 Béland and Martineau attended a lecture on the beluga by another government scientist, David Sergeant. At the end of the talk, Béland's secretary handed him a note. Someone had called the lab to report a dead beluga washed ashore a few miles from Rimouski. Béland rounded up Martineau and Sergeant, and they drove to the whale.

"Daniel Martineau had brought his little veterinarian kit. We looked at the whale for a while, and then he said, 'Well, let's open it up and see what it died of.' And he started cutting into it. None of us had ever done that. Daniel's first impression was that there must be something wrong with the heart—in proportion to the body it was far larger than any mammalian heart he'd seen." (They later learned that the beluga's heart is naturally immense, allowing it to survive pressure at great depths.)

The most critical decision the men made that day was to take samples of the whale's

ROBERT MICHAUD

blubber and send them off for laboratory analysis. That study turned up high concentrations of organochlorines, including PCBs, DDT, and Mirex, all so toxic that they had been banned in both the United States and Canada. Disturbed but fascinated, Béland and Martineau distributed posters all along the St. Lawrence shore, asking anyone who found a dead beluga to call the lab. In a single year the two men found fourteen dead belugas. Samples of blubber continued to show high levels of contaminants.

Perhaps it should not have come as a surprise. If some evil power had set out to design an environment and a creature perfect for toxification, it couldn't have done much better than the St. Lawrence and the beluga. Consider the following.

Item: Whales share with the rest of mammals various physiological traits, from the organization of bones to the structure and function of organs and nervous systems. Nevertheless, the beluga's chubby form is defined by an abundance of one class of body chemicals, the lipids—the creature is about 35 percent fat by weight. This blubber protects it from the chill of the northern depths and makes it buoyant.

Item: A phenomenally diverse catalog of man-made chemicals has entered the biosphere since the middle of this century. Uncounted tons of such compounds have poured into the streams and rivers of the Great Lakes watershed, into the lakes themselves, and into the St. Lawrence. New studies show that many exotic toxicants can travel thousands of miles with the winds, even volatilizing out of landfills.

Item: Although these man-made toxicants are usually not easily soluble in water, they are lipophilic—that is, they dissolve superbly in fat and will anchor themselves in the fatty tissues of animals. They also tend to concentrate as they move up food chains from simple invertebrates to longer-lived predators. A herring gull can carry in its fatty tissue more than 25 million times the concentration of toxicants found in waters where it catches fish.

Item: Belugas, tubs of lipids, are hungry, extremely long-lived, and the top predators in their environment; hence they are superb accumulators and magnifiers of toxic compounds. In short, St. Lawrence belugas are veritable barrels of hazardous waste.

By the summer of 1988, Béland, Martineau, and a growing group of colleagues had found some seventy-five dead belugas on the St. Lawrence shores. About thirty of those were in fresh enough condition to truck away and necropsy. The team discovered three patterns of disease. Four of the animals were deemed to have died of perforated gastric ulcers, a number that seems extraordinary for an ailment infrequently observed in marine mammals. A few others died of diseases, such as bladder cancer, never seen before in marine mammals. And a third group died of an assault by many illnesses: hepatitis, tumors, pneumonia, skin diseases,

and the blood poisoning septicemia, which suggests suppression of the immune system. One whale was apparently killed by nocardia, a bacterium found only in animals with suppressed immune systems.

The discovery of the bladder cancer, in 1984, gave rise to concerns that pollution from a huge Alcan aluminum plant in Chicoutimi (about ninety miles up the Saguenay) might be responsible for beluga deaths. A Canadian researcher had reported very high rates of bladder cancer in plant workers and had suggested that there were links between those illnesses and the plant's high emissions of benzo-a-pyrene (BAP), a proven human carcinogen. Sediment samples from the bottom of the Saguenay showed that tons of BAP had found its way into the river, either directly or from atmospheric fallout.

Unlike lipophilic organochlorines, BAP breaks down in animal tissues and becomes nearly untraceable. Luckily Béland hooked up with Lee Shugart, a scientist with the Oak Ridge National Laboratory in Tennessee and a specialist in tracing the metabolized altered forms of BAP in living tissues. Sure enough, Shugart found these altered forms of BAP in beluga brain tissue. They were not present, however, in belugas in the Arctic Ocean.

Béland points out that there is no clinical confirmation that the toxicants in the St. Lawrence are responsible for the deaths of all, most, or even any of the belugas. It is, to a large degree, another cigarettes-and-cancer issue, in which linking molecules of contaminants to specific damage—in this case in a huge, wild mammal—is nearly impossible. "But if you look at the literature," Béland notes, "if you look at mice or minks or pigs that have been fed PCBs and other organochlorine contaminants, they develop ulcerations, their immune system goes down, and they have reproductive problems. The levels of contaminants in the belugas are higher than in any of those animals."

Among the most striking findings have been, first, that males are more contaminated than females and, second, that even the very young can be greatly contaminated. The highest level of the banned pesticide Mirex was found in a whale just at the end of its nursing age. Béland's hypothesis is that a nursing beluga will transfer toxicants from her body fats to her extremely fat-charged milk, reducing her own toxic load while injecting her young with poisons.

Using his background as a population biologist, Béland has devised a scheme for assessing the status of the beluga population through elaborate mathematics involving the ratio of immature whales to adults. His analysis showed that the population is in slow decline.

"By 1987," Béland says, "I felt we had enough evidence to say this population is going down the drain, and there's good evidence that it's from contamination. I also felt that I had to say the government is not doing its job properly. If you work for the government, you're not allowed to say that. So I left the government." Béland is now the scientific director of the nonprofit research operation he and Martineau set up, the St. Lawrence National Institute of Ecotoxicology. Their first large contract came almost immediately, if ironically, from the Department of Fisheries and Oceans. After initial reluctance, Alcan—in cooperation with the World Wildlife Fund, Canada—agreed to help fund some of the institute's studies.

We saw no more belugas from the big schooner that fogbound day, although we glimpsed perhaps a dozen finbacks. The next day, from the Zodiak and still in moderate fog, we heard a whale blow in the distance, then closer. Béland, at the outboard, said, "That's a minke. And he's coming right toward us." In a few minutes the whale appeared dead ahead, dove, rose up again even closer, powered straight at us, then finally sounded into deep water, passing unseen beneath us. We hunted for miles up the fiercely cold and windy Saguenay, where the belugas will often make forays, but we saw not a sign of them.

As a species the beluga is not, by all appearances, another rhinoceros, on the brink of worldwide extinction. Although the white whale is listed as endangered by the Convention on International Trade in Endangered Species, the primary treaty controlling trafficking in vanishing creatures, it seems to be holding on strongly in Hudson Bay and other parts of its range. Still, the beluga has long been a biological hallmark of the St. Lawrence, the artery of Quebec, and its loss to the river would be a natural and cultural disaster of the first order.

There's something more. Recent studies in the Great Lakes Basin have consistently turned up evidence of damage ranging from cancer to genetic mutation to infertility in a wide variety of wildlife species, from terns to otters. For the St. Lawrence, and indeed for the entire Great Lakes system, the lipid-rich and hence toxic-assaulted beluga, once called the "canary of the sea," may also be the canary in the mine.

GAME LAWS WEREN'T WRIT FOR FAT CATS

TEXT BY TED WILLIAMS

The National Fish and Wildlife Foundation has it right when it reports that America "is the undisputed world leader in wildlife law enforcement." In this business, at least, the U.S. Fish and Wildlife Service doesn't mess around. Each year it cites something like 10,000 suspected poachers, of which about 9,400 are convicted. Agents have to be tough because no police work is as dangerous. And they have to be smart because the courts perceive wildlife crime in the context of, say, jaywalking. From all the big sting operations in the news these days, it is clear that the federal game cops are getting better all the time. No cheating hunter in this great land is beyond their reach—unless he is rich and powerful.

Consider first the marshes on the Eastern Shore of Maryland, which seem to draw more big shots from Washington, D.C., than ducks from the Atlantic Flyway. Duck-baiting is just as much a tradition here as it is in southern California, except that the state fish and game people don't pretend that it is salubrious. It is, in fact, prohibited by state and federal law. Still, lots of the nation's important business gets transacted in Maryland duck blinds. Bust the wrong hunter, went the old joke, and you get transferred to Okefenokee.

They understood that at Blackwater National Wildlife Refuge in Dorchester County until 1984, when Don Perkuchin took over as manager. He was appalled at what he saw going on around the refuge. Wealthy baiters had the place surrounded. They were sucking out birds, frequently onto "regulated shooting areas" where fat, pen-raised mallards acted as live decoys. With waterfowl populations crashing on a continental scale, Perkuchin went after violators in a big way, catching about thirty within a mile of the refuge his first season.

Then on January 8, 1985, Perkuchin made his first major mistake. He caught one J. D. Williams shooting over bait. According to a local who knows the scene of the crime, no self-respecting duck would go there for any purpose other than to swill grain dumped by humans. The place has the ambiance of a landfill, with old tires piled all about, and there isn't much water. As habitat, said the local, it compares unfavorably "with the worst feeding club you saw in California." J. D. Williams is one of the most influential lobbyists in Washington as well as a leading fund-raiser for the Democratic Party. It is difficult to find a waterfowler on the Hill who hasn't shot with him, and he has pals and connections everywhere in government. J. D. didn't like getting busted.

During his second year on the job, Perkuchin made another big blunder by nabbing C. Porter Hopkins. Hopkins is a traditionalist when it comes to gunning ducks on the Eastern Shore. This time he was shooting over bait. Hopkins also is big in Maryland politics, having served in the state legislature and run for the U.S. House of Representatives. He didn't like getting busted either.

Now the baiters rafted on the Hill, demanding that Blackwater staff be restrained from enforcing the law outside the refuge and that the job be left to the special agents who, with their superior training, would better be able to interpret the oh-so-complicated hunting regulations. It translated to this: "We've got one full-time enforcement agent for all of Dorchester County, and with the refuge staff off our backs, the likelihood that he is going to impede our illicit activities is zippo. What we want is a free fire zone."

Finally, in 1987, two Blackwater officers caught Stan Parris, the U.S. congressman from Virginia, shooting over bait. After writing the ticket, they called their regional headquarters in Boston. To their astonishment, the Boston office already knew about the citation. Two weeks later, Perkuchin and his staff were told to stay inside the refuge because there were certain high-powered politicos who weren't to be written up. So big-shot baiting continues on all flanks. However, it is perfectly okay for refuge personnel to help raid some distant, less sensitive shore—such as Tangier Island in the middle of Chesapeake Bay, where slob watermen are forever getting out of hand.

In 1988 Fish and Wildlife regional director

43

Howard Larsen and his deputy, Bill Ashe, were told to move Perkuchin out of Blackwater. When they replied that they liked him just fine where he was and would need written orders to make the transfer, they were reassigned. Now Larsen is counting flounders in Florida, and Ashe looks after Chesapeake Bay from Newton Corner, Massachusetts.

Perkuchin wouldn't talk to me, even off the record. But he was such a hit in Maryland, at least among honest sportsmen, that I had no trouble finding plenty of loquacious sources. Somewhere I had acquired his new telephone number, and when I rang him up a sweet voice answered. "Okefenokee," she said, sounding for all the world like Ma'm'selle Hepzibah. It really had happened! They'd disappeared him to Pogoland.

When Nathaniel P. Reed took over as Assistant Secretary for Fish, Wildlife, and Parks in 1971, Interior Secretary Rogers Morton, a resident of the Eastern Shore, told him he'd be getting lots of phone calls on Monday mornings from big-bore Maryland duck hunters who'd been arrested over the weekend. How did he intend to handle this? The answer, much to Morton's liking, became policy. Reed refused all the calls until Tuesday, at which point he would listen politely and say: "My, how interesting! Hire a good lawyer, and do let me know how you come out."

In the summer of 1988 a little bird told Reed that the Fish and Wildlife Service had warned Senator Phil Gramm of Texas that its own agents had his Eastern Shore farm under surveillance. The agents hadn't been hunting senators (or so they say). It was just that there was so much grain scattered about that they actually could see it from their airplanes as they flew hither and yon. Gramm was not seen breaking any law and, in fact, the agents say he wasn't even on his own property when, armed and in hunting attire, he approached his adjacent neighbor's bait and then retreated when he caught on to the stake-out.

"What's going on, Frank?" inquired Reed of Frank Dunkle, then FWS director. His answer, Reed told me, was that "evil people" in high places were making him do these awful things and that he'd warned Gramm because he was a "very useful senator." Now that all this is out, so is Dunkle as director. But Dunkle wasn't the disease, just a symptom.

The fact is that as Interior officials go, Reed and Morton were aberrant. G. Ray Arnett and James Watt, who occupied the same positions under Ronald Reagan, more closely fit the mold. Arnett allows that he'd

have tipped off Gramm, too. "Having wardens sitting around watching a pond with some corn in it because maybe they can catch a senator is misuse of resources," he declares.

In 1987, Arnett and his high-rolling hunting cronies were sitting around their duck club in California chewing the fat when suddenly it came to them that there was no group dedicated to defending hunters from all the ills that they are heir to—such as game wardens. Robert Petersen, who publishes hunting and gunning magazines, threw in the seed money. And recently the International Shooting and Hunting Alliance (ISHA) had four hundred members and an annual budget of over $900,000. It aims to preserve big shots, who it says are discriminated against, from "overzealous enforcement of game and gun laws." And toward this end it is calling for congressional oversight hearings on Division of Law Enforcement excesses. Further, it wants to require agents to get permission from the Interior Department Solicitor before serving search warrants, a process that would take about thirty days and effectively cripple any investigation.

ISHA's loudest mouthpiece is Don Causey, publisher of *The Hunting Report,* a newsletter that circulates to 35,000 subscribers, including me. Now that I have my first issue with Bill Clark's opinion that his $43,000 trip to the Soviet Union for Marco Polo sheep was "too expensive," I definitely shan't go. But there is still the $18,000 safari to shoot white-lipped deer on the Tibetan Plateau and the four-continent "Round-The-World Hunting Trip" at $30,000.

Basically, Causey thinks the suggestion that he is fawning for the fat cats is "a damned dirty disgrace," and he says he doesn't trust me to file a balanced report. "If *Audubon* paints me this way," he cried, "I have some of the wealthiest people and trial lawyers in the world on my subscriber roll. They support me one thousand percent. I will use the last nickel I have and pull every string I can to sue *Audubon.* I'm not kidding you. I can raise $200,000 in a week!"

The October 1988 issue of *Petersen's Hunting* magazine ran a piece entitled "Federal Wardens—Conservationists or Out-of-Control Cops?" Clearly they are the latter, explains author Don Causey. For example, this hapless big-shot real estate developer from Nevada named Sam Jaksick buys a special permit to kill a bighorn sheep in Oregon. Being short on both bighorns and cash, Oregon charges him $56,000. Enter the feds "with their bust-a-big-shot policy." Seeking only publicity for themselves, they set out

to "entrap, then harass and finally arrest" Jaksick on trumped-up charges of game harassment, etc., which, naturally, don't stick.

A 94 percent conviction rate means that 6 percent of all defendants beat the rap. Jaksick was among them. He was found not guilty, as the saying goes. But Causey left out some interesting details. To wit: The Fish and Wildlife Service had slipped an undercover man onboard Jaksick's helicopter to videotape the high-speed pursuit of bighorns. Anyone who views this tape is appalled. The panicked sheep are running their guts out in 100-degree heat over steep terrain. Their tongues are protruding, and you can see the helicopter's shadow and propwash on the ground. The case hinged on the tape, but the judge suppressed it because it was taken with a telephoto lens and, therefore, might be inflammatory. Not wanting a bighorn sacrificed, the U.S. Attorney opted instead to sacrifice physical evidence. He told FWS to move in when Jaksick appeared ready to kill a ram illegally. "Hey, sometimes you lose," says an agent who worked the case.

The story, however, does not end here. Nevada Congresswoman Barbara Vucanovich employs, as a legislative aide, the wife of Steve Robinson—the Fish and Wildlife Service's politically appointed deputy director. After Jaksick complained to Vucanovich, the FWS brass called in the Inspector General to investigate Dick Lichtenberg, the officer in charge of the Jaksick case. Lichtenberg, who has been enforcing federal law for more than twenty years, is highly regarded by his fellow agents, and the unprecedented move dismayed and demoralized them. The day after the Inspector General's report came out (which, by the way, confirms all the good things ever said about Lichtenberg), Vucanovich's office went after it with a Freedom of Information Act request. No one else knew it was available.

You can always tell the extra-important articles in Robert Petersen's *Guns & Ammo* magazine because the titles carry more than just one exclamation point. For instance: "New Sportsmen's Group in All-Out Battle for Shooting/Hunting Rights!!!" In this, shotgun editor Charles Riedy explains that without ISHA (which you may join as a charter member for $10,000) Americans are going to have constraints on "individual rights that would make even the Russians blush red." Of all his shocking disclosures, the most hideous is the case of the nameless duck hunter who was approached by a nameless warden in "northern California." The warden found shells loaded with lead shot twenty yards from the blind. They were of a different gauge and make than the steel loads in the hunter's gun and had been left there by someone else. But the warden said: "Well, these shells probably are not yours, but I'm going to write you up anyway just to see if it sticks."

I had no idea things had gotten this bad and wanted to dig into the story further. So I phoned Riedy. "Who was the arresting officer?" I asked. Riedy said he didn't know. "Yeah," I said, "but you talked to him, right?" Well, no; he hadn't actually talked to him. . . .

At this point I wanted to ask Robert Petersen if this kind of journalism was about typical for his publications and if he himself had had any run-ins with game cops that might have put him into his current snit. He wouldn't talk to me or return my calls, so I contacted the Fish and Wildlife Service. Petersen, I was told, had a record:

Nine years ago, on Alaska's Seward Peninsula, Petersen had killed a grizzly without waiting the required day after disembarking from a plane. Petersen, a guide, and the outfitter had tracked the bear from the air and landed ahead of it. Petersen and the guide got out, and the outfitter took off and illegally buzzed the animal, herding it toward his client.

That didn't work, so Petersen and the guide hopped back in the plane and got dropped off at another position. Again the outfitter, illegally directed by radio from the ground, herded the bear toward Petersen. When the bear came into range Petersen filled it with all six shots from his .44 magnum revolver. This didn't kill it. Nor did a shot fired by the guide, which only rolled the bruin down a hill and into a ditch. So Petersen delivered the coup de grâce with his .375 rifle. "And that," says Al Crane, the Fish and Wildlife agent in charge of the case, "is about as far into wildlife crime as you can get." Petersen was fined $1,000, but he didn't accompany the outfitter to prison. He cooperated with the government.

Then on October 25, 1986, while duck hunting near Stockton, California, Petersen was cited for wanton waste—that is, blasting birds out of the sky and leaving them where they fall. Given the choice of paying a modest fine or coughing up $2,000 for Ducks Unlimited and getting the charges dropped, Petersen chose the latter.

Ray Arnett had an unpleasant experience, also. He was caught trying to shoot rails in Virginia from a motorboat under power. He says he's heard the FWS was after him as a trophy to hang on its wall. But agent Don Patterson, who wrote the ticket, professes to have been flabbergasted to find Arnett in the boat. "We go looking chiefly based on a complaint [in this case from a Fish and Wildlife Service airplane 2,500 feet above the marsh]. We wrote probably eighteen people that day, and Arnett just happened to be one of them."

A lot of the problem, according to Don Causey, is that anti-hunters have infiltrated the Division of Law Enforcement. In *The Hunting Report* Causey writes that he "is seeking confidential input from U.S. Fish and Wildlife enforcement agents that will help us document the rise of anti-hunting sentiment among enforcement personnel."

But the agents aren't coming forward, so he's having to document it himself. "This agent (a woman) was quoted as calling duck hunting a 'dastardly deed,'" he reveals in a recent issue.

"Did you say duck hunting is a dastardly deed?" I asked the agent, whose name is Marcia Cronan.

"No," she said, "I support it. It's a legitimate, frequently necessary management tool."

"Well, then, were you quoted as calling it dastardly?" I demanded.

"No," she said. In 1976, when she worked for the National Park Service police, she'd been borrowed by the Fish and Wildlife Service for its first big undercover operation. Being a woman and a good watercolorist, she had a marvelous cover. The experienced outlaws on Tangier Island suspected every stranger in pants and were extremely camera-shy. So Cronan just sat in the lovely marshes and painted "the hunters doing their dastardly deeds." Which is exactly what she told *The New York Times* and exactly what it reported.

My study of ISHA's noise and gas left me wondering if the organization really is a threat to anything save the already shaky credibility of the hook-and-bullet press. Do functionally intelligent hunters really believe this stuff? "Russians blushing red," and so forth? Do they even read it? Should conservationists and law enforcement people worry or laugh? I decided to poll other hunting organizations.

"Is ISHA legitimate?" I inquired of Warren Parker, first vice-president of Safari Club International.

"Yes," he said, then started telling me about this "horribly harassed" sheep hunter named Jaksick.

Next I put the question to Jim Glass, president of the Wildlife Legislative Fund of America. ISHA is fine, he told me, and his organization is going to join it in the good

fight because "systematic abuse of the law by enforcement agencies is as damaging to the conservation of wildlife as no enforcement at all."

One might suppose that ISHA would approve of the Fish and Wildlife Service taking time from big-shot busting to bust instead 108 non-personae in Colorado's impoverished San Luis Valley and beyond. But no. "They went in there with helicopters and flak suits," Arnett told me. "It looked like a SWAT team maneuver. These people are citizens of the United States. They aren't drug dealers." Causey calls the operation "classic entrapment."

Locals and the media agree. From the newspaper and TV coverage, it certainly appears that the government was duplicitous and heavy-handed. It landed on March 6, 1989, with 275 agents (albeit in an area stretching from Denver to Phoenix to Albuquerque). And for two-and-a-half years before that its undercover man had played serpent to the locals' Adam and Eve, posing as a taxidermist and meat processor. "He just forced us to do it," lamented convicted eagle seller Jose F. Carson, who on an entirely different matter (firewood) reportedly has threatened to kill the sheriff.

"Maybe if we had ten violent criminal offenders escape from prison, that kind of an operation might have been justified," complained State Senate Minority Leader Larry Trujillo, who in 1967 had been fined for illegal possession of deer after a spotlight beam and muzzle flash were seen emanating from the car he was in at about two o'clock on a November morning.

"Do we really want to be this heavy-handed over wildlife?" inquired State Senator Robert Pastore of Monte Vista.

"Times are hard here. Hunting year-round is a way to put animal protein on your table to feed your family," remarked San Luis pastor Patrick Valdez.

"I feel it was racially motivated," opined the mayor.

"I could have taken six men out there and done the whole thing without traumatizing every woman and child in the county," observed the sheriff.

"I did not know there was going to be this kind of force concentrated in one place," exclaimed Colorado Governor Roy Romer, who appointed a commission to investigate the raid.

The *Denver Post*'s Tomas Romero accused the Fish and Wildlife Service of "taking fathers from wives' and children's arms."

All this, then, is basically what the public knows about the San Luis raid. The real story, of this raid, however, is less heartrending.

The U.S. Attorney had ordered the Fish and Wildlife Service to keep a lid on the investigation, so the media had to be spoon-fed at a post-roundup news conference. It made them feel nonessential, and they threw a temper tantrum.

Nowhere in America is there enough wildlife to serve as extra, year-round welfare when "times are hard." But it wasn't being used for this in the San Luis Valley. Arnett's pronouncement notwithstanding, many of the suspects were believed to be drug dealers. The valley has long been a den of organized drug activity, and much of the money garnered from the illegal taking of wildlife, including at least twenty-five eagles, was used to sustain habits rather than families. Other proceeds went to purchase weapons.

As for the wildlife market supposedly created by the undercover agent, it was dwarfed by existing traffic. Although he bought 14 tons of elk, 2.5 tons of deer, 0.5 tons of bear and antelope, he turned away more than 80 percent of the animals offered.

The Fish and Wildlife Service pulled off the raid without a single bruise to any suspect, bystander, or agent. Perhaps it was "heavy-handed," but you don't clean up places like the San Luis Valley with a carload of metermaids. For example, it is common practice for the citizenry to issue death threats to game wardens, shoot at them, vandalize their cars, and poison their dogs.

Among the people under surveillance were numerous felons, some violent. The sheriff's house gets shot up fairly regularly, and in 1987 it was firebombed off the map. Last year a sheriff's car was torched in front of the jail. According to the town fathers of San Luis, the rumors among non-Hispanics that it is dangerous for them to enter the valley will have to be dispelled "before the tourist trade can grow dramatically."

With shots flying around the sheriff's house once again, the Fish and Wildlife Service thought it prudent to issue him a flak jacket. And the sheriff thought it prudent to publicly distance himself from the operation, condemning it and announcing that he didn't even know it was going down.

The reason he didn't know, at least according to the government, is that it was concerned for his safety. But there might be another explanation that doesn't get talked about: The sheriff's deputy—whose "addiction to poaching," to use his own words, included jacking deer out of his cruiser with his girlfriend holding the spotlight—has been cited for twenty-nine game violations and indicted by a federal grand jury on seven counts of wildlife felony. And the mayor's son has been charged for the alleged sale of elk meat. Further—although family trees in the area are shrouded in mist—deputy, mayor, son, and sheriff all are named Espinoza.

The Fish and Wildlife Service agent who must bear ultimate responsibility for disrupting commerce in the San Luis Valley is Terry Grosz of the Denver office. What made him tick, I wondered? He probably gets paid less for doing this sort of thing than the average reader of *The Hunting Report* spends on wine. Was he in it for publicity? Was he insane with power? Did he have a vendetta against the very rich and the very poor? Did he require restraining?

Grosz claims that all he wants to do is protect wildlife. "We really don't have a lot of time left," he told me in his throaty cowboy voice. "Even at best I think we're sliding backwards. I guess what bothers me most is when I sit on a quiet rim somewhere in Montana or on a saddle of a horse or in a marsh early in the morning or late in the evening and realize the changes that have taken place just since I was a kid. What we're trying to do, however successful we are, is not enough. And it never will be enough until the American people jump in and support us so it's not a fight all the time to save things for them and their children."

Maybe he's lying, but I think not.

II
BIRDS OF MANY FEATHERS

MAKING SENSE OF SEXUAL NONSENSE

TEXT BY J. P. MYERS · PAINTINGS BY LARS JONSSON

Sandpipers come to the tundra north of tree-line in early June each year. They come from estuaries south. Some have traveled from nearby wintering areas, perhaps a thousand miles away. Others have been far more am-bitious in their journeys. Sandpipers are among the world's greatest migrants.

Spring sweeps them northward, north from the pampas of Argentina, the desert coast of Chile, the palm swamps of Paraguay,

the muddy basins in Venezuela and Suriname. They come by the millions, pausing en route at staging sites along U.S. coastlines, and from there pouring out over the tundra's expanse.

They come to reproduce. Breeding begins in earnest almost on arrival, for the tundra's brief summer season places a high penalty on procrastination. Roughly three, at most four, weeks stand between arrival and the period of peak surface-insect abundance, the ideal time for sandpiper chicks in search of calories. Incubation alone represents an irreducible two-and-a-half to three-and-a-half weeks, so time for finding a mate, building a nest, and laying the clutch must be compressed into a week.

Despite all this haste, style seems not to have suffered, for sandpipers have found more ways to organize their social lives than virtually any other group of birds. At one conservative extreme lie the monogamous mating habits of the dunlin, a large sandpiper that is dun-gray in winter but strikingly red-backed and black-bellied in spring. At the opposite extreme strut the outlandish and unrepentently promiscuous male buff-breasted sandpipers, pectoral sandpipers, and ruffs.

Most sandpipers are monogamous. Males defend the territory, build the nest, and help incubate. Females bear the energetic burden of making an egg and also alternate with males in incubation. Even monogamous species, however, show subtle and unexpected variations that affect each species' life-style and migrations. For example, in most species only one parent stays longer than a few days after hatching. The other, usually the female, quickly packs up and leaves the Arctic, heading south in the first leg of migration. Often that means she spends a scant four to five weeks on the tundra during her brief breeding effort.

There is more. In most species, by the time the offspring fly with complete competence, both parents have departed south. Young sandpipers of all species leave their nests within hours of hatching. They feed themselves by picking insects off the tundra's surface. Only during the first few days, and then just for warmth and protection from predators, are they completely dependent on an adult.

The challenge faced by young birds deepens during migration. Juveniles scarcely one month old must migrate south on their own, negotiating the distance, direction, and hazards without parental guidance. For some species that may demand only a gradual drift from estuary to bay and beach along well-marked coastlines. But for others—birds like semipalmated sandpipers that fly nonstop from the Bay of Fundy to Suriname, or lesser golden plovers traveling from the Aleutian Islands toward some minor mid-Pacific atoll —it is an astonishing feat, covering thousands of miles over open water.

Beyond monogamy, several sandpiper species show characteristics that ornithologists have begun to recognize only recently. Perhaps the Victorian ancestry of ornithology as a science prevented full recognition and acceptance of traits and behaviors so explicitly non-Victorian.

The first step in this direction is shown by sanderlings, those wind-up toys that run up and down in front of waves and are familiar

A male pectoral sandpiper skims low over the tundra with his pectoral sac throbbing, hooting two or three times a second as he passes over a female.

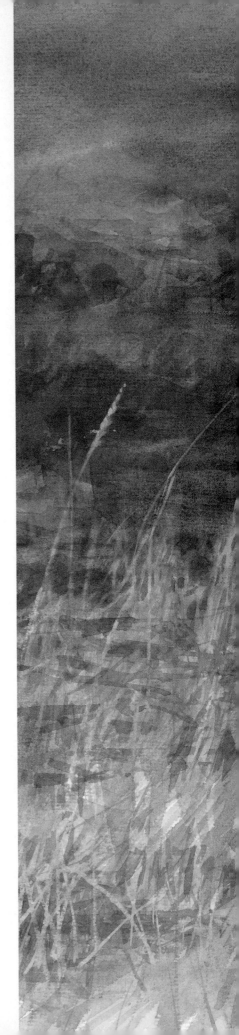

The male buff-breasted sandpiper is the flasher of the tundra.

to all beach-goers in late summer, fall, and winter. Sanderlings indulge in so-called "facultative sequential polyandry." At some times and places, for example in the Greenland Arctic, this species behaves as any good monogamous sandpiper should. Farther to the west, however, some of the females abandon their mates as soon as the last egg of a clutch is laid and go out searching for another male. To the scientist, this makes it polyandry, where one female mates with more than one male. It is sequential polyandry, because it doesn't happen all at once; the female finishes a nest with one mate before starting the next. And it is facultative because sometimes (and in some places) she does, and sometimes she doesn't.

Sanderlings occasionally employ one additional twist in their mating organization: Instead of abandoning her first male after completing the clutch, the female remains with him, but both then leave the clutch for several days, letting it sit exposed on the tundra while they mate again and produce another clutch. Each nest, incidentally, contains four eggs, no more. Once this second clutch is out, one of the pair remains to incubate it while the other returns to the first. Despite days of exposure, despite sitting in a nest cup lined with only a few strands of lichen and dead grass only inches above the permafrost, these eggs remain viable and eventually hatch four young sanderlings.

In white-rumped sandpipers the female limits her attention to but one male. The male, by contrast, is polygynous, spreading his parental role between several mates, all present on his territory simultaneously. Thus a male white-rump fathers the young of several females. For none of his mates, however, does he do more than defend the territory and build a nest. He plays no role at all in raising the brood. Indeed, by the time they hatch he usually has left the tundra, headed south toward wintering grounds in the marshes of Uruguay, Paraguay, and Argentina. The female stays on. She must do all the incubation and care for her young. But she too departs before the young have fledged.

Pectoral sandpipers carry the white-rump's life-style one step further. Both males and females in this species are promiscuous. The males defend very large territories, acres in size. Perched astride a tundra mound, imperiously surveying his domain for intruders, a male pectoral displays at virtually anything that resembles, even remotely, a female of his own species, no matter its true age or sex or species. This indiscriminate attitude is known in other animals as well, but only in

A male sanderling near its nest. A pair of sanderlings occasionally will leave their first clutch of four eggs for several days while they mate again and produce a second clutch. One bird remains to incubate the second clutch, while its mate returns to the first nest. The eggs are still viable despite being exposed to the elements in a cup of lichens and grass only inches above the permafrost.

elephant seals does it reach the proportions regularly recorded in journals of Arctic ornithologists. For another, smaller species of sandpiper to move innocently across the tundra past a pectoral male's mound is to risk hybrid progeny.

Though they nest within the territory of one male, female pectorals consort with several before the clutch is complete. In view of their treatment by males, this seems strange. At the peak of the breeding season, mid-June, any female pectoral taking flight is chased immediately—first by one male, the local territory holder, and then by all his neighbors. Together, this gaggle hounds the female for minutes on end. As she gathers height and flies farther, the first males peel away from the group to return to their own grounds. New ones replace each departing male as the group passes over other territories. If she lands, the males land on top of her, fighting among themselves and attempting to mount her. They stay down only a few moments, for she usually flies off again immediately. The pursuit continues until at last she eludes them. Surely monogamy has benefits, if only those of peace and quiet.

No one familiar with pectorals merely in migration could anticipate the behavior a male employs to attract his mates on the tundra's surface. Few displays in the bird world seem better evidence of the occasional capriciousness of natural selection. Picture the vision confronting a female pectoral feeding quietly beside a tundra pond once a local male begins his nuptial display in earnest:

From her viewpoint, the only obstructions above the horizon have been a few nearby stems of dull-brown sedge or grass left standing from the previous year, or perhaps a bit more distant, the top of a tundra mound. Even these scarcely limit her field of view, and it is still too early in the season for vegetative growth to begin, much less interfere. Such peace concerns the male not at all. He booms in from afar, skimming low over the tundra with wings pumping and pectoral sac throbbing, all the while hooting an unworldly *oooah-oooah-oooah* two to three times per second as he passes barely over her. The male's sac makes the display. Filled with fat, jutting out even as he stands alert, in display it inflates with air and bounces pendulously so far down it must challenge the aerodynamics of flight.

On North American Arctic tundra, the only shorebird more extreme in its mating system than the pectoral is the buff-breasted sandpiper. Each male displays from a small territory that is clumped beside the display sites of up to a dozen or so other males. The females visit this arena, or lek, in ones or twos, and somehow select among competing males. They travel from one male to another, then back again, inspecting the physical characteristics of each.

The male's finely marbled underwings are a focus of attention. The white flash of wing lining is what first brings in the females. Late at night, when the tundra sun is low but still above the horizon, the wing-up displays of several nearby males on their lek can be seen

These vignettes show how a male buff-breasted sandpiper lures females—as many as six at a time—by flashing his white wing linings. Having inspected the minute details of his underwing, the females may stay to mate—or simply walk away.

for miles, puffs of white against an ocher land still somber before the mid-June flush of new plant growth.

At times up to six females may gather around the display court of a single male, some in front, some behind, perhaps sharing notes about the quality of this primary covert or that arch of wing. The male makes almost no sound. Instead, as the females approach, he first hulks over, ruffling his back feathers and starting a quickened tread. Abruptly he rears back, thrusting his head up and wings out, keeping his bill parallel to the ground while marching in place. Only now does he vocalize, a subtle *tic-tic-tic* timed to match the slow footsteps taken in place. As a crowning gesture he draws his neck in and throws his bill back, gazing catatonically toward the Arctic sky. The females crowd forward, inspecting minute details of his underwing.

One of three things happens now. The first fulfills the male's desire: The females stay to mate. More often than not, however, they depart without so much as a by-your-leave, stealing away while he remains in full display. The third event is unexpected, at least for someone who has never watched a buff-breast lek. In truth it occurs quite frequently: A neighboring male bursts in upon the scene, mounts the resident displaying male, viciously pecks him on neck and head, attempts to copulate. This effectively breaks up the courtship, and he flies back to his own territory followed quickly by the first male's female visitors.

This pattern of display and interruption may continue for an hour or more on end. Females move from one male to another and back again, each time with their show disrupted by the intruding neighbor whose own role switches between disruptor and disruptee.

There is one variation on this parade. I once watched a male displaying to six females for over an hour. It was late at night, perhaps two o'clock in the morning, and despite the date—June 6th—the temperature hovered just below freezing. A second male had gained entry to the group of females, and each time the resident entered the final stages of display, the interloper upset the show by mounting him. Every time this happened the resident broke off the display and chased the intruder away. But once he chased the intruder off, the resident made a stereotypical, low flight around the periphery of his territory, some thirty meters in diameter; while he was away, the other male stole back. Calmly, it stood beside the display post and tucked its bill, only to wait for the onset of the next display. Why the resident didn't learn the ruse I'll never know. But one curious thing about this species is that in most other birds that display on leks, the males are far more brilliantly colored than the females. In the buff-breasted sandpiper, the sexes are virtually indistinguishable by plumage.

Just as with white-rumped sandpipers, buff-breasted and pectoral males play no part in incubation or rearing the brood. They do even less, for in neither species do males even help build the nest. Soon after the eggs are laid, they depart in migration toward the marshes and grasslands of southern South America. I doubt buff-breasted males even know where the females' nests are, for these may be several kilometers distant from a given lek. At least in the case of the pectoral, females usually build their nests within or near the male's territory.

Sandpipers such as these make the tundra tundra. Their song evokes Arctic wind and midnight sun and craneflies crawling over lichen ridge. Their social style provokes disbelief, wonder, and perhaps relief that pectoral males weigh but ninety grams. I certainly wouldn't venture out late at night if they weighed much more.

OREGON ROBINS

TEXT BY GLEN MARTIN • PAINTING BY LAWRENCE B. McQUEEN

When I first took note of them some years ago, my eye idly registered them as robins. I'd only glimpsed dusky shapes hurtling through the thickets of laurel and madrone, and even then they were usually at the corner of my eye.

It was only after I'd flushed one from the litter and humus directly in front of my feet in a thicket of black oaks that I saw the distinctive orange wing bars. It was shaped like a robin, and it flew like a robin. And indeed, like the robin, it was a thrush: a varied thrush, to be precise.

In my part of northern California, old-timers still refer to varied thrushes as Oregon robins. And to the casual observer the two species seem almost identical, at least in flight. It is only through leisurely examination of birds at rest that the differences are apparent to most of us. The varied thrush has a charcoal mask that surrounds orange stripes accenting the eyes, while the robin displays a simple cowl of gray. The robin has a rather lovely striped throat that the varied thrush lacks; the varied thrush sports chevrons of orange along its pinions that are missing in robins. Yet the different coloration almost seems like a kind of taxonomic *trompe l'oeil;* in silhouette or in flight, the birds look remarkably alike.

Robins and varied thrushes belong to different genera. Robins are classified as *Turdus,* and varied thrushes are in *Ixoreus.* Yet their immediate ancestor was a common one, and some of their traits and characteristics are shared in common as well: an acute appetite for madrone berries, for one.

November is a fat month for the wildlife sharing the mountain I live on. The oaks are heavy with acorns, there are still some grapes for the gleaning in the numerous hillside vineyards, and the moribund orchards of long-dead homesteaders are dropping their apples. The top branches of the madrones droop with clusters of rich, scarlet berries. Everything from band-tailed pigeons to cedar waxwings avail themselves of the fruit, but no birds are more avid in their admiration of madrone berries than varied thrushes and robins. Yet they express their lust for the fruit in different ways.

Robins usually go for madrone after they've stripped the vineyards of the last vestiges of leftover grapes. By mid-November they are present on the mountain in great cacophonous flocks. They swoop onto the madrone clusters en masse and gorge without restraint. There are always some robins on the mountain, but their numbers are augmented considerably in the fall by migrating individuals from the north. Varied thrushes are also migratory, their numbers gradually increasing until a walk through any stretch of woods will flush a goodly number. Never, though, do they congregate like the robins; at the most, I've seen five or six in loose association on the forest floor. When they feed on madrone berries, they evince far greater caution than do robins. Wont to feed in a solitary fashion, they insinuate themselves among the leaves and berry clusters. But though they are wary, they gorge just as rapaciously as the brazen robins; they simply look over their shoulders a lot more.

At one time there was some testy Linnaean squabbling among ornithologists on the subject of varied thrushes and robins; some felt they should both be classified in the same genus. But most are now satisfied with the way things stand. Along with obvious differences in markings and coloration, there are other subtler (yet significant) dissimilarities between the two birds. For one thing, they lead different lives. Some authorities have opined that varied thrushes and robins once shared the same range, since much of North America was forested with a thick, climax growth prior to its settlement by Europeans. As the forests were cleared, it was then assumed, robins moved into the meadows and farmlands and claimed them as their own, while varied thrushes stayed behind in the woods. But the varied thrush is so tenacious in clinging to the crepuscular world of the thicket and deep forest that the matter seems to go beyond mere predilection. What, after all, kept them from following the robins to the meadows, vineyards, and orchards, where fat larvae and ripe fruit were abundant?

Perhaps it was light. It's possible that varied thrushes possess more retinal cones (the photoreceptors that enhance vision in darkness) than robins. This could mean that their eyesight in dim environments is especially acute, giving them a distinct edge over other species when it comes to foraging in the forest understory. Or it could mean that they

57

find direct sunlight excessively dazzling; perhaps they stay in the brush not because they're particularly well suited to it, but because they are *not* suited to the wide-open, well-lit spaces. Research on the ocular structures of both varied thrushes and robins is scant, in any event, so all conclusions must remain theoretical. Yet if robins did make the leap from one preferred habitat to a dramatically different one, it was a trick the varied thrushes couldn't match. Varied thrushes are cousins to the robin, no more; *Ixoreus* they are, and *Ixoreus* they shall remain.

Varied thrush migrations appear to be cyclical, at least as to their numbers and in my part of northern California. Ornithologists at the California Academy of Sciences in San Francisco observe that the birds are in every woodland thicket in Golden Gate Park some years, and are quite rare in others. On my mountain, the winter population waxes and wanes with the madrone berry crop. This may reflect population distribution more than numerical population; the birds are apt to be dispersed to a greater degree in the absence of a centralized food source such as a grove of heavily laden madrones. It's a safe bet that a large crop of ripening madrone berries in August is a portent of a lot of varied thrushes in November; if the trees fail to set a good fruit load, I'll see fewer birds. Still, I'll always see *some* varied thrushes in the November woods, and their appearance will be sudden and dramatic. One day, the madrone thickets will be unpopulated save for Steller's jays, gray squirrels, and the occasional pileated woodpecker. The next day will find the dim light of the understory pierced by luminous bars of orange flashing from beating pinions. The air will resound with throaty, quavering cries, and I'll know that the varied thrushes have returned.

Not all birds that prefer the seclusion of the thicket exhibit the honed perceptions of varied thrushes. Brown towhees, for instance, seem so blithely oblivious of their surroundings that a rancher I know has tagged them

with the sobriquet "cat food." But the thrushes—most of them anyway—rate pretty high on my avian IQ scale. Even the brazen robin will become skittish and retiring in short order, given a legitimate reason. When the grapes are ripening, local growers hereabouts set out sonic alarms and propane cannons; the robins become acutely sensitive to any human presence during these times, and they display a lot of the same behavioral devices as their varied thrush cousins: most notably, the use of cover and foliage as a screen to hide evasive flight. Generally, robins will fly up and out of a vineyard when disturbed. But when they know they are being deliberately harassed, they dart among the vine rows in a manner that accents their similarity to varied thrushes to a remarkable degree.

Still, few birds—not even such notoriously shy thrushes as the Swainson's and the hermit—exceed the varied thrush in studied reclusiveness. Varied thrushes are fairly large birds and not particularly rare within their range, especially during their seasonal migrations. But they are difficult to observe; they must be sought in the deep brush, and the seeking must be conducted quietly and without haste.

Winter is mild in northern California, but it is still a distinct season. The hills are green with new grass, the days are crisp and clear; dramatic squalls full of rain and wind blow down from the Gulf of Alaska. Succulent edible fungi such as chanterelles and various species of *Boletus* poke through the duff. Like chanterelles, the varied thrushes are harbingers of winter. And, also like chanterelles, they are hard to find—but worth the effort. Each season and place has its good things, and a thicket full of varied thrushes must be accounted one of the modest pleasures of November and December in northern California. It serves to reassure me: Varied thrushes under the madrones make me realize that we've once again muddled through another year, and that things are more or less well with the world.

The varied thrush resembles its thrush cousin, the robin, in flight. But it bears distinctive markings and ranges only along the West Coast. Unlike the robin, the varied thrush remains a forest recluse.

BACK FROM THE ARGENTINE

TEXT BY ALDO LEOPOLD • PHOTOGRAPH BY GARY R. ZAHM

When dandelions have set the mark of May on Wisconsin pastures, it is time to listen for the final proof of spring. Sit down on a tussock, cock your ears at the sky, dial out the bedlam of meadowlarks and redwings, and soon you may hear it: the flight-song of the upland plover, just now back from the Argentine.

If your eyes are strong, you may search the sky and see him, wings aquiver, circling among the woolly clouds. If your eyes are weak, don't try it; just watch the fenceposts. Soon a flash of silver will tell you on which post the plover has alighted and folded his long wings. Whoever invented the word "grace" must have seen the wing-folding of the plover.

There he sits; his whole being says it's your next move to absent yourself from his domain. The county records may allege that you own this pasture, but the plover airily rules out such trivial legalities. He has just flown 4,000 miles to reassert the title he got from the Indians, and until the young plovers are a-wing, this pasture is his, and none may trespass without his protest.

Somewhere nearby, the hen plover is brooding the four large pointed eggs which will shortly hatch four precocial chicks. From the moment their down is dry, they scamper through the grass like mice on stilts, quite able to elude your clumsy efforts to catch them. At thirty days the chicks are full-grown; no other fowl develops with equal speed. By August they have graduated from flying school, and on cool August nights you can hear their whistled signals as they set wing for the pampas, to prove again the age-old unity of the Americas. Hemisphere solidarity is new among statesmen, but not among the feathered navies of the sky.

The upland plover fits easily into the agricultural countryside. He follows the black-and-white buffalo, which now pasture his prairies, and finds them an acceptable substitute for brown ones. He nests in hayfields as well as pastures, but, unlike the clumsy pheasant, does not get caught in hay mowers. Well before the hay is ready to cut, the young plovers are a-wing and away. In farm country, the plover has only two real enemies: the gully and the drainage ditch. Perhaps we shall one day find that these are our enemies, too.

There was a time in the early 1900s when Wisconsin farms nearly lost their immemorial timepiece, when May pastures greened in silence, and August nights brought no whistled reminder of impending fall. Universal gunpowder, plus the lure of plover-on-toast for post-Victorian banquets, had taken too great a toll. The belated protection of the federal migratory bird laws came just in time.

FDR: BIRDWATCHER

TEXT BY GEOFFREY C. WARD • PAINTING BY CHRISTOPHER MAGADINI

Franklin Roosevelt's open blue Ford moved steadily across a muddy field near Springwood, his family home at Hyde Park, New York. The President was behind the wheel, skillfully negotiating the rough terrain with the special hand controls his paralysis required, and as he drove he chatted amiably with his friend and advisor on forestry, Nelson C. Brown, sitting to his right.

Three big cars filled with Secret Service agents moved warily along the rough forest road that skirted the field, their occupants nervous that the man they were there to protect had left the road and driven onto boggy ground where their heavy, bulletproof vehicles could not follow. They knew that Roosevelt often chafed at their perpetual presence but was especially resentful of it here, deep in the woods he'd known and loved since boyhood; and if his protectors got too far from him, they never knew when he would try to lose them altogether, laughing as he careened down one or another of the rough tracks that honeycombed his forest.

The President halted his car at the edge of the field and appeared to be staring intently into the trees. The Secret Service men stopped too, hands on the handles of their revolvers, straining to see what the President clearly saw.

Then Roosevelt beeped his horn. The agents leaped from their cars and pounded into the muddy field, pistols in hand, ready to eliminate whatever menace had made "the Boss" sound an alarm.

When they reached the car, FDR was roaring with laughter. There was nothing to worry about, he explained, as they holstered their weapons and fought for breath.

He had been peering into a clearing in the woods beyond the field's edge, he said, when he noticed the head of a large bird just visible through the blowing grass.

"What's that bird?" he had asked his companion.

Brown said he wasn't sure, "but if you sound the horn very lightly we will soon find out."

Startled by the horn—and the shouting of anxious agents that followed it—a ring-necked pheasant disappeared into the woods, feathers blazing in the afternoon sun.

As the agents stumped back to their cars, the mud sucking at their polished shoes,

FDR started up his Ford and moved off again, still grinning, his cigarette holder at an especially jaunty angle.

Roosevelt's interest in birds began in early boyhood. Few presidents—few Americans—have led a more comfortable and sheltered existence than did Franklin Roosevelt during his first years. His father, James Roosevelt, was almost twice his mother's age but a lively, vigorous presence in his son's life, inculcating in him his own serene Episcopalianism, his sturdy sense of a wealthy citizen's duty toward those less fortunate than he, his love for trees and the land. But Franklin's day-to-day activities were left to the loving but determined care of his mother, Sara Delano Roosevelt. He was her only child, and she poured into his raising all of her formidable energy. Few boys have ever received more maternal devotion—or had to grow up under more intense scrutiny. His mother picked his books and toys, screened his infrequent playmates, oversaw his games, even stood at the side of the tub while he took his baths until he was at least eight.

About that time he began to show an interest in the rich variety of birds that fluttered in and out of the great trees in which he had been taught to take such pride. It is probably no coincidence that his newfound scientific interest gave him his first legitimate excuse to stray a little way from the house in which he was watched so ceaselessly.

Like most birders of his generation, he started as an oologist—a collector of eggs and nests. The daughter of the Episcopal rector at Hyde Park remembered that as a little girl she attended a Springwood Easter party at which her small host arrived late; he emerged slowly from the woods, inching his way across the lawn, oblivious of his guests, a brilliant blue robin's egg cupped in his small hands.

His father insisted that only a single egg ever be taken from a nest and that no nest could be collected until the winter, but several drawers in Franklin's upstairs bedroom were quickly filled with fragile specimens, and he began to read everything about birds he could get his hands on, demonstrating for the first time his extraordinary ability to read and remember prodigious amounts of material.

At eleven, he laboriously wrote an essay on "Birds of the Hudson River Valley," filled

At the enthusiastic urging of his mother, Franklin began giving lectures on birds to patient relatives, delivering one so impressively that his grandfather took him to the American Museum of Natural History to meet the ornithologist Frank M. Chapman.

63

with the special scorn only a young hobbyist can summon for those less knowledgeable than he:

Many people do not know what a great variety of birds we have. They can always point out a robin but probably could not tell the difference between a Fox Sparrow and a Song Sparrow and will think that a nuthatch is a woodpecker.

At the enthusiastic urging of his mother, Franklin began giving little lectures on birds to patient relatives, delivering one entitled "The Shore Birds of Maine" so impressively that his grandfather gave him a life membership in the American Museum of Natural History and took him there to meet its curator of paleontology, Henry Fairfield Osborn, and the great ornithologist Frank M. Chapman, who let him poke through the trays of bird skins.

Franklin spent the summer of 1893 abroad with his parents and was desolated to find that a business appointment in London forced them to cancel a long-planned visit to Osberton-in-Worksop, the Nottinghamshire seat of the Earl of Liverpool, Cecil Foljambe, one of England's most knowledgeable bird fanciers, whose collection of mounted birds was unmatched outside of museums.

"Mummie, can't I go without you?" Franklin begged.

"You mean you'd visit people you had never met?" she asked, genuinely surprised. Until that moment she had thought her sheltered son well mannered but awfully shy.

"I'd go anywhere to see those birds," he answered, and his parents nervously allowed him to take the train alone, so that the elderly earl and his eleven-year-old visitor could spend the afternoon together talking about birds and gravely examining the brightly colored exhibits in their glass cases.

The Foljambe birds dazzled Franklin—he would later take his bride, Eleanor, to see them on their honeymoon—but there was another collection almost as spectacular much closer to home, just up the Albany Post Road, in fact, on the sprawling Hyde Park estate of Colonel Archibald Rogers of Standard Oil. Rogers' British butler, Arthur Bloomfield, was an entirely self-taught ornithologist whose collection of hundreds of stuffed and labeled specimens, amassed while traveling with his peripatetic employer from one stately home to another, had grown so large that the colonel eventually built him a little stone building just to house it all. Young Franklin liked to go there whenever Bloomfield had a few moments free from his duties in the main house.

In any case, as soon as Franklin got home from Europe in the autumn of 1893, he began lobbying his parents for a shotgun. Nests and eggs were no longer enough for him. He wanted to shoot and mount his own collection. His mother was appalled—her son was far too young, too delicate, for firearms, she said—but his father acquiesced, presenting him with a gun on his twelfth birthday, January 30, 1894. With it came yet another set of rules, which if not obeyed, meant confiscation: There was to be no shooting during the mating season; nesting birds were off-limits; only one member of each species was to be collected.

That shiny new gun meant many things to Franklin. It enabled him to create a collection of stuffed birds, first of all. But ornithology, in turn, licensed him to kill; to stalk Springwood's forests at dawn, alone and unwatched; to affect things directly on his own and out from under his mother's anxious love. Something of the feeling of liberation that shooting gave him can be read in a schoolboy essay called "Guns and Squirrels":

Many Mamas think guns are very dangerous things & think they will go off without cartridges or without being cocked, but if properly handled they are not dangerous... It is great fun shooting...and it is not very easy.

For Franklin it seems never to have been very hard. In shooting, as in most things, his assumption always was that he would find a way to bring home any prize he sought. One of his mother's favorite stories had him strolling in from the river side of the house, requesting his shotgun. She asked him why he needed it.

"There's a winter wren up in one of those big trees down there," he said. "I want to get him."

His mother unlocked the cabinet in which the gun was kept. "Why do you think the wren is going to oblige you by staying there while you come in and get your gun?"

"Oh," said Franklin, shouldering his shotgun. "He'll wait."

He did, and the young hunter returned a few minutes later with another addition to his collection.

He became an "insatiable" hunter, his mother recalled, and in his small "Bird Diary" for 1896 kept a running tally of kills and sightings:

January 31. *Shot 3 Pine Grosbeaks and saw 18 others. Sent the birds to T. Rowland, one to be stuffed & 2 to be skinned.*

February 14. *Saw about 50 Pine Grosbeaks while driving on the avenue. I noticed a blue-gray bird fly out of a pine tree and im-*

mediately a pine grosbeak fell to the ground. It was still warm, though dead. I suppose that the blue-gray bird was a Great Northern Shrike.

February 18. *New York. Went to Museum [of Natural History] & Mr. Frank M. Chapman put me up for Associate membership of the A.O.U. I am to send about 1 dozen grosbeaks to Museum for Local Collections. Mr. Chapman gave me a card of introduction to Mr. L. S. Foster, publisher of "Auk," etc. as I intend to buy back no's of the "Auk." Mr. [Arthur] Dumper [Franklin's tutor] reported some grosbeaks at Hyde Park.*

February 19. *(In snow—15 degrees) Shot a Pine Finch. The bird was alone in a small pine tree, & he appeared very shy. Had great difficulty in shooting him.*

February 25. *Shot 1 male Pine Grosbeak for Museum and saw 30 others . . . Mr. Dumper saw a woodchuck & I smelt a skunk.*

March 7. *Saw red-shouldered hawk.*

April 15. *Cowbirds at Newburgh.*

April 16. *Cooper's hawk near Staatsburgh. He flew up quite close to me and appeared to be tame.*

April 18. *Saw near Barrytown about 100 red-winged Blackbirds.*

April 25. *Shot a barred owl at 5 P.M. in Newbold's Gully [a declivity in the woods between his house and his neighbor's, next-door.]*

May 7. *Shot a Scarlet Tanager. Also an Indigo Bunting.*

May 8. *Shot a red-headed woodpecker.*

By the age of fourteen he had collected and identified more than three hundred different species native to Dutchess County. The next year the American Museum gratefully acknowledged his gift of ten carefully prepared pine grosbeak skins.

In collecting, as in so many other things, Franklin received additional inspiration from the example of his celebrated cousin, Theodore. TR, too, had been a voracious collector of specimens as a boy, and he had relished the noisome hobby of taxidermy, as well, although it made the lives of his parents and siblings and servants quite miserable.

In the end Franklin found he could not stomach the stench—it made him "green," his mother recalled—and after trying two or three times to stuff his own trophies, he asked to have his skins sent off to professional taxidermists in Poughkeepsie and New York. His ever-indulgent parents agreed. (His mother considered his birds too precious for anyone but herself to dust, and when Springwood was greatly enlarged in 1915, she had a special glass-fronted case built for twenty-seven of his best specimens in the front hall,

where they remain today, a little the worse for wear, but each still labeled in Roosevelt's boyish hand. A harrier hawk hung from a wire nearby, and a prominent place was also found in the living room for her son's largest prize, a green-backed heron.)

The acclaim Franklin's ornithological knowledge and shooting skill elicited from his proud parents and pleased relatives evidently inspired him to compose "The Spring Song" for *The Foursome,* a typed magazine gotten up by FDR and three of his contemporaries who lived at Tuxedo Park. It's possible the article has not seen print in its entirety since 1896:

Listen! The bugler has come. A few shrill notes and a trill, and we see our friend the Song Sparrow.

In quick succession the Robins and the Bluebirds arrive. This is the advance guard.

A few days more, and Blackbirds appear. Hear their juicy note, which reminds you of strawberries and cream, but, venture too close, and they will be off, with a cheery "can't catch me." You see the Robin on your lawn, busily engaged in grubbing, but you would be surprised to hear that he eats about seventy worms every day. If those worms were laid end to end, their length would extend fourteen feet. The American Robin is an entirely different species from the English Robin Redbreast of Nursery tales. The latter is smaller, in form resembling our Bluebird.

The Bluebird, the color-bearer of the Spring Army, is gladly welcomed as a harbinger of Spring, as, flitting about the orchard, his mellow note mingles with the Spring Chorus.

Walk now along the Creek and, with angry rattle, a Kingfisher will startle you from revery. There you will also see a lazy Heron, slowly flapping his way from pond to pond. With neck drawn in, and legs dangling, he will remind you of Japanese Screen pictures.

Suddenly, a loud "tapp, tapp," will ring out on the clear air, and you will see a fine red head stuck out inquisitively from behind a branch. A black-and-white body will follow as the Wood-pecker climbs into view.

But what is that soberly clad bird hopping about near the Spring? You will soon see, as, when he faces about, his spotted breast will come into view, and you will know that a Wood Thrush has arrived.

Now will come numbers of small birds, known as Warblers. Their song is feeble and they are very shy, only staying a few days.

A little brown bird is seen hopping about the patch; this is the chippy or Chipping Sparrow. Always cheery, he will be with you all summer, but an even smaller and browner bird will attract your attention. The House Wren, for it is he, will scold from the start, but we will put it down to a disagreeable wife.

The Peabody-bird, or White-throated Sparrow, comes at this time, and he will stay with us until driven southward by the cold, when sitting on a fence-rail, he bids us, "Farewell."

How much of this essay was his own work, how much that of the nanny who presumably typed it up for him, and how much may have been cribbed from someone else's article we will probably never know. (It has something of the weary tone of the overwrought outdoor writers whom his cousin Theodore dismissed as "Nature fakirs"; nothing else Franklin wrote at the same age has anything like the clarity of this essay.)

Franklin entered Groton School at fourteen that fall, perhaps the only new boy ever to boast a complete set of bound volumes of the *Auk*. But birdwatching was not thought robust enough a sport for Groton. The enthusiasms of its resolutely manly headmaster, the Reverend Endicott Peabody, ran toward football (which Franklin was too light to play well), boxing (at which he was no better, having had his nose bloodied by a far smaller boy in his only known public match), and baseball (which he also played poorly, finding at least a measure of compensatory success as manager of the team in his senior year). And so he began to keep his enthusiasm about birds mostly to himself, at least when among his schoolmates, although he did lecture about them once more: At his cousin Muriel Robbins' request, he spoke before her settlement-house class of Irish immigrant boys from the mean streets of East Boston. The call of the Peabody-bird was a very long way from the daily concerns of his listeners, and the enthusiasm of this slender, overeager young man for such things must have been at the very least a novelty.

He never lost his interest completely, however. Eleanor Roosevelt was often surprised in the early years of their marriage by the curiously selective keenness of his eyesight, chiding him gently when he blamed nearsightedness for failing to recognize an acquaintance on the street. "That," she explained, "has always seemed strange to me. For as long as I have known him, Franklin could always point to a bird and tell me what it was."

During the summer of 1907 Franklin, two Harvard friends, and his younger brother-in-law, Hall Roosevelt, left Eleanor behind in the Roosevelt cottage at Campobello and sailed north to Oak Island off Nova Scotia, intent on digging up Captain Kidd's pirate treasure, rumored to be buried there. They found no treasure, but on the way back Franklin spotted a cormorant's nest at the top of a tall tree on a small rocky island. Hall, then sixteen, was sent ashore to bring it down. He clambered up the tree and returned with the nest and the four baby birds it held, so that Franklin could send them to the American Museum. The nest and its contents reeked so, Eleanor remembered, that when the expedition got back to Campobello, Hall "had to take off all his clothes and leave them on the beach and scrub himself before he could enter the house."

Although the hectic public career that began with Roosevelt's election to the State Senate in 1910, and only accelerated after his appointment as Assistant Secretary of the Navy in 1913, kept him apart from his family much of the time, he seemed anxious to pass on his hobby to at least the eldest of his children. Anna Roosevelt treasured all her life her memories of the times when he would swing her up onto the saddle in front of him and canter off into the Hyde Park woods, identifying each bird they scared up along the forest path.

As with a good many enthusiasts of his time, birdwatching and birdshooting remained inseparable in Roosevelt's mind. He took a shotgun with him on a semi-official horseback inspection tour of Haiti in 1917, shot a dove and had himself photographed with it, then liked to explain to friends who saw the picture that he had really bagged a "Great Haitian Shrink Bird," a big exotic species, measuring four feet from wing-tip to wing-tip, which had dwindled after death because it had not been immersed in boiling water.

Almost his first thought after James M. Cox and he were spectacularly trounced for President and Vice-President by Warren Harding and Calvin Coolidge in 1920 was to head south for a week of wildfowl-shooting in Louisiana. He was photographed there, too: In just one noisy morning in the flooded canefields he and seven friends accounted for some sixty ducks and geese.

Infantile paralysis struck Roosevelt down in the summer of 1921, leaving him unable ever again to take a step unaided, threatening to end forever his political hopes. He stayed out of politics for seven years, struggling with marginal success to recover the use of his wasted legs and forced to fall back on sedentary hobbies—collecting stamps, books, naval prints—to stave off the boredom and depression that might have crushed a less resilient and resolute man.

Hunting birds was now virtually impossible for him, of course—although he did once try shooting driven quail at Warm Springs, Georgia, banging away at the tiny targets hurtling over his head, the brakes on his wheelchair locked so that the recoil would not send him rolling backwards. And the twisting forest paths around Springwood he had prowled as a boy in search of birds were closed to him as well—at least until, in the late twenties, he began widening some of them for his hand-controlled automobile.

But, his son Elliott remembers, even as president, wherever he was and whenever he had the opportunity, FDR enjoyed identifying the birds that came within range, keeping binoculars near at hand at Hyde Park and Warm Springs and sometimes halting the conversation to identify a distant song. Even when cruising aboard warships, he kept an eye out, and at least once—at St. Joseph Island off Texas in 1937—he had himself carried onto the beach so that he could get a better look at shorebirds.

One day during the winter of 1942, Margaret Suckley, his wife's distant cousin, told him that she and two other members of the staff of his newly created Franklin D. Roosevelt Library at Hyde Park planned to take part in the annual census of Dutchess County birds in the spring. Would he like to come along? To her surprise "he said he would love it," James L. Whitehead, another bird enthusiast on the staff, remembered, "and so we made our plans."

Those plans were not universally popular with the President's entourage: "The Secret Service men not enthusiastic," his secretary Bill Hassett noted, "when they learned the President plans to leave home at four o'clock Sunday morning to go with friends...to hear the spring bird notes." But the President was almost pathetically eager to go—he had not been able to indulge his boyhood passion for more than twenty years. Just as soon as Whitehead and the others drew in front of a still-darkened Springwood before dawn on Sunday, May 10th, "the door to the 'Big House' opened, and there sat the President in his wheelchair, all ready to go. He had evidently been ready before we got there, and this was only shortly after four o'clock."

Roosevelt was lifted into the car and seated in the back alongside Miss Suckley and Ludlow Griscom of Harvard, the author of *Birds of the New York City Region* and one of the preeminent authorities on bird identification. Library staffer Allen Frost sat up front with the Roosevelt chauffeur. Five sleepy Secret Service men rode in a second car behind. "I'm sure they thought us all crazy—the President included," recalled Whitehead, whose car brought up the rear.

It was a chilly, wet morning, and it took almost an hour to reach the census site, Thompson's Pond near Pine Plains in the northern end of the county, but halfway there Roosevelt asked the driver to stop and fold down the roof so that he could hear the night sounds—whip-poor-wills, sparrows, a catbird.

The small convoy reached the pond just after five, Whitehead recalled, and "stopped on a little road built right through the center of the marsh—reeds and grasses growing thick on both sides." Everyone but FDR got out in the gray light and stood around his car to listen to the marsh birds greet the dawn. The Secret Service men, "all of them bored," stood in a cluster a little distance away.

The chorus was so "awe-inspiring," Whitehead noted, that even FDR spoke in half-whispers. At first Roosevelt seemed a little bewildered by the variety of calls and songs —Whitehead was afraid that "the President knows little now of birds"—but with Ludlow Griscom's help "lots of it came back to him," and the birders heard or saw Virginia rails, American bitterns, northern flickers, eastern meadowlarks, cedar waxwings, scarlet tanagers, and seventeen separate species of warbler. The President himself filled out the checklist in his bold hand: "Total for day 108 species. Franklin D. Roosevelt."

A soft but steady rain began to fall around seven o'clock, and the cars pulled beneath the trees for shelter. Roosevelt sipped hot coffee, ate sandwiches, and told stories of his boyhood pursuit of birds, of the blue heron that came year after year to the marshy riverbank below the house and the robins he used to tease by tying a string to a branch.

About eight the President said good-bye and headed back for Springwood. He had to see to his house guests, the crown prince and princess of Norway, and could not be away long from the special phone that linked his country home with the White House.

Despite the early hour at which he'd risen and the time he'd spent in the damp cold, he seemed "fit as a fiddle and full of enthusiasm" when Bill Hassett saw him shortly after noon. "His face lighted up when he related how at the break of the day he heard the note of a marsh wren, then a red-winged blackbird, after that a bittern. All told, he recognized the notes of twenty-two different birds."

Roosevelt told Miss Suckley he'd like very much to go birding again, if it wouldn't be too much trouble. But then the war closed in around him, and he never again could quite find the time.

Infantile paralysis struck Roosevelt down in the summer of 1921, leaving him unable ever again to take a step unaided. The twisting forest paths he had prowled as a boy were closed to him—until he began widening some of them to accommodate his hand-controlled automobile.

EMPTY THE SKIES

TEXT BY PETER STEINHART

John Cowan, who managed Gray Lodge refuge for thirty-two years, remembers the swales and potholes he hunted as a boy in the Sacramento Valley. "If you fly over all that good habitat today," he says, "you'll see nothing but ricefields and channelized ditches."

On November evenings, John Cowan likes to stand in the marsh on the sunset side of California's Gray Lodge Wildlife Area and watch one of the great spectacles of American wildlife. Through clumps of tule and rush, Cowan can see clusters of pintail, wigeon, and mallard and lines of elegant white snow geese on the water. There is the sound of splashing as masses of ducks and geese preen and wash. Over the rush of water come the cries of the geese, the nasal cranks of the mallard, the whistles of the pintail, and the squeaky exclamations of the wigeon. It is impossible from the noise to tell how many thousands of birds are crammed into this marsh.

Minutes after the sun goes down, however, there is a sudden roar, like the sound of a jet aircraft taking off. From the marsh rise twenty or thirty thousand snow geese. The white of their wings flashes pink in the glow of the sunset, and they circle, sideslip on the wind, and return to the marsh. Smaller groups take off and circle, as if urging the mass to join them. As the sky darkens, the ducks, too, begin to rise in groups of two or

five or twelve. Wigeon whistle overhead. Pintail fly so low that one can hear the wind lisping through gaps between wing feathers. As the twilight grows murky, the shapes loom out of the marsh like bats. They rise and break apart, clusters of them, then waves, then clouds. The rush of wings and the din of squawk and whistle fill the air. The birds boil up out of the marsh, now by the hundreds, now by the thousands. Within twenty minutes there are nearly a million birds in the air.

It is lavish abundance. It is the lively energy of large birds, clean against the rising moon, full of will and purpose. "Seeing that evening flight is just the greatest thrill," says Cowan, who for thirty-two years was the manager of Gray Lodge. Today he watches the night flight and thinks about how things must have been before California's Central Valley, the broad plain between the Coast Range and the Sierra Nevada, was turned into an agricultural fiefdom. Then the valley had 4 million acres of wetland in which the rivers flooded in winter and spread out over the valley floor into lakes and swamps

and inland seas. All that water spawned aquatic plants and invertebrates, which, in turn, drew wintering ducks and geese and shorebirds in unimaginable numbers. Early settlers said flocks blackened the skies, that geese covered the ground completely for miles at a stretch. In the 1890s Dr. Hugh Glenn employed twenty to forty goose herders at a time on his Sacramento Valley wheat farms to shoot geese out of his fields. He spent $13,000 a year just supplying the ammunition.

Today such spectacles as Gray Lodge's night flights are rare. You see them at Gray Lodge during the hunting season because the birds have crowded into this refuge to escape the guns of hunters, and at dusk, when hunters must stop shooting, they fly off to feed in neighboring grainfields. Over most of the state, the great flocks of waterfowl are gone. They have gone because the wetlands have gone.

Most of California is arid. To quench thirsty fields and factories and keep dust off its suburban streets, the state has sponged up water wherever it ponds, funneled it into ditches and canals, and husbanded it narrowly to human purposes. California once boasted some 5 million acres of wetlands. Today 92 percent of that is gone. Of the orig-

inal 4 million acres of Central Valley wetlands, 96 percent is gone. Tulare Lake, once a vast sea in winter, today is planted almost entirely in cotton. Most of the original great blue heron rookeries in the valley are gone. There were once white pelican colonies all up and down the valley; today there are none.

As a boy, Cowan hunted the bypasses and tule marshes of the valley. "There were swales," he says. "There were potholes. The birds had a lot of places to go." Today the Sacramento River and its tributary creeks have been corseted in levees. The trees have been torn from the bottomlands to make room for crops. The farmlands have been so leveled by laser-guided tractors that rainwater finds no place to pond. There are 550,000 acres of ricelands, almost all of them so flat a beachball dropped to the ground wouldn't know which way to roll. "If you fly over all that good habitat today," says Cowan, "you'll see nothing but ricefields and channelized ditches. Farms come right up to the edge of the river."

Habitat for migrating birds is perilously small. "I can take you up in an airplane and in a couple of hours show you the entire wintering habitat," says Daniel Connelly of the California Department of Fish and Game. In the Central Valley, it is compressed into

Tule marshes at the Sacramento National Wildlife Refuge are among a mere 80,000 acres of Central Valley waterfowl habitat saved by state and federal agencies.

69

100,000 acres of state and federal refuges and wildlife management areas and 300,000 acres of private lands, most of which are owned or leased by duck-hunting clubs. Half the duck-club lands are rice farms that are flooded after harvest and leased to the hunters.

Rice-farm stubble fields provide food for the birds in the fall, but rice farms are diminishing. As foreign competition has pushed California rice farming into a depression, the fields have been converted increasingly to almond and pistachio orchards, which offer nothing to wintering birds. And as the members of the hunt clubs age, younger hunters who can't meet the inflated prices of land and management have sold out, returning club lands to agriculture or turning them into industrial parks. California's wintering duck population plummeted from 7 million birds in 1980 to 2½ million in 1989. The quality of the wintering grounds is at least part of the reason.

The decline in waterfowl is not just California's loss. California winters 60 percent of the ducks and geese of the Pacific Flyway, a fifth of the entire continent's waterfowl population. The Central Valley alone hosts 84 percent of the flyway's pintail, 70 percent of its shovelers and gadwalls, 80 percent of its snow geese, 70 percent of its white-fronted geese, and 70 percent of its tundra swans. Some species, such as Ross' goose and the Aleutian Canada goose, winter only in the Central Valley. Wetland losses in the Central Valley thus will affect waterfowl populations throughout the Pacific Flyway.

Not only waterfowl suffer from wetland losses. As the wetlands go, so do the phalaropes, grebes, sandpipers, egrets, herons, and rail. And so too do the fisheries. The Sacramento–San Joaquin Delta once hosted a dozen fish canneries as well as thriving commercial fisheries in salmon, shad, perch, and sturgeon. Because these species need wetlands for feeding and other activities, today the canneries are gone, and the delta has only sport fisheries. Salmon fishermen from San Francisco must now fish in Oregon and Washington waters for Columbia River stocks.

As wintering grounds shrink, the quality of the remaining areas declines. Crowding of ducks and geese on limited refuge wetlands encourages epidemics of botulism and avian cholera. At times refuge personnel must go out and stack corpses like cordwood and burn them. Moreover, as the October to January hunting season wears on, hunter bags show a declining number of young birds and an increasing proportion of adults, an indication that the hunt cuts into the breeding

MAP: JOE LEMONNIER; PHOTO: GARY R. ZAHM, SOURCE: U.S. FISH AND WILDLIFE SERVICE

NO ROOM FOR DUCKS

Wetlands in 1850

Present Wetlands

Redding

Sacramento Valley

Sacramento

Sacramento River Delta

San Francisco

San Joaquin Valley

Bakersfield

Los Angeles

Salton Sea

stock. Heavy human activity also occurs in and around the wintering grounds. Airplanes and helicopters whine overhead. Mark Strong, wildlife biologist at the Sacramento National Wildlife Refuge, says, "A helicopter coming over at legal altitudes will put every goose in the air." Sightseers and birdwatchers driving through the refuges also put birds to flight.

A serious adversity is the change in food available to the wintering birds. "Forty years ago," says Ed Collins, manager of the Sacramento refuge, "there was enough variety out there that the birds could go out and choose what they needed." But with the conversion to farmland and channelization of the rivers, the choices have thinned out. There are no natural wetlands left in the valley. All remaining ponds are fed by ditches and canals rather than by floods or seeping groundwater. As a result, Cowan says, some 80 per-

Above: The marshes of a duck-hunting club are leveled for crop production—the fate of most California wetlands.

Opposite page: Diking ricefields—once marshlands—in the Sacramento Delta.

71

cent of the plants in the valley are now non-native species such as star thistle. "I'm sure ducks can't use that," he says. "We have developed a monoculture of ricefields, and you don't have the diversity of aquatic plants that grow in those potholes and riparian habitat."

Ricefields are often considered a boon to waterfowl. In fact, ricefields were established on Sacramento Valley refuges in part to relieve farmers of crop damage by providing ducks and geese with their own rice. The birds also feed in rice stubble after harvest, and duck clubs continue to plant rice to attract ducks.

But rice is not enough. At the Sacramento National Wildlife Refuge, biologists Mickey Heitmeyer and Dennis Raveling of the University of California, Davis, have been looking at what ducks eat to get through winter. Between September and March the birds must not only fuel their bodies through the pre-alternate molt (which gives pintail their long tails and mallard their green heads) and then through courtship and a pre-basic molt (which gives the hens their camouflage plumage), but also must fatten up for the northward migration. Each of these tasks requires its own nutritional strategy, and the ducks therefore change their feeding behavior several times during winter. Wigeon, for example, feed on submerged plants in October, then switch to moist-soil seeds and rootstocks, and finally, late in winter, switch again to feeding on grasses in upland areas. Mallard eat moist-soil seeds in the fall, switch in midwinter to high-energy foods such as acorns or row crops, and later move on to a diet of invertebrates. "What we're finding out is that birds don't eat just one thing in winter," says Heitmeyer. "They eat a whole bunch of things. It's important that they get the right resource at the right time."

To complete its molt a bird needs protein. Row crops provide a lot of energy, but ducks can't assimilate protein from them, Heitmeyer says. The birds instead get protein from moist-soil seeds and invertebrates. Heitmeyer calculates that mallard need three to five grams of protein daily just to get through a molt. "Say they only get half that per day: They can take the needed protein out of their muscle mass, or they can delay the molt." One recourse will weaken the bird and make it more vulnerable to predators. The other will delay migration and reduce the bird's chances of breeding.

The biologists conclude that natural marshes are essential to the birds. But most of the remaining wetlands are flooded only in the hunting season and therefore don't grow the moist-soil plants and invertebrates that ducks require. "Most of our duck clubs are loafing and resting areas," says Cowan. "They don't provide very much feed." Mark Strong spends much of his time trying to convince duck-club members to manage for natural plant foods, but few duck clubs want to pay for the year-round water management needed to sustain natural ponds. Cowan urges the state and federal refuges to keep at least 10 percent of their areas in permanent ponds, but even they fail to meet this quota. Permanent water is hard to find in this valley.

Even the duck-club ponds may be in trouble. As fewer ducks come down the flyway, the hunting season is shortened to reduce the hunters' take, and the hunt-club fields are drained even earlier. Moreover, as fewer ducks return each autumn and hunters have a harder time filling their bags, the number of duck hunters declines. In 1970, 2.5 million ducks were harvested in California by 187,240 hunters. In 1980, 1.4 million ducks were harvested by 106,600 hunters. By 1989 there were only 672,000 ducks harvested by 72,000 hunters. As the hunters decline, the number of duck clubs declines. Duck clubs in the Sacramento Delta are being sold to become industrial parks and farms. Each year more private wetlands are dried out. Each year the fate of the migrants rests more heavily on the state and federal refuges.

But the refuges have problems of their own. Virtually all of the water delivered to the nine federal refuges in the Central Valley is provided by the Bureau of Reclamation from the Central Valley Project on an if-and-when-available basis. The refuges have no legal rights to that water, and since the bureau doesn't recognize wildlife as a beneficial use of project water, it will not bind itself to contracts for delivery. Kern and Pixley national wildlife refuges in the southern San Joaquin have no water rights. Kern floods only 2,300 of its 10,500 acres. Sacramento, Delevan, and Colusa refuges in the Sacramento Valley have been getting 105,000 acre-feet yearly at the pleasure of the Bureau of Reclamation but have no contractual rights to any of it. The bureau soon could start awarding that water to farmers instead of to the refuges. Agricultural demand for water is growing in California at the rate of one percent per year, but new supplies are unlikely to be developed because farmers can't pay the $400- to $500-per-acre-foot cost of newly developed water, and the public no longer wants to subsidize farmers by building dams. Conservation is not likely to solve the problem. Rice farmers have reduced consumption about 20 percent, which might make more freshwater available to the refuges. But it would come at the cost of water to the private wetlands, most of which flood their fields with water that has already passed through agricultural fields.

The refuges depend heavily on the ability to manipulate what water they get. To manage for native marsh vegetation, which in the West is adapted to cycles of drying and flooding, they must flood and drain ponds several times each year. Flooding is also the most effective means of keeping tules and other weeds from choking out the ponds. But the refuges rely on irrigation districts to conduct federal water to refuge ponds. And because they get water on an if-and-when-available basis, they get it only when the irrigation districts have the capacity to deliver. Says Strong, "When we are first starting to put water on the ground for the rice crops, that's when all the farmers are putting water on their ricefields. We're at the end of the ditch. We have to wait our turn in line."

Sometimes the turn doesn't come in time. Gary Zahm, manager of the Kesterson, Merced, and San Luis refuges near Los Banos, once asked the irrigation district to deliver water needed for a germinating millet crop. The company told him it would be ten to twelve days before he could have the water, and while he waited, the crop simply dried up. Things get even harder in winter, when the birds are in the refuges, because the irrigation districts shut down their reservoirs and canals for maintenance work.

The refuges lack their own delivery sys-

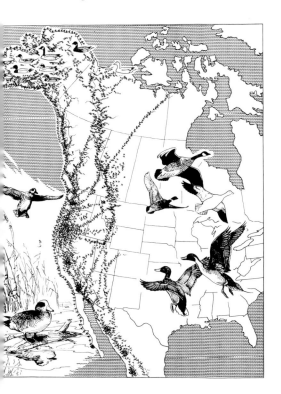

tems. They once pumped water from their own wells but today find the energy cost is too high. San Luis refuge pays seventy-five cents an acre-foot for water delivered through the irrigation district's gravity-flow canal. It costs eleven to sixteen dollars to pump an acre-foot of water from the refuges' own deep wells. Cuts in refuge funding simply don't allow the refuges to spend that kind of money. "We've taken some of these wetlands out of production mainly because we just couldn't afford to do it anymore," says Zahm.

The state waterfowl management areas have the same problem. In order to save water, managers at the Los Banos Wildlife Area grow swamp timothy instead of watergrass, even though the birds normally feed on watergrass in December and January because it provides the protein they need to get through the cold winter months. Gray Lodge has been flooding its fields later in the year, and in consequence producing less food. At Honey Lake Wildlife Area, managers have stopped pumping water in the fall and started to manage chiefly for spring nesting populations instead.

If water quantity is a problem, water quality may prove a disaster. All the Central Valley refuges and most of the duck clubs use agricultural wastewater to flood their fields. It is water that has run through farm fields and collected in drains and ditches. Often, it carries loads of salts, pesticides, and toxic chemicals.

In 1965 the Bureau of Reclamation began to deliver Central Valley Project water to new farmlands west of Fresno. Under much of that land are impervious clay barriers that keep irrigation water from dribbling down to the water table and cause it to puddle under the fields like water in a dish. When the puddled water reaches the root zone, it poisons the crops with salts accumulated while percolating through the soil. Farmers have installed tile drains under their fields to collect and bear away the water, which is too salty to be used on other fields. To dispose of the water, the bureau planned to construct the San Luis Drain, a concrete ditch 180 miles long, and dump the waste into San Francisco Bay. Along the ditch, northwest of Los Banos, the bureau built temporary holding ponds. The ponds subsequently became Kesterson National Wildlife Refuge. Before it extended the drain beyond Kesterson, however, the bureau ran out of money. So Kesterson became the end of the ditch.

The bureau began ponding drainwater at Kesterson in 1972. In 1983 the Fish and Wildlife Service began finding dead and de-

Central Valley wetlands are critical to waterfowl of the Pacific Flyway, in winter serving over 70 percent of the Flyway's pintails, lesser snow geese, gadwalls, white-fronted geese, and northern shovelers.

formed birds on the refuge. In 1984, 40 percent of the nests of certain species held dead embryos, and 20 percent held embryos with missing eyes and deformed beaks, legs, or wings. It was clear that selenium, leached off the fields west of Fresno by the drainwater and accumulating in Kesterson's plants and invertebrates, was poisoning the birds. The State of California declared Kesterson a toxic pit, and a citizen sued the bureau and the Fish and Wildlife Service on charges that they violated the Migratory Bird Treaty Act by subjecting migrants to toxic chemicals. The Department of the Interior, which oversees both agencies, then agreed to close the drain and clean the ponds.

Shutting down the drain doesn't solve the problem. Kesterson's pollution resulted from the drainage of 40,000 acres of Westlands Water District farmlands. But Westlands alone comprises 600,000 acres, and there are dozens of other districts in the valley. The drainwater they release contains not just selenium but arsenic and boron, which also are toxic to wildlife. It is expected that over the next century 40 percent of those lands will require tile drains. The San Joaquin River is already 75 percent agricultural wastewater in summer months. Salt Slough, which runs into the river and is supposed to provide the

Left: Whitefronts flare off against a goose-filled sky over the Sacramento Valley. A biologist at the Sacramento refuge, Mickey Heitmeyer (shown) says, "Birds don't just eat one thing in winter." That is, wigeon need watergrass or millet for protein, but wildlife areas often are denied the water needed to grow essential crops.

Pages 76–77: Pristine, privately owned wetlands (inset) survive on the delta where the Sacramento and San Joaquin rivers meet. (Both photos by Tupper Ansel Blake)

GARY R. ZAHM

TUPPER ANSEL BLAKE

75

Dredge spoil dumped on a salt marsh on San Francisco Bay angers California Fish and Game biologist Paul Kelly (above). The California clapper rail (near right)—an endangered species— clings to survival on a rapidly vanishing fringe of saltgrass and pickleweed, for 75 percent of San Francisco Bay's original wetlands has been filled. Clapper rails scour mudflats at low tide for fiddler crabs, shrimp, snails, and worms and hide their platform nest, containing as many as fourteen eggs, under an arched roof of grass. Kelly fears agencies that are charged with protecting the bay are doing an inadequate job.

78

San Luis refuge with water, is at least 12 parts per billion selenium. If the refuge managers use that water, selenium will accumulate in plant tissues, the cells of invertebrates, and, eventually, the tissues of birds. Grassland Water District, 51,500 acres of duck-hunting clubs next to Kesterson, has selenium levels approaching those at Kesterson even though it does not take water from the San Luis Drain. Thousands of acres of drainwater evaporation ponds dot the landscape south of Kesterson. Says Gary Zahm, "Some of them are worse than Kesterson. They've already found birds down there with liver damage and selenium levels as high as those of the birds at Kesterson."

Even without selenium or arsenic, the saltier wastewater has changed the character of the landscape. The refuges of the San Joaquin Valley can no longer provide the winter habitat they once did. On an October afternoon, Gary Zahm is standing beside Salt Slough on the San Luis National Wildlife Refuge. A vee of forty tundra swans flies overhead. Zahm looks up wistfully, but the swans don't stop. Says Zahm, "There used to be more swans. One of the reasons there are fewer is the loss of the sago pondweed. As the habitat gets saltier, horned pondweed and wigeon grass replace it. The type of water quality needed to produce the plants swans feed on just isn't around."

Things don't get much easier on migrants when they move over the Coast Range to California's shoreline. Only five percent of the Pacific Flyway's waterfowl winter on the coast, but some are exclusive visitors such as surf scoters and black brant. And shorebirds winter on coastal tideflats and salt ponds by the millions. San Francisco Bay is a major wintering ground for western sandpipers, short-billed dowitchers, marbled godwits, black-necked stilts, and avocets. However, most of the state's human population has settled along the coast and in the process has drained and filled the wetlands. Humboldt Bay and other north-coast estuaries are silted in by logging operations and road construction upstream. Orange and Los Angeles counties buried 90 percent of their marshes under housing, industrial parks, airport runways, and dredge piles. San Diego County once had 32,000 acres of wetlands but today has only 3,000.

San Francisco Bay is the state's largest estuary. "It's the major refueling and resting place for birds on the Pacific Flyway," says Roger Johnson, formerly manager of the San Francisco Bay National Wildlife Refuge. But housing, military bases, airports, harbors, and garbage dumps have already filled 75 percent of the bay's original wetlands, and dikes separate most of the shore from tidal inflow. With the lost wetlands have gone bald eagles, peregrine falcons, wood ducks, bitterns, yellow rail, and hooded mergansers. Wetlands are still going under pavement, especially in the south bay, where developers covet baylands for housing tracts and industrial parks. Oakland Airport is expanding, and the state highway department has plans for new freeways. Profits for developers can be enormous. A single undeveloped wetland acre near San Jose recently sold for a million dollars.

Paul Kelly is a biologist with the California Department of Fish and Game. He is much concerned with the effects of this building boom on the bay's wildlife. On a December morning, during one of the year's highest tides, he is out on the bay in an airboat counting California clapper rail. The high tide flushes the small birds out of their haunts in the saltgrass and pickleweed, and they mutter along on exposed islands of *Grindelia* wondering whatever happened to privacy. The airboat roars over the water. The rail dive as it approaches and hold themselves under by clinging to submerged plants. It is a rail nightmare, this snarling beast racing at them with all hiding places gone.

The clapper rail is an endangered subspecies, victim in part of the conversion of low-lying salt marsh to commercial salt ponds. Kelly estimates that only 500 rail remain. And he fears that the needs of rail and other south bay wildlife are not adequately looked after by the agencies charged with protecting the bay.

The Bay Conservation and Development Commission has jurisdiction over bay shores up to the mean high-tide line and over adjoining wetlands. It requires developers who wish to fill wetlands to provide substitute wetlands in mitigation. But since all the lands of the south bay are either already in public ownership or being held for future development by speculators, no mitigation lands are available there. The sites most threatened by development are the seasonal wetlands behind the dikes. The commission has little jurisdiction there, and the U.S. Army Corps of Engineers regulates their filling. Under the terms of the Clean Water Act, the Corps requires a developer who wishes to build on these wetlands to get a permit.

The lands behind the dikes are particularly important to migratory birds, says Kelly. They may be dry for ten months of the year, but when rains come they pond, spawning billions of aquatic plants and invertebrates, and suddenly fill with birdlife. "Ecologists always portrayed the salt marsh as the ultimate ecosystem," says Kelly. "Certainly for herring and crab and fish it is the ultimate. But the needs of the birds are more diverse. I could take you to a salt pond and show you 10,000 eared grebes and thousands of dabbling ducks. You'd never see anything like that in a salt marsh. Some bird species don't even use the bay. They just use the seasonal wetlands. Phalaropes, white pelicans, avocets, stilts, eared grebes, Bonaparte's gulls, they use the salt ponds, not the bay. By far the majority of dabbling ducks are on the salt ponds. Most of the diving ducks are on the ponds. That's where we see the snowy plovers when we see them by the bay. We have more waterbirds on nontidal areas than on tidal areas, more in numbers and kinds."

The seasonal wetlands are especially important in winter, when high tides crowd shorebirds off the mudflats and high winds set up waves that batter them. "Shorebirds have a metabolism something like a shrew's," says Roger Johnson; "they're feeding all the time." Says Kelly, "They don't have the luxury of waiting for the next low tide like the big guys. You see western sandpipers perched on boards on the open water, feeding on brine flies." They also feed in the seasonal ponds behind the dikes.

Bay conservation commission regulations thus far have checked conversion of wetlands in the tidal areas. But the Corps of Engineers, faced with a land rush behind the dikes, has been both understaffed and undercommitted. The Corps has only three staff members to try to affect compliance with permit requirements and wetland fill laws. When developers have applied for permits to fill seasonal wetlands, Corps officials have sometimes failed to process the requests. Corps officials also have given verbal permission to proceed with projects without visiting the site to see whether it is a wetland. And developers have found ways to get around Corps procedures. The Corps determines whether a building site is a wetland by looking for water or for aquatic plants. So, developers drain and disc the land, actions the Corps doesn't construe as filling but which effectively remove the aquatic vegetation. Once the plants are gone, the developers maintain the site no longer qualifies as a wetland under Corps definitions, and they go ahead and fill.

Having succeeded with this dodge, developers have proposed projects on virtually every remaining acre of seasonal wetland in the south bay. Some projects have been built without permits. In some cases, the Corps has simply granted a permit after the fact.

Kelly and Fish and Wildlife Service officials have joined with members of local Audubon chapters to insist that the Corps stop such activities. "The position of the Fish and Wildlife Service is that there should be no more losses of wetlands in the bay," says Johnson. They have produced old photos of disputed sites showing levees, flood gates, and other water-management structures which prove the land was once subject to tidal action. Local conservation groups have sued to block airport expansion plans. They have urged the Environmental Protection Agency to challenge Corps wetlands determinations. All these efforts have increased public concern about the fate of south bay wetlands to the point that the Corps announced it would prosecute developers who filled without a permit. But developers continue to destroy wetlands.

The 17,000-acre San Francisco Bay National Wildlife Refuge lies in the middle of all this fill activity. Bay-area residents pushed for its establishment after the Leslie Salt Company disclosed plans to build a city of 50,000 inhabitants on the site. When the refuge was authorized in 1972 it took the lands slated for development first. But it took in almost no seasonal wetlands. "When we were putting together the refuge, we erred in assuming that some of the open agricultural land was going to remain vacant forever and a day," says Johnson. Today nearly every acre of wetland around the refuge is slated for development. Kelly and Johnson feel the refuge needs additional lands to protect freshwater and brackish open water, an abandoned salt pond that has the largest snowy plover nesting area on the south bay, meadow wetlands that once served as duck clubs, and seasonal ponds that provide essential winter habitat for migrants. A Citizens Committee to Complete the Refuge has convinced Congress to expand the refuge by 20,000 acres.

The birds of the Pacific Flyway face tough times elsewhere in California. East of the Sierra Nevada, along the fringe of the Great Basin, is a chain of lakes that serves as a third important migration corridor in California. The lakes, three hundred to five hundred miles apart, have no outflows to the sea and so are highly saline. But they breed luxuriant blooms of brine shrimp and brine flies, which make them important staging areas for ducks, geese, grebes, and shorebirds. They range from Goose Lake on the Oregon border through Honey and Mono lakes to the Salton Sea. Each one has its troubles. Mono Lake is shrinking as Los Angeles diverts the water that once flowed into it from Sierra streams. If Los Angeles has its way, the lake may become too saline to support life.

The Salton Sea, five hundred miles south of Mono Lake and on the edge of the Mojave Desert, is smoky blue, the color and texture of windowpanes on a hazy day. It is dotted in winter with thousands of grebes, ruddy ducks, scaup, and pintail. Willet, godwits, and western sandpipers scurry over its mudflats. The desert sun is intense. Brine flies swarm in the mud. Great blue herons croak from rookeries in drowned mesquite trees a few hundred feet from shore.

The Salton Sea is an accident of water engineering. In 1905 the canal built to bring Colorado River water to the Imperial Valley broke, and for two years the Colorado bled into the California desert. The break was repaired, but irrigation water from the Imperial and Coachella valleys has been drained into the sea ever since. By the 1970s the entire flow of the Colorado River was being diverted, and the river's outflow into the Gulf of California, once a lush wintering ground for migrants, had dried up. The Salton Sea has provided the migrating birds an alternative habitat.

As irrigation increased, the sea grew. It grew so much that the original shoreline of the 35,000-acre Salton Sea National Wildlife Refuge, established in 1930, is now submerged a quarter of a mile beyond the present shoreline. Some 2,400 acres of the refuge are still above water, protected by levees on the southern shore. There, ponds host pintail, Canada geese, and snow geese in winter. But the flooded acres also are productive. The sea holds astonishingly high populations of marine fish, including orangemouth corvina, sargo, and gulf croaker (bairdiella) transplanted from the Gulf of California. With the fish came marine worms, copepods, barnacles, herons, cormorants, pelicans, and grebes. "There are some pretty staggering wildlife populations here," says refuge manager Gary Kramer. "Well in excess of 1½ million shorebirds will use the area at one time."

But the Salton Sea is changing yet again. A successful effort to conserve irrigation water in the Imperial and Coachella valleys has reduced the amount of water entering the sea. More water is evaporating than is draining into the sea, and as the sea shrinks, it grows saltier. It is already saltier than seawater, and eventually it will grow too salty to support the invertebrates that now feed the enormous bird and fish populations. The wildlife refuge will still flood ponds with freshwater to support wigeon and pintail and

snow geese in winter, but increasing salinity will doom the herons, pelicans, and cormorants, which feed on fish. Grebes and phalaropes may all but vanish. Shorebirds will be hard pressed.

Both the U.S. Fish and Wildlife Service and the State of California have long been aware that California's wetlands are disappearing. But they have been unable to find ways to stop the trend. The state pledged in 1952 to provide more adequate waterfowl habitat, bought four parcels, and ran out of money. Since then, no funds have been provided.

The Fish and Wildlife Service is trying to buy up easements on thousands of acres of duck habitat in the Central Valley, most of it in the Butte Sink and Grassland area. The easements would bind duck clubs or farmers to flood their fields through most of the winter. But since farmers won't sell easements lest they reduce the value of the land as bank-loan collateral in better times, duck clubs are really the only takers. And the program doesn't address the water-delivery and water-quality problems that beset the refuges. Since 1983 the service has petitioned the Bureau of Reclamation to secure rights to at least some portion of the 550,000 acre-feet needed to manage the state and federal waterfowl areas in California. Although the bureau has a million acre-feet of unappropriated water, it has opposed the petition. A bill before Congress seeks to secure at least some of that water.

A willet flashes over a salty shallow.

JEFFREY RICH

81

C. G. KELLEY

In 1979 the California Legislature resolved that the state should protect all its remaining wetlands and, by purchase or easement, add 50 percent to the existing total. Some funds were made available from the state's Wildlife Conservation Fund, and in 1984 voters approved a bond measure aimed at saving wetlands. A second ballot initiative in 1988 authorized millions more in bonds for wetland purchases. But the money doesn't come close to the $481-million price tag the state put on the goal in 1983.

Meanwhile, staff cutbacks have reduced the Department of Fish and Game's ability to manage its own waterfowl management areas. For example, at the Imperial Wildlife Area on the Salton Sea the maintenance crew was cut from twelve to six, and manager Chris Gonzales worried that cattails would take over much of the habitat. At Honey Lake Wildlife Area the staff was cut 50 percent. Said area manager Kit Novick, "Right now we have a number of lands which are idle because we don't have the manpower." Budget cuts in 1990 leave the future of these and other areas uncertain.

Private organizations have stepped in to help. The California Waterfowl Association hired its own biologist and started a "high-density nesting project" to breed more mallard at the state's Grizzly Island Wildlife Area in Suisun Marsh. The Nature Conservancy and National Audubon Society have both made efforts to purchase critical wetlands in California. The Nature Conservancy already has projects under way on the Cosumnes River on the edge of the Central Valley and on the Carrizo Plain, a large soda lake in San Luis Obispo County that hosts large numbers of wintering sandhill cranes. National Audubon manages the Ballona wetlands in Los Angeles and last year acquired 780 acres of valuable wetlands near Modesto that will be the start of a new San Joaquin National Wildlife Refuge. A joint venture under the North American Waterfowl Management Plan seeks through such efforts to protect 80,000 acres of existing wetlands and add 120,000 acres to the wetlands of the Central Valley.

However, even combined with state and federal activities, these efforts don't stop the overall loss of wetlands. No one expects this trend to reverse itself. Says Mark Strong, "The long-term trend is way down. There's no question there will be a continuing trend to convert more wetlands into croplands. We're fighting for every acre here. But I think we've already lost so much that we can't take care of the waterfowl populations we once had."

Under the intense desert sun, great egrets nest in drowned mesquite trees on the Salton Sea.

83

IN MEMORY OF
MARTHA AND HER KIND

TEXT BY DAVID WILCOVE • PAINTING BY JOHN DAWSON

*"Against hawks,
raccoons, foxes, and
opossums, the passenger
pigeon's strategy was a
spectacular success.
Against* homo sapiens, *it
was a fatal mistake."*

*First the legend. It is September 1, 1914, a
hot, muggy day in Cincinnati. Summoned
by telegram and letter, eminent ornithologists from across the country have gathered
at the city's zoo, where they now cluster in
front of a large, metal aviary. Joining them
are a handful of reporters and a crowd of
onlookers. Their hushed voices are almost
lost amidst the incessant droning of the summer cicadas. Inside the aviary, a lone pigeon
lies huddled on the floor, a listless ball of
feathers. This is Martha, the world's last passenger pigeon, and she is dying. The grand
old men of ornithology have gathered to witness the passing of her race. The oldest
among them remember a time when clouds
of wild pigeons swept across the skies of a
wilder nation. Now, in Martha's final hours,
they sense their own mortality. Martha is
motionless, but the steady blinking of her
beady, dark eyes betrays life. The blinks grow
longer, until the eyes no longer open. An elderly gentleman extracts a pocketwatch from
his vest. It is 1:00 P.M.*

*Now the reality. Martha was indeed the
last passenger pigeon, and she died on September 1, 1914. But her death was witnessed
not by a gathering of eminent graybeards,
but by her keeper and his son. The press
essentially ignored the event, save for a short
obituary in the* Cincinnati Enquirer. *A day or
two after her death, she was taken to the Cincinnati Ice Company plant, suspended in a
tank of water, and frozen in a three-hundred-
pound block of ice. Martha was then shipped
to the Smithsonian and promptly stuffed.
She resides there today, sharing her glass case
in the Hall of Birds with a great auk, a Carolina parakeet, and other spectral companions.*

Over three-quarters of a century has passed
since Martha's death, and while other species
have vanished in the interim, none has
seemed so tragic and inexplicable a loss as
that of the passenger pigeon, once the most
abundant bird on Earth. The passenger
pigeon remains a subject of lively speculation
and research among scientists. In fact, ornithologists at the turn of the century witnessed the process with little more than be-

wilderment. It is time to give Martha the
obituary she deserved.

Martha was part of a small colony of passenger pigeons at the zoo. The colony had
been started in 1878 or 1879 (the record is
unclear) with the purchase of four pairs of
wild pigeons from Michigan. What prompted
the zoo to buy pigeons will never be known,
but it paid handsomely for them—$2.50 a
pair at a time when dead ones were selling for thirty-five to forty cents a dozen in
Chicago. The decision proved a wise one, for
within two decades, the passenger pigeon
was extinct in the wild.

The Cincinnati Zoo housed its pigeons in
an outside aviary where, it was hoped, they
would prosper. They didn't. A few young
were produced, but never enough to make
up for the loss of older birds, and over time
the colony dwindled. Other zoos were even
less successful at breeding these pigeons. By
spring 1909 the Cincinnati flock, now totaling just three individuals, was all that
remained. A year later, only Martha was left.

She would live for four more years, an
aging dowager sharing her aviary with a
handful of mourning doves. During her last
months, Martha was too weak to fly up to her
perch and spent her time huddled on the
cage floor. Now a celebrity, she drew crowds
of onlookers who were probably disap-
pointed by the inert little bird they saw. On
Sundays, in fact, the keepers had to rope off
the area around the cage to keep the public
from throwing sand at her to make her move.
At her death she was reputed to be twenty-
nine years old, a remarkably advanced age
for a pigeon.

Captive propagation has saved other species, most notably the Socorro dove of Mexico
and the pink pigeon of Mauritius, so why
didn't it work with the passenger pigeon? No
one knows for certain, but the most plau-
sible explanation is simply ignorance. Zoos
today go to extraordinary lengths to maintain
healthy bloodlines among their animals.
Stud books, DNA "fingerprinting," computer simulations, and the like are routinely
used to minimize inbreeding and genetic
bottlenecks among zoo animals. A century

ago, however, captive propagation was more a matter of benign neglect than science: Put a few pigeons of both sexes in a cage, feed them, protect them, and let nature take its course. Nature did, but one suspects the result was increasingly unfit pigeons.

Far more difficult to comprehend is how the passenger pigeon ever ended up in such a precarious state, from billions of wild birds at the start of the 19th Century to a handful of captive ones at the close. People were convinced the species was all but indestructible, and the answers usually put forth to explain its demise—overhunting and the clearing of forests—simply don't add up. True, millions of pigeons were killed, but the numbers taken were at best a small fraction of the total population. And while forest destruction contributed to the extinction, the birds disappeared far more rapidly than the trees. To understand why the pigeons vanished, one must first understand how they lived and, in particular, their unique relationship with beech, oak, and hickory trees, whose mast they devoured.

Prior to the arrival of European settlers, most of eastern North America was covered by these mast-producing trees. Their large, nutritious nuts sustained the great flocks of pigeons. The trees and pigeons shared a survival strategy: safety in numbers. As anyone with an oak or hickory in the backyard learns, these trees do not produce a steady crop of nuts year after year. Instead, all of the oaks, hickories, or beeches in a given area produce an enormous crop of nuts only once every few years. This synchronous and unpredictable production of mast is designed to overwhelm hungry squirrels, bears, blue jays, and other seed eaters, giving at least a few acorns, hickory nuts, and beechnuts the chance to become saplings.

The passenger pigeon responded to this trick by adopting a nomadic life-style. During the fall and winter, flocks wandered through the eastern forests in search of masting trees, sometimes traveling hundreds of miles a day. With the coming of spring, they formed immense nesting colonies in areas where large crops of nuts from the previous autumn remained on the ground. Like their food trees, the pigeons were following a strategy of overwhelming abundance: nesting aggregations so vast that local predators could not wipe them out. One such colony in Wisconsin was estimated to cover more than 750 square miles and contain some 136 million birds. Because the colonies were such an ephemeral phenomenon, switching location from year to year and dispersing as soon as nesting was over, predators were not able to build their numbers enough to have a serious impact on the birds.

Against hawks, raccoons, foxes, and opossums, the passenger pigeon's strategy was a spectacular success. Against *Homo sapiens,* it was a fatal mistake. The colonies were a magnet for professional hunters eager to supply urban markets with pigeon meat. The resulting carnage has been described and redescribed many times, but it bears repeating. Young birds were knocked from their nests with poles; "stool pigeons," tethered birds whose eyelids had been sewn shut, were used to lure other pigeons to the ground where they could be netted; trees filled with nests were cut down or set afire; and sulfur was burned beneath nesting birds to suffocate them. From a single nesting colony near Grand Rapids, Michigan, hunters shipped 588 barrels—more than 100,000 pounds—of pigeons to market.

By the 1700s observers along the eastern seaboard could see that the flocks were thinning, the nesting colonies disappearing. "Some years past they have not been in such plenty as they used to be," wrote one naturalist in 1770. "This spring I saw them fly one morning, as I thought in great abundance; but everybody was amazed how few there were; and wondered at the reason." The last major nesting in New England occurred near Lunenburg, Massachusetts, in 1851. A decade later the big flocks were gone from coastal New York State and Pennsylvania. The declines were noticed, but little was done to save the pigeons. A few states passed laws to protect nesting colonies, but they were rarely enforced.

By the latter half of the 1800s the northern Lake States had become the last stronghold of the passenger pigeon. Here the birds fell victim to two seemingly unrelated advances in technology: the expansion of the railroad and the invention of the telegraph. In 1830 there were only twenty-three miles of railroad track in the United States; by the Civil War, the total had risen to more than 30,000 miles. This railroad network allowed commercial pigeon hunters to reach even the most distant colonies and ship birds to urban markets hundreds of miles away. The telegraph enabled hunters everywhere to learn quickly of the discovery of new nesting colonies. Exposed and vulnerable, the wild pigeons evaporated like ether. In 1878 their total population was estimated at about 50 million. By 1887 only one large nesting aggregation was left, located in Wisconsin. The birds abandoned this colony just two weeks after starting to nest, probably because of hunters. A few scattered pigeons were sighted here and there throughout the 1890s, but they were little more than the dying embers of an extinguished firestorm. On March 24, 1900, the last wild passenger pigeon was killed in Pike County, Ohio, leaving only Martha and her aging zoo colleagues.

Why the pigeons disappeared so rapidly— from tens of millions in 1878 to virtually none twenty years later—has long puzzled natural historians. Recently, two ornithologists from the University of Minnesota, David E. Blockstein and Harrison B. Tordoff, came up with a compelling explanation. During this critical twenty-year period, they argue, hunters managed to disrupt or destroy every major nesting colony. The birds were prevented from breeding for a period of time exceeding several pigeon generations, and the population crashed as entire cohorts died without replacing themselves.

Although the vast majority of passenger pigeons nested in a few immense colonies, a small proportion regularly chose to nest solitarily or in little groups. These birds were never exploited as ruthlessly as those in the colonies, yet they too disappeared. Blockstein and Tordoff believe that without the numerical protection provided by the large colonies, these lone pairs and little groups rarely produced fledglings. Their conspicuous twig nests and fat squabs were easy targets for a host of predatory animals.

The loss of the passenger pigeon was an ecological event of profound significance, altering the lives of predators and prey, shifting and changing the pathways of nutrients and energy flow in ways we will never fully understand. With the great flocks gone, the very oaks and hickories whose limbs once snapped under the weight of feasting pigeons now stood empty. Nuts once destined to be turned into pigeons fell to the ground, where they were hoarded by squirrels and blue jays. And for animals that once ate squab, the end of the nesting colonies meant a long, difficult search for other foods.

The passenger pigeon was a phenomenon of numbers. "Yearly the feathered tempest roared up, down, and across the continent," wrote Aldo Leopold, "sucking up the laden fruits of forest and prairie, burning them in a traveling blast of life." From an ecological perspective, the extinction of the passenger pigeon is best defined not by the death of the last individual (a lone, decrepit bird in a metal cage) but by the disappearance of the flocks. Thus, if ecologists rather than historians were in charge of such things, we would know 1887—the year of the last great nesting aggregation—as the true date of extinction for the passenger pigeon.

No one alive today remembers the autumn skies as they appeared darkened by pigeons; no one can recall the flashes of blue and russet as the flocks wheeled and turned before diving into the trees. The captive birds, however, lasted long after the wild flocks were gone, and as the seventy-fifth anniversary of Martha's death approached, I began to wonder whether anyone alive today remembered Martha, whether that tenuous and final link still endured. Was there a young child growing up in Cincinnati in the early years of this century with an incipient curiosity about birds, who might have visited the local zoo? Would seeing the very last passenger pigeon stick in a child's memory, and persevere through the ups and downs of seventy-plus years?

In the winter of 1987 I published a notice in several ornithological journals, asking anyone who had seen Martha before her death to contact me. I received only one reply, a brief letter from a gentleman named Merrill Wood. He wrote:

> I remember when I was six years old, my parents took me to the Cincinnati Zoo in the summer of 1914 (June, July, or August, probably August) to see the last living Passenger Pigeon, kept in a large enclosure with some Mourning Doves. My mother (no ornithologist) said she did not see much difference in the two species of doves. In September my father read to me from a newspaper that this famous bird had died.

Mr. Wood identified himself as a retired professor of zoology "now age seventy-eight and probably will soon join that bird."

I wish Professor Wood good health for many years to come, but I also know he is right: There cannot be many other people left who saw a living passenger pigeon, and sometime in the not-too-distant future there will be none. The passenger pigeon will face another extinction, this time from memory.

By the year 2014, the centennial of Martha's death, our only remaining links to the passenger pigeon will be a handful of historical accounts and the mounted specimens that stare vacantly into space from the security of their museum showcases.

The land itself will show no signs the wild pigeon was ever here, except perhaps in the names we have bestowed upon a few landmarks—places like Pigeon Creek in Pennsylvania or Pigeon Swamp in New York. If there are alternative explanations for these names, I prefer not to know them. We name bridges and buildings after famous people. We can also name a few creeks and swamps after the remarkable bird we destroyed.

III
NATURAL PHENOMENA

MATCHSTICKS!

TEXT BY FRANK GRAHAM JR.   •   PHOTOGRAPHY BY LARRY CAMERON

In the fall of 1989, that old cliché was heard again and again in South Carolina after Hurricane Hugo had devastated the Low Country's forests—"trees snapped like matchsticks," or "big pines scattered every which way, like handfuls of matchsticks." But the mundane little word, metaphor or simile, hardly reflects the horror of the reality, mile after mile of shattered wood, decapitated and dismembered giants standing over oceans of debris.

A thousand journalists have chronicled the human misery. Homes in splinters, the roofs of others heaved aslant, like the caps of tipsy soldiers. Twenty-six lives were lost. (The toll of dead and injured in the cleanup is said to have surpassed that of the storm itself, as amateur loggers were brained by falling trees or maimed by their new-bought chainsaws.) An elderly woman, asked to describe Hugo, burst out: "He was a *bitch!*"

But what was nature's impact on nature itself? It will be months, even years, before all the consequences reveal themselves, but here follows the report of an *Audubon* writer on Hugo's grim trail.

Norman Brunswig, manager of the National Audubon Society's Francis Beidler Forest Sanctuary, some forty miles northwest of Charleston, had kept track of the hurricane's approach for a week as it smashed through the Caribbean islands.

"It wasn't clear what it was going to do as it approached the South Carolina mainland," Brunswig said. "We kept hoping it would change direction—not to sandbag somebody else, but just turn out to sea, or maybe lose force."

But those hopes were dashed on Thursday morning, September 21st, when Hugo not only headed straight for Charleston but also picked up speed and power. Winds accelerated to 135 miles an hour. Before closing the Beidler visitors' center, Brunswig supervised the taping of windows and the filling of the sanctuary's canoes with water to hold them in place. Then he left to board up the windows at home, casting a worried glance at the tumbling menace of the sky.

"We had bought our house because of the large pines that surrounded it," he said. "Now the trees were a real danger, and late in the day we accepted our neighbor's invitation to sweat out the storm at their place, which is in the middle of a field."

Hugo struck at 11:30 that night. No one slept as the storm tore at the building, shaking it almost without letup and drowning out with its shrill keening the smashing of trees in the nearby forest. At dawn, and al-

Here, the loblolly pines of South Carolina's Francis Marion National Forest, before and after Hurricane Hugo.

90

most reluctantly, Brunswig and his wife, Beverly, returned to their house. Twenty-six of the big pines in their yard had fallen, three of them hitting their house. But a new roof and some touching up where water had seeped in undid most of the damage, meaning that the Brunswigs had fared better than many of their Low Country neighbors. The scene at the sanctuary, however, was to depress Brunswig for weeks.

The 5,819-acre Beidler Forest, in the rambling Four Holes Swamp, holds Earth's largest remaining virgin stand of bald cypress and tupelos. (Some of the cypresses are believed to be more than six-hundred years old.) It is an aqueous forest, the big trees standing in three feet of black swamp water. River otters, bobcats, water moccasins, alligators, turtles, white ibises, and prothonotary warblers are among the wild creatures that inhabit the sanctuary. Before Hugo hit, visitors walked into the swamp on a boardwalk 6,500 feet long, immersing themselves in the shaded grandeur of another world.

Norm Brunswig found that world in tatters once the staff had cut a way into the visitors' center through a jumble of fallen trees. Miraculously, the center itself was intact. The wind had taken down dozens of trees just behind it, but they had fallen into the swamp or across the boardwalk. The boardwalk was in ruins for most of its length. Oaks, with their shallow root systems, were

This page: The boardwalk at National Audubon Society's Francis Beidler Forest, near Charleston, before and after Hugo. Next page: Ruined beach houses on Folly Island after the storm.

toppled, the muck clinging to the roots where trees lay in windrows on their sides. Many of the tall, slender pines were snapped like—well, like matchsticks. But the huge cypresses, supported by their buttresses, lived to fight again.

There was little satisfaction even of that kind at the Medway Plantation, a 6,800-acre showplace twenty miles closer to the coast. Brunswig (also assistant director of National Audubon's Sanctuary Department) has worked closely with the Medway staff for some time, and seven hundred acres of the plantation have already been donated to the society by its owner. There the ruin was on a greater scale than that suffered at Beidler Forest.

"The lights went out when the storm came on," Robert Hortman, Medway's manager, told Brunswig afterward. "Even through the boarded windows we could hear the loblolly pines snapping: *Tsss-chuck! Tsss-chuck!* When the eye of the storm passed over and everything was strangely quiet for a while, I went out and shined my flashlight up into the trees, and there was nothing there!"

Hortman and his staff were trapped in the interior of the plantation for five days while emergency crews worked to open the tree-clogged access roads. The old plantation house somehow stood up to the storm, the uprooted live oaks and other ancient trees piled around it, like a precious egg packed in its nest.

What made the privately owned plantations like Medway special was that they weren't under the commercial gun. There was no need to squeeze every penny from the forest. Their managers could be selective, in

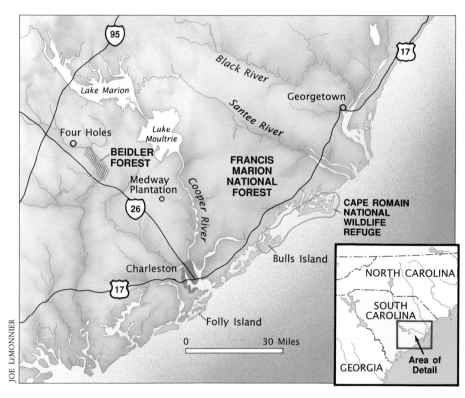

JOE LeMONNIER

the old-fashioned European way, letting the pines grow for ninety years or more, producing "perfect" trees. The most valuable timber is usually found in the first, or bottom, log, but at Medway the pines were snapped off in that lower portion or, if the tree broke higher, everything below was often structurally damaged.

"In some areas there aren't enough trees left to regenerate the forest, so we'll have to do a lot of planting," Hortman reported. "The wildlife? I've seen foxes wandering

93

around like they were dazed, and wild turkeys limping or with broken feathers. Because the forest canopy is gone, the warblers are confused, and there are birds in the understory I've never seen before."

Brunswig might exult in the survival of the giant bald cypresses and tupelos in Beidler Forest. But the splendor around them was gone for now, replaced by the stench of rotting vegetation in the water, and by hordes of mosquitoes that hatched after the storm from puddles where their normal predators could not get at them. Many of the standing loblolly and longleaf pines showed ugly scars, their bark ripped away by the glancing blows of their stricken neighbors as they fell.

"This spring the fresh greenery in the swamp will hide part of the destruction," Brunswig said. "But there may be profound consequences of the storm here. Pine bark beetles find scars to be inviting points of entry, so we could have a beetle epidemic that will finish off a lot of the trees that Hugo didn't get. And it looks as if we lost almost all our oaks and hickories, the trees that deer, squirrels, and our big wild turkey population depend on for mast. They'll have a feast this fall, perhaps, but in future years there's going to be famine."

As soon as Hugo began its rampage through the Caribbean, wild areas and their inhabitants took beatings:

• The Puerto Rican parrot, down to only thirteen birds in the wild in 1971, had responded to affirmative-action programs launched by interagency biologists in the Caribbean National Forest (its only known home), and counts earlier last year turned up forty-seven individuals. After Hugo demolished large areas of the forest, computer projections estimated that half the wild population had been wiped out. A few days later, preliminary surveys in the field found only twenty-four parrots. Fortunately, another fifty-four of them were safe in an aviary maintained for a captive-breeding program.

• Sixty-five miles of South Carolina's dunes took a fearful beating when the hurricane made its landfall. Federal, state, and private funds were used to scrape sand into new protective dunes, efforts that were criticized by some scientists who predicted that the artificially steepened slopes would only cause waves to break farther inland. Under state law, some two hundred beach houses carried away in the storm surge cannot be replaced. Their location would now be on the seaward side of the "critical line," where future erosion can be expected to occur.

• Shellfish beds along parts of the South Carolina coastline were closed because runoff from Hugo's heavy rainfall overburdened sewage plants. The resulting overflow contaminated shellfish, posing "a threat to public health."

• Enormous numbers of fish died when leaves and bark blew into lakes and rivers, rotting there and robbing the water of oxygen. Further oxygen was lost when organic muck, churned up on lakebottoms, decomposed. "The turtles are feasting," an observer said.

Bulls Island, just north of Charleston, was one of South Carolina's glories. On its nearly 5,000 acres grew the finest maritime forest of the Atlantic Coast—a green, densely textured tangle of live oaks, pines, and palmettos. The island, a component of the Cape Romain National Wildlife Refuge, also proved suitable for the experimental release of red wolves as a part of the federal program to restore that species to the wild.

A visitor last fall had ample warning of what to expect on reaching the island. Mile after mile of forest along Route 17, the coastal highway, had simply ceased to exist, now resembling isolated fenceposts with chewed-off tops. Refuge headquarters at Moore's Landing, in the mainland village of Awendaw, had also ceased to exist. The scene put one in mind of a wartime outpost, after the bombs have gone off and the survivors have crawled from the mud to try to carry on as before.

Men and women, wearing U.S. Fish and Wildlife Service insignia, walked among the trailers and campers hastily installed on the headquarters site. Waiting on the remains of a dock for a boat to take them to Bulls Island were George Garris, the refuge manager, and Warren Parker, the leader of the red wolf recovery team.

"It wasn't the wind that wrecked us," Garris was saying. "A surge of water nineteen feet high came ashore at this spot, picking up trees and mud and smashing everything in its path. The visitors' center and headquar-

ERWIN AND PEGGY BAUER

ters was built well—it would take a million dollars to put up one like it today—but it's gone. So are fifty years of refuge records, our books, our color slides. One of the staff hasn't even found the remains of his desk."

Parker expressed his amazement that the wolves had somehow lived through the storm on Bulls Island.

"We had a pair of wolves out there that produced a litter of five pups last spring," he said. "An alligator got the female and one of the pups—we found the radio the female was carrying in some gator droppings! When we flew over the island after the storm, we saw the male and the four remaining pups still together. We dropped carnivore logs—they're big chunks of horse meat like the ones they feed to tigers in zoos. The wolves may not be able to move around enough now to capture prey. I'm going out there today to see if we ought to take them off the island."

Scientists believe the red wolf evolved here in the New World. (The gray wolf is a larger European animal that apparently came to North America over the Bering land bridge.) Restricted to what became the southern United States in recent times, the red wolf declined precipitously after the arrival of European settlers. By the 1970s the remnants of the population were hybridizing with coyotes. Only a handful of pure-bred red wolves were left, prompting the Fish and Wildlife Service to capture all of them. The red wolf, like the California condor, became extinct in the wild.

"This is the first time an 'extinct' animal has been reintroduced," Parker said. "We now have a small population living free on the Alligator River National Wildlife Refuge in eastern North Carolina. Wolves that are born in captivity don't do well when they're released. They usually live only six or eight months, at best. But they are valuable if they can produce and rear pups during that time, as they've done on Bulls Island. The pups learn from them and can make it in the wild."

Garris and Parker joined several other men in a small boat that headed through the offshore marshes toward the island.

"These marshes were full of clapper rails," Garris shouted above the roar of the twin outboards. "Some of them survived that big surge of water and got carried inland. I've seen rails up there, headed back toward the marshes."

The men landed at a battered dock on Bulls Island. Its maritime forest lay in untidy layers, the horizontal trunks forming an almost impassable barrier. The palmettos, deprived of their lush neighbors, were nothing

Cape Romain National Wildlife Refuge was hit hard by Hugo. A 19-foot storm surge destroyed the refuge headquarters and ravaged the finest Atlantic maritime forest, but radio tracking confirmed the miraculous survival of endangered red wolves on Bulls Island.

Because of heavy damage to old pines in Francis Marion National Forest—trees that sustained a rare growing population of red-cockaded wood-peckers—the U.S. Forest Service rushed to provide 800 artificial cavities like the box being installed by Sheryl Sanders, below.

but frayed and upended broomsticks. Huge army-surplus front-loaders and other equipment, operated by emergency crews sent from refuges all over the Southeast, were opening rudimentary roads through the debris.

"Here are some tracks!" called Parker, who was standing only a few feet from the dock. "It's the big male, and the tracks are fresh."

Garris nodded. "Before the storm the male came here every night," he said. "This is where he landed, and maybe this is where he thinks he's going to get off."

"We use Bulls Island to acclimatize wolves to life in the wild," Parker said. "There isn't enough room here to sustain a growing population, but it gives a young wolf a taste of what freedom is like."

As Garris and Parker followed a path opened by the cleanup crews, they found more distinct tracks in the muck. The wolves were moving, and so were raccoons, squirrels, even deer. Parker, climbing a metal observation tower left standing by the storm, wasn't able to pick up signals from the radios carried by the wolves, but he was more than satisfied with his inspection tour.

"The wolves are probably up at the north end of the island, and we know now that both the wolves and their prey can get around," he said. "We'll leave them on the island until late winter, then take them off and either release them at Alligator River or use them in the captive-breeding program. The male is a marvelous animal. This is the second year in a row he has lost the female to gators, but in both years he reared the pups by himself. We'll bring out another female in February."

Bulls Island's maritime forest may take a century to recover, but life goes on in the ruins.

A Forest Service worker, wearing a hard hat and protective eyewear, climbed a metal ladder that was propped against a pine in the Francis Marion National Forest. At the foot of the ladder another forester started a chainsaw, then hoisted the chattering machine to her on a light rope. In a moment she was cutting into the tree, hollowing out a deep, rectangular cavity.

"We can't afford to wait," said Robert G. Hooper, a Forest Service research biologist who was standing nearby. "The biggest threat to the red-cockaded woodpecker is habitat destruction, and Hugo destroyed a large part of the habitat here. The birds nest in old pines. They seldom accept nest boxes, and so we're trying to give them a focus for establishing new colonies."

Few areas of South Carolina were ransacked quite as thoroughly by Hugo as the 250,000-acre Marion National Forest. Perhaps 50 percent of the trees were knocked down, a loss in lumbermen's terms amounting to anywhere from 700 million to 1 billion board feet. (A forester calculated that the downed timber was the equivalent of a board, one by twelve inches, long enough to circle the globe seven times.) The blow was compounded by the circumstance that this forest sustained an increasing population of the red-cockaded woodpecker. Under the Endangered Species Act, the little woodpecker is a priority item wherever it breeds on public lands.

"We had about 475 colonies," said Hooper, who is assigned by the Forest Service to red-cockaded protection work. "These woodpeckers live in family groups, from two to nine birds, including the breeding pair, young of the year, and older siblings that hang around as helpers. Each colony may excavate three or four cavities and defend them against other family groups. We're trying to create about eight hundred artificial cavities now because we estimate that 80 percent of their old nest trees went down."

Hooper and his colleagues may be optimistic in preparing such a high number of woodpecker homes. Early surveys disclosed that 75 to 95 percent of the birds survived in areas of the forest escaping heavy damage, but only 40 percent were detected elsewhere.

"I've actually found only one dead red-cockaded," Hooper said. "It was in a tree that broke, like so many did, right at the cavity. The tree had hinged over, and I could see the bird's feathers sticking out. We don't know exactly what happened to most of the missing birds. They would probably fly out as the tree went down. They could have been beaten to death in the storm or maybe blown fifty miles away."

The woman on the ladder had finished carving out a hollow in the tree. Hooper held up a rectangular piece of wood that would fit neatly inside the new hole. It was a portable woodpecker nest, coated with a sealant to keep out the tree's resin and itself hollowed out with a woodpecker-sized cavity. In the event that other birds or mammals enlarge the cavity for their own purposes, biologists have designed a metal "restrictor" that can be fitted over the entrance, bringing it back down to red-cockaded size. The forester, after coating the inside of the hollowed tree with glue, pounded in the plug with a mallet. Everyone hoped it would not remain long untenanted.

There will be trying times ahead for the Francis Marion National Forest. With sawmills glutted by the unexpected harvest everywhere in the region, much of the fallen timber may rot in the warm climate before markets can be found for it. Threats of fire and insect infestation will grow, once spring arrives. Either occurrence, by prematurely removing more trees, would further cloud the woodpecker's future.

"It will take a very long time for the forest to recover, and at least several decades before the red-cockaded population can return to pre-hurricane levels," Bob Hooper said. "But the woodpecker will be a driving factor in whatever decisions are made affecting this forest in the future."

The Montana conservationist Les Pengelly once described selective logging as the practice of selecting a forest and then logging it. In the aftermath of Hurricane Hugo, one might be excused for wondering what the fuss made by forest preservationists is all about. Perhaps the advocates of clearcutting are right: Why not cut the trees as soon as they are "harvestable," rather than let them rot where they stand, or be reduced to rubble in a violent storm?

Such thoughts may have troubled Norm Brunswig when he saw the trees strewn across Francis Beidler Forest. But if they did, they soon flickered out, submerged by his plans for rebuilding the sanctuary's boardwalk so that it will be ready to lead curious and wondering visitors into the swamp again this spring.

"Our job at the sanctuary is to preserve natural systems," Brunswig told a friend several weeks after the hurricane. "The species of plants and animals at Beidler evolved in a disaster-prone ecosystem. We're not here to log the forest or salvage the downed timber. We're here to let events play themselves out in good times and bad, and tell the story to the public."

97

CHRISTMAS CACTUS

PHOTOGRAPHY BY THOMAS A. WIEWANDT

Once every ten or fifteen years, several inches of snow falls on the foothills of Arizona's Tucson Mountains. Falls on saguaro and prickly pear, on ocotillo and sotol, briefly transforming the Sonoran Desert into a bizarre rendition of a traditional New England greeting card.

TRANS-ALASKA PIPELINE IN THE BROOKS RANGE BY GEORGE HERBEN

IV

THE CONSERVATIONISTS

UNTRAMMELED BY MAN

TEXT BY T. H. WATKINS

Above: Wolf track on Isle Royale in Lake Superior. Opposite page: Vermilion Cliffs Wilderness, Arizona.

It's now over a quarter-century since President Lyndon B. Johnson signed the Wilderness Act of 1964. It set the stage for the creation of a system of preserved wilderness that today has grown to include more than 90 million acres in 474 units of national parks, national forests, national wildlife refuges, and other federal lands. In sizes ranging from the six acres on Florida's Pelican Island National Wildlife Refuge to the 8.7 million acres on Alaska's Wrangell–St. Elias National Park and Preserve, these areas are places to be kept inviolate, where vehicles are forbidden and all but the most benign of human contacts proscribed. No other nation has ever done anything like it; no other nation has even thought of doing anything like it. Like the Omnibus Civil Rights Act signed earlier in 1964 and the Voting Rights Act signed a year later, the Wilderness Act was nothing short of revolutionary—an attempt to enshrine in law a principle designed to change the way we live on the Earth. Unlike those other two great statutes, however, which were fashioned in an attempt to ensure that the rights and dignity of one group of citizens were not violated by the ancestral cruelty and ignorance of another, the Wilderness Act was an effort to ensure the protection and preservation—at least in part—of the Earth itself, from all citizens. What is more, unlike the other two laws, which were written in the blood and anger and sorrow of the streets then forced upon a reluctant government, the Wilderness Act was the child of the system whose deepest traditions it would turn on end.

The sometime schoolteacher and essayist Henry David Thoreau first gave voice to the concept a century earlier. In "Walking," a long essay written in 1861, the peripatetic philosopher of Concord, Massachusetts, etched a thought that has since become part of the national memory: "The West of which I speak is but another name for the Wild," he wrote, "and what I have been preparing to say is, that in Wildness is the preservation of the World." Thoreau knew, by instinct and observation, what the whole weight of

science has since proved: The roots of human survival are nourished in primeval soil. He knew, and John Muir knew, and a few others with them and after them knew, but even as they formed their convictions and gave them voice, the wildness itself was disappearing all around them. The great dark woods of New England had been felled twice over and were being felled again. The last groves of ancient hardwoods were being ripped down and carried out of the Appalachians on railroads that curved like entrails through the smoky forests. The piney woods of the Great Lakes country were stripped, rough-cut into lumber, cobbled into rafts the size of a village common, and floated down the swift midwestern rivers to market. In California the redwoods of the Coast Range and sugar pines of the Sierras were vanishing. In Oregon and Washington the Douglas fir and Sitka spruce were under assault. The enormous prairie of the Ohio and Mississippi river valleys had gone over to the inferior grasses of corn and wheat and barley. Coal mines gouged the hills and hollows of Appalachia, gold and silver and copper mines pocked the crags and saddles and hanging valleys of the Rockies. Mills and smelters shattered the long silences and stank up the blue distances of southwestern deserts. Cattle and sheep packed the rich grassy swales of mountain meadows and river valleys from the High Plains to the Kaibab Plateau. Mountain slopes were brutalized, tortured with erosion, wetlands were sucked up, dredged, filled, built upon. Everywhere rivers were polluted and channeled and dammed; everywhere wolves and bears and butterflies died.

In a struggle that pitted the Industrial Age against everything else, philosophy was poor armament. By the turn of the century the hope of the remaining wildness was in law, not philosophy, no matter how eloquently delivered—in law and in the government that gave it substance. Already the machinery of law had moved to create a National Park System—although with only four parks and, with no overriding legislation to administer them, precious little system. It had also established, in 1891, the National Forest Re-

The Crab Orchard Wilderness, Illinois.

serves, vast areas withdrawn by presidential decree from untrammeled use and exploitation—providing you could keep out or catch those who were bent on destruction. To do that, law would give the reserves the U.S. Forest Service in 1905, and President Theodore Roosevelt would put Gifford Pinchot at its head. Pinchot was no wilderness visionary, had no understanding of and less sympathy for those who would have saved wild country for its own sake; but as the patron saint of utilitarian conservation, he was at least a steward who would tolerate no unseemly wreckage. Law also would give the national parks the National Park Service in 1916, and President Woodrow Wilson would put Stephen T. Mather at its head. Mather preserved scenery, not wilderness, but he loved his parks and made them grow, and when he left in 1929 the National Park System, like the National Forest System, was firmly in place as an inextricable part of the American bureaucracy. And it would be in these two bureaucratic systems that the idea of wilderness as law would be conceived and slowly, agonizingly, nurtured at least partway toward birth.

For quite a while it looked as if bureaucracy would prove barren ground. In 1892 John Muir had joined with a few other Cali-

fornia mountain-lovers to form the Sierra Club. One of the club's principal achievements was the addition of the glorious valley floor to Yosemite National Park in 1905. The small but energetic organization also became an early voice for the creation of forest reserves, an advocacy that brought Muir the friendly acquaintance of Gifford Pinchot and Theodore Roosevelt, and Muir's was one of the earliest and most influential voices urging Roosevelt to establish the Forest Service and to appoint Pinchot the first chief forester.

However friendly at the outset, the relationship between Muir and Pinchot probably never could have flourished. A chasm of perception lay between the two, a difference suggested by Pinchot when he told of the time they had encountered a tarantula on the rim of the Grand Canyon during a trip in 1896. Muir, Pinchot wrote in bemusement, "wouldn't let me kill it. He said it had as much right there as we did." In any case, whatever chance there might have been for a permanent friendship was effectively stifled shortly after the Sierra Club's victory in achieving an expanded Yosemite National Park. In 1905 Pinchot eagerly endorsed San Francisco's plan to build a dam on the Tuolumne River in a portion of the park called

108

the Hetch Hetchy Valley. The project, the city's spokesman said in a claim sure of a sympathetic hearing in a Progressive-minded era, would free San Francisco from the grip of monopoly in the delivery of its water supply and in the generation of its electricity. But it also would flood the Hetch Hetchy Valley, destroying a place whose beauty many people—including John Muir—considered the equal of Yosemite Valley's.

The Hetch Hetchy affair was the first (though by no means the last) pure conflict between the two schools of conservation thought—use and preservation—and it pitted Pinchot and Muir against each other with precision. Eight years they fought, but in 1913 Interior Secretary Franklin K. Lane had a bill to take Hetch Hetchy introduced in Congress, and late in the year it was passed and signed into law. "The destruction of the charming groves and gardens, the finest in all California," Muir wrote to Sierra Clubber William E. Colby, "goes to my heart. But in spite of Satan & Co. some sort of compensation must surely come out of this dark damn-dam-damnation."

Muir died the following year, and with his passing much went out of the life of the preservation movement. Even in the Sierra Club there had been a painful split between those who opposed the damming of Hetch Hetchy and those who felt it more politic to let the city have it, and in the years that followed the club gradually subsided into an agreeable association of amateur mountaineers and naturalists. Outside the government the pursuit of the primitive was now pretty much confined to Robert Sterling Yard's National Parks Association, an organization started when Yard had been the main publicist for the National Park Service under Mather. Since then Yard and Mather had fallen out over the question of concessions, roads, and tourist facilities—Mather was generally for them, Yard violently against them—and Yard spent the tiny resources of the group in a storm of newsletters, broadsides, petitions, and pamphlets in complaint of what he perceived as the degradation of the primeval qualities of the national parks under the management of Mather and his successor, Horace M. Albright. It was a showy effort, but almost entirely the work of a single man.

Within the government, however, something was beginning to grow—in spite of the fact that the boom years of World War I and the Stuttering Twenties would seem to have been a poor time for something as abstract as wilderness preservation to have sprouted. Even more remarkably, the sentiment had developed deep in the lower ranks of the Forest Service, that temple of Pinchot's firm utilitarian prejudices. In 1919 Arthur Carhart, a young professional landscape architect, joined the Forest Service as a "recreational engineer," and the following year he was given the assignment of developing recreation plans for Trappers Lake in White River National Forest, Colorado. After several months of studying this untouched wild place, he concluded that the best thing to do with it was to leave it alone. His recommendation came to the attention of Aldo Leopold, the assistant forester for District 3 (an area that encompassed most of the Southwest), who had been thinking about the idea of wilderness preservation in the forests for some time. They met and talked, and Leopold persuaded Carhart to put their conclusions in writing. The problem, Carhart wrote in the consequent memorandum,

Arthur Carhart, 1919: Hired by the Forest Service as a "recreational engineer."

Aldo Leopold: "The Commanding General of the Wilderness Battle."

est use," and its criterion, "the greatest good to the greatest number," which is and must remain the guiding principle by which democracies handle their natural resources.

Pinchot's promise of development has been made good. The process must, of course, continue indefinitely. But it has already gone far enough to raise the question of whether the policy of development (construed in the narrow sense of industrial development) should continue to govern in absolutely every instance, or whether the principle of highest use does not itself demand that representative portions of some forests be preserved as wilderness.

"By 'wilderness,'" he went on, "I mean a continuous stretch of country preserved in its natural state, open to lawful hunting and fishing, big enough to absorb a two weeks' pack trip, and be kept devoid of roads, artificial trails, cottages, or other works of man." In October 1922 he recommended to his superiors that a 540,000-acre segment of Gila and Datil national forests in New Mexico be set aside as the Forest Service's (and the nation's) first administratively designated wilderness area, "in order to preserve at least one place in the Southwest where pack trips shall be the dominant play." And on June 3, 1924, a few days after Leopold left Albuquerque to become director of the Forest Products Laboratory in Madison, Wisconsin, District 3 forester Frank Pooler put into place the recreational working plan that established the Gila Wilderness Area.

The idea first promulgated by Carhart and Leopold slowly began to take on a bureaucratic dimension. In 1926 L. F. Kneipp, chief of the Forest Service's Division of Lands and Recreation, did a survey of roadless areas in the forests similar to the Gila Wilderness, found seventy-four tracts totaling 55 million acres that qualified, and helped to formulate what came to be called the "L-20 Regulations"—administrative directives that allowed the Chief Forester to encourage the designation by district foresters of "primitive areas" within their forest regions, areas that were to be kept wild in their "environment, transportation, habitation, and subsistence." By 1932 the list of primitive areas had grown to sixty-three, embracing 8.4 million acres.

This was not good enough for another young forester. His name was Robert Marshall, a graduate of the New York State College of Forestry, the holder of a Master of Forestry degree from the Harvard Forest School (a forestry training center owned and operated by Harvard University), and a PhD in plant physiology from Johns Hopkins University. One of a small group of incipient reb-

was, how far shall the Forest Service carry or allow to be carried manmade improvements in scenic territories, and whether there is not a definite point where all such developments, with the exception perhaps of lines of travel and necessary sign boards, shall stop. There is a limit to the number of lands of shoreline on the lakes; there is a limit to the number of lakes in existence; there is a limit to the mountainous areas of the world, and in each one of these situations there are portions of natural scenic beauty which are God-made, and the beauties of which of a right should be the property of all people.

Carhart's recommendation with regard to Trappers Lake was endorsed by his superiors, and the area was left unmarred. Two years later Leopold outlined his own thinking on the subject of wilderness in an article in the *Journal of Forestry:*

When the national forests were created the first argument of those opposing a national forest policy was that the forests would remain a wilderness. . . . At this time, Pinchot enunciated the doctrine of "high-

els within the Forest Service establishment, he also was the son of the highly successful New York lawyer Louis Marshall, who had been instrumental in establishing New York State's Adirondack Forest Preserve in the 1880s and who had imbued his children with both a powerful love of the outdoors and equally vigorous liberal instincts. In Robert these were swiftly translated into an affection for socialism and a suspicion of rank capitalism that discovered grounds for complaint in what free enterprise had done to the forests of the nation—and was still doing. He became a true disciple of Leopold's wilderness gospel, and in one of the first letters between them, early in 1930, he had called Leopold "the Commanding General of the Wilderness Battle." In February of that year Marshall outlined his own thinking in "The Problem of the Wilderness," an article published in *The Scientific Monthly*. America was losing its wild country, he warned his readers: "Just a few years more of hesitation and the only trace of that wilderness which has exerted such a fundamental influence in molding American character will lie in the musty pages of pioneer books and the mumbling memories of tottering antiquarians." It was necessary, right now, he said, to undertake a thorough study of the nation's wilderness needs and to be forthrightly radical in designating additions to the tiny resource already established by the Forest Service—"because," he said, "it is easy to convert a natural area to industrial or motor usage, impossible to do the reverse; because the population which covets wilderness recreation is rapidly enlarging; and because the higher standard of living which may be anticipated should give millions the economic power to satisfy what is today merely a pathetic yearning."

As young and relatively inexperienced as he was (he was twenty-nine in 1930 and had spent comparatively little time in the field), Marshall's thinking was provocative, and his influence and contacts were such that he was asked to contribute a chapter on forest recreation needs in the so-called Copeland Report of 1932, an analysis of the nation's forests that Congress had requested in a resolution introduced by Senator Royal Copeland of New York. The report, "A National Plan for American Forestry," completed after the elections of 1932 and one of the first documents approved and passed on to the new president, Franklin D. Roosevelt, was radical in its own right, declaring that private ownership of forests had led to widespread degradation of watersheds and soil depletion and that state and federal governments should

MABLE MANSFIELD (THE WILDERNESS SOCIETY)

Bob Marshall in Montana, 1935: One of the true disciples of Leopold's wilderness gospel.

join in a program of acquisition that would place a total of 224 million acres of forestland in public ownership. Marshall's contribution pointed out that in 1931 the national forests had drawn more than 8 million recreation visitors and the national parks and monuments more than 3 million, that wilderness recreation was growing in popularity, and that

a greatly increased amount of journeying in the wilderness may fairly be expected. It would seem reasonable, therefore, to establish as wilderness areas all tracts for which no definitely higher present utility exists. If in the future the use of these tracts does not justify their retention as wilderness areas, it will always be possible to cut them up with additional roads. But once roads are built, it will be very difficult to restore the wilderness.

111

FRED WHITEHEAD

*Cumberland Island
Wilderness, Georgia.*

Marshall went on to recommend that 10 million acres of designated wilderness be added to the current system of primitive areas at once—all that he apparently felt could realistically be put forth in an official proposal. In *The People's Forests,* his own radical dream for the future published in October 1933, however, he was a good deal more ambitious, not only advocating the public ownership of no less than 562 million acres of forests but raising the wilderness ante to 27 million acres.

Though polemics and burrowing from within were useful, Marshall felt, something more was needed. As early as his 1930 *Scientific Monthly* article, he had been persuaded that "there is just one hope of repulsing the tyrannical ambition of civilization to conquer every niche on the whole earth. That hope is the organization of spirited people who will fight for the freedom of the wilderness." In January 1935 he joined with Aldo Leopold, Robert Sterling Yard, and a handful of other "spirited people" to found the Wilderness Society. The other founders asked Marshall to serve as president of the society. He decided to clear the idea with his boss, writing him that the organization was designed to fight "the propaganda spread by the American Automobile Association, the various booster organizations, and innumerable chamber of commerces, which seem to find no peace as long as any primitive tract in America remains unopened to mechanization," and that he did not feel that the presidential position would interfere with his government job. His boss disagreed; he suggested that it would be better for Marshall to do the work but let someone else carry the title. Marshall

concurred, officially remaining in the background, while funding the organization largely from his own pocket and effectively dictating its policies.

The boss in question was Harold L. Ickes, Secretary of the Interior, who had hired Marshall away from the Forest Service to work at the Bureau of Indian Affairs. Ickes was a veteran of the nasty saloon and streetside politics of Chicago; a Bull Moose Progressive and Illinois campaign chief; a fighter of utility magnates such as Samuel Insull and corrupt urban bosses such as Mayor William Hale ("Big Bill") Thompson; and, as administrator of the Public Works Administration, one of the most powerful bureaucrats in the world, a man spending billions of dollars to build dams, roads, hospitals, schools, and sundry other projects—surely the most unlikely candidate imaginable as the first Cabinet-level wilderness advocate in history. But he was that—and what's more, he would be the last for almost thirty years.

On the morning of November 19, 1934, all of the country's national park superintendents, many of their assistants, and various other park personnel gathered in the auditorium of the old Interior Building on E Street in Washington, D.C. They were there for a conference on the problems and prospects of the National Park System, and the first speaker to be heard from was their boss: the Secretary of the Interior. "Gentlemen," Ickes told them, "I do not have any formal remarks to make; I just have some general observations which may give you something to discuss and to think about. As you will observe, I am sitting down instead of standing." Then, sitting down, the Secretary proceeded to extemporize a few general observations that took up the better part of an hour and effectively summarized his own conclusions on a subject to which he had given considerable thought. "I suspect that my general attitude on what our national parks ought to be is fairly well known," he said. "I do not want any Coney Island. I want as much wilderness, as much nature preserved and maintained, as possible. . . . I recognize that a great many people, an increasing number every year, take their nature from the automobile. . . . But I think the parks ought to be for people who love to camp and love to hike and who like to ride horseback and wander about and have . . . a renewed communion with nature."

Four months later, standing up this time, Ickes addressed a Conference of State Park Authorities in the Interior Department auditorium and defied those (including Roosevelt) who wanted to extend the Blue Ridge

Parkway through Great Smoky Mountains National Park in what was billed as a "Skyline Drive." The beautiful Blue Ridge, choreographed by the Interior Department's National Park Service, built by the Interior Department's Bureau of Public Roads, and financed entirely by funding from the Interior Department's sister agency, the Public Works Administration, was just under construction as one of the showcase parkways of the New Deal. Ickes liked it well enough, but believed that it should go no farther than the northern boundary of Great Smoky Mountains National Park, and said so at the State Park Authorities meeting in a statement that neither Robert Marshall nor Aldo Leopold would have been reluctant to endorse:

> I do not happen to favor the scarring of a wonderful mountainside just so that we can say we have a skyline drive. It sounds poetical, but it may be an atrocity. . . . I think we ought to keep as much wilderness area in this country as we can. It is easy to destroy a wilderness; it can be done very quickly, but it takes nature a long time, even if we let nature alone, to restore for our children what we have ruthlessly destroyed. . . .
>
> There ought to be many exceptions when it comes to dealing with wilderness areas, with regions of natural beauty. We ought to resolve all doubts in favor of letting nature take its course. In a field where nature is preeminently the master artist, where nature can do much more than we can do with all our cleverness, with all of our arts and with all of our best efforts, we can not improve but can only impair if we undertake to alter.

This was in the way of a manifesto, and he meant every word of it. Because of his stubborn opposition, the Great Smoky Mountains portion of the Skyline Drive was never constructed, and he consistently resisted the building of highways where he felt highways had no business being built. "We are making a great mistake in this generation," he told a group of road-builders in his office early in 1937. "We are just repeating the same mistake in a different form that our forefathers have made. Instead of keeping areas . . . which will add to the wealth, health, comfort and well-being of the people, if we see anything that looks attractive we want to open up speedways through it so the people can enjoy the scenery at sixty miles an hour."

Bandelier Wilderness, New Mexico.

Congaree Swamp Wilderness, South Carolina.

ership in the country. "There seem to be two policies on the part of the . . . administration," Benton MacKaye, a planner with the TVA and co-founder of the Wilderness Society, wrote Robert Marshall in May 1935. "One of these, which is somewhat sketchily expressed by the higher authority, Mr. Ickes, appears to be one with our own objective; the other, being put to tangible operation . . . just the opposite of our objective."

Robert Sterling Yard tended to agree with MacKaye, particularly when a Wilderness Society and National Parks Association proposal for the designation of a special class of park—the national primeval park—was spurned by Cammerer. These special enclaves would be carved out of entirely roadless and undeveloped regions and would be managed in much the same way as today's National Wilderness Preservation System—no roads or vehicles of any kind allowed, no permanent structures, no commercial use whatever.

On the face of it, this proposal precisely matched Ickes' own interpretation of what a proper national park should be. Yard and his allies would have done well to confront Ickes directly, but they could not bring themselves to do that. As one part of his announced ambitions for the Interior Department, Ickes wanted the national forests taken out of the Department of Agriculture and given to him. Most of the preservationists had affection for and strong ties to the Forest Service in those years (four of the founders of the Wilderness Society, for example, were foresters by profession). Moreover, they remembered the day not too long before when Interior Secretary Albert B. Fall had exercised his stewardship of the public lands by turning over the oil reserves of Teapot Dome for a bribe of $100,000. They despised the Interior Department, did not trust the Park Service, and regarded Ickes' yearning after the national forests much as they would have the slavering of a rapist. This was perhaps inevitable, but it was a pity; if such organizations as the Wilderness Society had been able to put aside their mistrust of the secretary's motives and his agency long enough to recognize his commitment to preservation and support him in the attainment of his highest ambitions, they might have forged an alliance that could have transformed the history of public land management in this country.

In the meantime, and getting little credit from them along the way, Ickes did what he could. In August 1933 he and his Commissioner of Indian Affairs, John Collier, had persuaded Robert Marshall to leave the Forest Service and come into the Bureau of Indian Affairs to head up forestry, grazing, and

Unfortunately, in the day-to-day operations of the system, the fondest objectives of the secretary were consistently undercut by the lack of commitment (or even sympathy) on the part of many at the top of the Park Service—including its director, Arno B. Cammerer—who had gotten their training and philosophy from the first director, Stephen Mather. Mather's principal goal had always been to popularize the parks in order to build a constituency that could be called upon to influence Congress in the proper disposition of such matters as additions to the system and appropriations to the Park Service. This meant keeping the customers happy and comfortable, not inordinately exposed to the wonders of wilderness—a policy that had encrusted into tradition and was echoed in the field by most park superintendents. The situation inspired confusion in at least some of the conservation lead-

wildlife management on the Bureau's Indian reservations. Marshall's most lasting contribution in this job was the administrative designation of sixteen wilderness areas with a total of 4.8 million acres on the Indian reservations (although the designations would be rescinded in the 1950s by the Eisenhower Administration). He then returned to the Forest Service in 1937 to become chief of the Division of Recreation and Lands. Here, before his sudden death in November 1939 at the age of thirty-eight, Marshall continued to pursue the designation of wilderness on the national forests, helping to formulate the "U Regulations," which used the term "wilderness" as an official designation for the first time, and prohibited timbering and road construction in any established wilderness area. (Appropriately, the first major wilderness area under the U Regulations was the million-acre Bob Marshall Wilderness of Montana, which was established by administrative order in 1940.)

Ickes was not about to let the Forest Service steal the march on him. His was one of the loudest voices in securing specific wilderness directives for Everglades National Park. The act of May 30, 1934, spelled it out precisely when it authorized the Secretary of the Interior to accept state deeds to about 2,000 square miles of the Everglades in Dade, Monroe, and Collier counties, Florida (which deeds were forthcoming in 1935): "The said area or areas shall be permanently reserved as a wilderness, and no development of the project or plan for the entertainment of visitors shall be undertaken which will interfere with the preservation intact of the unique flora and fauna and the essential primitive conditions now prevailing in this area." The essentially primitive condition of 559,960 acres of Joshua Tree National Monument in southern California, established by executive order in 1936, would not have been argued by anyone, nor did management practices established at the Secretary's direction seriously alter that quality. Ickes participated actively in the long fight that finally saw Washington's 900,000-acre Olympic National Park authorized in 1938 —and instituted management policies designed to keep the park primitive. In 1935 he initiated new efforts to establish Kings Canyon National Park in California, directing specifically that "this park will be treated as a primitive wilderness," and while he could not get Congress to agree to its designation as the John Muir National Wilderness Park, the word "wilderness" remained in the title of the authorization act when the

Aleutian Islands Wilderness, Alaska.

*Columbia
Wilderness, Oregon.*

half-million-acre park was established in 1940—and he saw to it that the park was managed as such.

While an effort in the late 1930s to add more than 4 million acres of essential wilderness in southern Utah to the National Park System failed, other essentially primitive units were added to the system during Ickes' tenure. Land purchases and exchanges for Michigan's Isle Royale National Park—a 115,643-acre wilderness island in Lake Superior, authorized in 1931—were completed in 1938. And Organ Pipe Cactus National Monument, a 330,689-acre desert enclave in southwestern Arizona, was established by executive order in 1937. North Carolina's Cape Hatteras National Seashore—the first national seashore—was authorized as a 30,319-acre "primitive wilderness" in 1937.

By the beginning of World War II, then, the Forest Service—with more than 14 million acres administratively designated or effectively managed as wilderness—and the National Park Service—with one major official wilderness park, three that were wilderness parks in all but name, and other units managed essentially as wilderness—had endorsed the wilderness idea. Bureau-

cracy had embraced revolution. But as Harold Ickes was among the first to point out, all the wilderness except that established in the Everglades was subject to the administrative whims of the agencies in charge. What the Secretary of Agriculture had given, the Secretary of Agriculture could take away—as could the Secretary of the Interior, for that matter. Early in 1939, then, Ickes was moved to have drafted and submitted to Congress the first wilderness bill in history, introduced in the Senate by Senator Alva B. Adams of Colorado and in the House by Congressman Rene De Rouen of Louisiana. This legislation would have empowered the President to set aside, by proclamation, wilderness areas in national parks and monuments, places in which roads, automobiles, commercial developments, hotels, cabin camps, or any other permanent human structures would be banned—just as specified by Robert Sterling Yard's dream of primeval parks. "Under this proposed legislation," Ickes declaimed in a speech before the Commonwealth Club on February 15, 1939,

a proclamation by the President will establish a wilderness area, and once it is estab-

Wichita Mountains Wilderness, Oklahoma.

lished, only an act of Congress can change its status. . . . In asking Congress for the passage of this bill to set aside wilderness areas, I am requesting that the discretionary power of my own department be cut down. . . . I want these wilderness areas so protected that neither I, nor any future Secretary of the Interior, can lower their guard merely by signing an administrative order.

The Secretary did not get his Wilderness Act, which died quietly in the public lands committees of the House and Senate later that year. The Congress of the United States was not yet ready to accept the revolution the bureaucracy of the United States was prepared to offer up.

But a seedling at least had been planted. In the year of the Ickes park-wilderness bill, Kenneth Reid, executive director of the Izaak Walton League, echoed the concern expressed in the Secretary's speech: Forest wilderness areas, he said, were disappearing, and, "There is no assurance that any one of them or all of them might not be abolished as they were created—by administrative decrees. They exist by sufferance and administrative policy—not by law." In comment-

ing on Robert Marshall's passing, Harvey Broome, a fellow founder of the Wilderness Society, wrote to a colleague in 1940, "Since his death I have been wondering just how permanent and legally inviolable are the various wilderness areas in this country. . . . What is to hinder some future secretary from abrogating those regulations? Do you think wilderness would have more permanence if there were some new status, established by congressional enactment?"

Good question, and it soon became an integral part of the discussion. Not merely because the idea of wilderness as law was the best one, but because after World War II it was the *only* one. The bureaucracy that had given birth to the idea of wilderness preservation had suddenly turned on its creation, and it was becoming increasingly clear that Congress now would have to step in to save the remnants of a wilderness past if they were going to be saved at all.

The Forest Service, caught up in the frenzy of a postwar building boom, began to eye its resources more often as commodities to be exploited than as systems to be preserved. The process of reclassifying the 8.4 million acres of primitive areas established by the

117

Collegiate Peaks Wilderness, Colorado.

L-20 Regulations of 1929 as official wilderness under the more specific U Regulations of 1939—begun with such enthusiasm just before the war—now moved with glacial deliberation. By the end of the 1940s only 2 million acres had been authorized as administrative wilderness. What was more, Forest Service planners were beginning to show a curious bias: In more than one instance, while the total acreage of a primitive area might remain the same under reclassification, boundaries were adjusted so that nicely timbered stream valleys and lower mountain slopes somehow disappeared from the protected acreage, and treeless crags and alpine meadows took their place—leading one cynic to comment that the Forest Service had instituted a firm preservationist policy of "no timber harvesting above timberline." In the meantime, areas not covered by either the L-20 or the U Regulations were being steadily cut, roaded, or otherwise rendered unfit as wilderness (one estimate had it that no less than 35 million acres of roadless forestland had been given the treatment between the middle of the 1920s and 1960).

It was exciting stuff, being in at the ground floor of a swiftly growing industry, and the Forest Service made the most of it, sending a small army of Willie Lomans in Smokey-the-Bear hats out into the boardrooms of lumberyard America. In 1952 assistant chief forester Christopher Granger told the readers of *American Forests* that the splendid growth in the timber industry could be ascribed to "the initiative of the Forest Service men going out and getting business." Growth indeed: In 1951, 1.5 billion board feet had been taken off the national forests; in 1961 the figure was 8.3 billion. And wilderness? Well, maybe later. And maybe there was enough put aside already.

For its part, the National Park Service fell in love with recreation in the decade of the fifties, persuading Congress to authorize up to a billion dollars to bring the roads, facilities, and amenities of the parks up to snuff, ready to meet the needs and demands of 80 million visitors a year by 1966. This was pretty exciting, too, and the Park Service called it "Mission 66." There was little to be heard now about primeval parks and even less about wilderness. The Interior Department as a whole—Harold Ickes long gone, Douglas McKay, the car salesman from Oregon, flapping about now in shoes he could not begin to fill—embraced another kind of excitement: reclamation, flood control, hydropower.

Dams.

In 1950 two of the biggest were proposed for Echo Park and Split Mountain Canyon on the Green River, Utah, both or either of which would have wrecked much of Dinosaur National Monument by flooding it. A very bad idea, as it turned out—not only generically bad but tactically bad. "This," Wallace Stegner wrote in *This is Dinosaur,* "is a country as grand and beautiful as any America can boast; and if the dams are built as they have been proposed, at Echo Park and in Split Mountain, almost all of . . . this river-veined and marvelous wilderness will be wiped out." Such a wholesale and unsubtle assault on the sanctity of the national park idea—and the wilderness idea contained within it—was too direct and damaging to be endured; for the first time in history all the major conservation organizations in the country joined in a phalanx to protect a single wilderness. And they won; the public pressure they were able to generate was enough to move the lumbering beast of Congress to refuse to authorize the dams. But even while the fight was in its earliest stages, this singular demonstration of how far the bureaucracy had fallen from grace persuaded the preservationists outside the government that administrative assurances were no longer enough, if they ever had been.

On March 30, 1951, Howard Zahniser, a former bureaucrat himself in the editorial ranks of the U.S. Bureau of Biological Survey (one of the predecessors of today's Fish and Wildlife Service) and by now executive secretary and editor of the Wilderness Society, gave the banquet address at the Second Wilderness Conference held under the auspices of the Sierra Club in Berkeley, California. His words were not only a call to action for the preservationists in the room, but an implied rebuke to those minions of the Park Service and the Forest Service who were also in attendance. "It behooves us to do two things," Zahniser said.

> First we must see that an adequate system of wilderness areas is designated for preservation, and then we must allow nothing to alter the wilderness character of the preserves. . . .
>
> As soon as we have a clear consensus of conservationists we should most certainly press steadily for the maximum security possible; that is, congressional establishment of a national wilderness system

JAMES MARSHALL (THE WILDERNESS SOCIETY)

backed up by an informed public opinion.

> A bill to establish a *national wilderness preservation system* should be drawn up as soon as possible with the joint cooperation of the federal land-administering agencies and conservation organizations. . . .
>
> Let us try to be done with a wilderness preservation program made up of a sequence of overlapping emergencies, threats, and defense campaigns! Let's make a concerted effort for a positive program that will establish an enduring system of areas where we can be at peace and not forever feel that the wilderness is a battleground!

There it was, then, spelled out for the first time. Now all they had to do was make it happen.

The fight to prevent the construction of the Dinosaur dams (not to mention such other items as an attempt by the Forest Service to cut nearly 200,000 acres from the Gila Wilderness, power company proposals for dams in Kings Canyon National Park, and efforts by local timber interests to open Olympic National Park to salvage logging) kept the idea of a wilderness bill on the back

Howard Zahniser in the Idaho wilderness: A call to action in 1951.

Great Sand Dunes
Wilderness, Colorado.

burner until 1956, when Zahniser, taking up his own challenge, finally was able to sit down and begin composing the legislation he had called for in his 1951 speech. A first draft was swiftly done, and following his own dictum that consensus must be reached among those in the conservation community, he sent it off to a raft of people, including David Brower of the Sierra Club, Ira Gabrielson of the National Conservation Committee (and Zahniser's former boss at the Bureau of Biological Survey), and Charles Callison and Stewart Brandborg of the National Wildlife Federation. The bill, after going through another eighteen drafts, was offered up to Senator Hubert Humphrey of Minnesota and Representative John P. Saylor of Pennsylvania, both of whom introduced it in their respective houses in June 1956, then reintroduced slightly modified versions in the new Congress in January 1957.

In the Senate the bill was co-sponsored and consistently championed by a number of Hubert Humphrey's colleagues, chief among them such westerners as Clinton Anderson of New Mexico, Frank Church of Idaho, Henry ("Scoop") Jackson of Washington, and Richard Neuberger of Oregon; co-signers in the House of Representatives included Lee Met-

calf of Montana and George Miller of California among its most vigorous proponents.

No one expected that the bill would get through without amendment, and very little in Zahniser's first version did not get fiddled with during the course of the next seven years, including the language that defined exactly what it was that was meant by the term "wilderness." A wilderness, early drafts declared with poetic emphasis, "in contrast with those areas where man and his own works dominate the landscape, is hereby recognized as an area where the earth and its community of life are untrammeled by man, where man himself is a member of the natural community, a wanderer who visits but does not remain and whose travels leave only trails." In the final version the last phrase was reduced to "where man himself is a visitor who does not remain," depriving the statement of some philosophical weight and lyrical character, perhaps, but possibly making it easier for your average congressperson to understand it. There were sixty-six other changes in the final bill, almost all of them painstakingly written into the legislation by the incomparably dogged and patient Zahniser himself, each of them crafted to satisfy one special interest or another which felt itself threatened, foiled, or subverted by the idea of wilderness preservation.

So it was that the provision for the revival of wilderness areas on Indian reservation lands was stricken from the final version, as was the National Wilderness Preservation Council, a central body that would have been the oversight agency for all matters regarding the system, including recommendations for additions and expansions. So was the provision that enabled the president, acting upon those recommendations, to establish wilderness areas by executive order; as revised, only by an act of Congress, following the usual legislative process, could wilderness areas be established. Other compromises included the continuation of grazing in areas in which it had already been taking place, the authorization of water projects in wilderness areas by presidential decree if deemed in the national interest, and a provision that wilderness areas be open to the various mining laws until January 1, 1984.

None of these substantial changes, of course, won the hearts of the stock-raising industry, the mining industry, and other commercial interests who would have been pleased only by a bill that would have institutionalized their exploitation. Nor did compromise inspire the affection of the Forest Service and the Park Service, both of whom tended to look upon this congressional intrusion on "their" turf with injured self-righteousness.

What the revisions did do, however, was make it increasingly easier for the bill's sponsors in Congress to persuade their fellow lawmakers that every effort possible had been made to satisfy a bewildering gaggle of interests, that any remaining opposition was nothing more than a kind of generic resistance to the very idea of wilderness, and that the political danger of voting for the legislation was consequently minimal. This contention was further strengthened by a veritable explosion of support from the bulk of the American press: For one of the few times in American history, most of the nation's newspapers were in favor of a piece of conservation legislation, a unanimity normally reserved for declarations of war or resolutions condemning flag-burning. If a newspaper such as the *Denver Post,* subsisting in the heart of the opposition's homeland, could come out in support of wilderness, could *The New York Times* be very far behind? And the *Post* was right in there, all right, reservedly but unmistakably. "This newspaper," it said in the space reserved for its daily allotment of Revealed Wisdom, "after an examination of the over-all picture, believes that the wilderness legislation should be passed. . . . There is positive value in wilderness—to science, to people, and to the future."

On September 6, 1961, the United States Senate mirrored public sentiment by passing S. 174, "an act to establish a National Wilderness Preservation System for the permanent good of the whole people," by a vote of 78 to 8. Attention then moved to the arena of the House Committee on Interior and Insular Affairs, in whose care the House version of a bill had been placed.

By then the band of wilderness advocates inside and outside Congress had acquired a friend in court. Secretary of the Interior Stewart M. Udall, appointed by President John F. Kennedy early in 1961, became only the second Cabinet-level officer of government to both understand and champion the cause of wilderness. "The public has demanded assurance that the wilderness remnant will be protected for the recreation and re-creation of the American people," Udall wrote in the Spring–Summer 1962 issue of *The Living Wilderness.*

UPI/BETTMANN NEWSPHOTOS

Interior Secretary Stewart Udall (left): An important friend in court.

121

122

A national program for wilderness preservation involves a great and enduring benefit at remarkably low cost. . . . America has yet to prove that she is willing to balance material abundance with spiritual benefits. Our people deserve both. Friends and enemies and the uncommitted throughout the world watch with anxiety, fear, and hope. The demonstration will be made on many frontiers. Through preservation of wilderness, there is within our grasp a lasting testament to the maturity of our society and a lasting legacy for the well-being of our people.

And at Secretary Udall's urging, John F. Kennedy became the first president in history to promote the wilderness idea, making it Camelot's own in a conservation message to Congress on March 1, 1962: "We must protect and preserve our nation's remaining wilderness areas. This key element of our conservation program should have priority attention. I therefore strongly urge the Congress to enact legislation establishing a National Wilderness Preservation System."

Big guns were at work in the battle, now, but not quite big enough to blast a bill out of the House Committee on Interior and Insular Affairs, whose chairman, Wayne Aspinall of Colorado, was reasonably certain that his constituents wanted nothing to do with wilderness. If he was going to put his neck on the line, Aspinall made it clear, there was going to have to be some dealing done. And there was. One of the done deals had been the agreement to keep wilderness areas open to entry under the mining laws until January 1, 1984. A lesser-known deal may also have taken place, according to Robert Wolf, who was then a young forester working for the Senate Interior Committee. During conversation one day, Wolf remembers, Aspinall told him that he intended to introduce legislation to create a Public Land Law Review Commission—a body that would review and make recommendations regarding the more than 3,000 land laws still on the books. Aspinall would need support in the Senate, of course, but when Wolf carried the news back to Senators Henry Jackson and Alan Bible, both responded negatively. Bible said, "We don't need that—and besides, it would cost a lot of money."

Senator Clinton Anderson's reaction was more subtle. "He leaned back in his chair," Wolf remembered, "put his hands behind his head, and said, 'Bob, you think Wayne really wants that bill?'

" 'Yes,' I replied.

" 'Well,' Anderson said with a smile, 'I really want a wilderness bill.'

"I went back to my office and told a colleague: 'We've got a wilderness bill!' "

Wolf says he can't prove that a deal was done, but it was not long after this incident that Chairman Aspinall indeed reported a wilderness bill out of committee on June 18, 1964. It included a provision excluding the San Gorgonio Wild Area of southern California, but this irritant was soon removed by amendment, and on July 30th the House voted 373 to 1 for passage. The Senate, in the meantime, had passed another, revised, version of its own bill in 1963, and after differences between the two pieces of legislation were rationalized in conference committee, a finished bill was sent to the White House. (And, a few days later, so was the Public Land Law Review Commission Act that Aspinall had wanted.)

Zahniser, who, Brower said later, had used up "his last energy" in a "tireless search for a way to put a national wilderness policy into law," was not there on the afternoon of September 3rd when Anderson, Aspinall, Udall, and two dozen other dignitaries gathered in the Rose Garden of the White House to watch President Lyndon B. Johnson scrawl his signature across a sheet of sunlit paper called the Wilderness Act. On April 27th Zahniser had appeared for the last time before the House Subcommittee on Public Lands. "In our own far beginnings on this continent," he told the committee,

the wilderness was everywhere, and . . . man himself was both in and of the wilderness. . . . Now, over much of the earth . . . man has so changed and developed the primeval scene that he himself and his own works dominate the landscape. The areas where the earth and its life community are still untrammeled by man are only remnants. . . . Preservation of wilderness should be one of our established public-land policies. If it is so declared by Congress, if the agencies that now have the custody over our areas of wilderness are authorized to continue to manage them . . . in such a way as to preserve their wilderness character—then we can well expect to have a living wilderness indefinitely, perhaps forever.

When Zahniser died on May 5th, a great bureaucrat was deprived of the chance to witness the final moment when the poetry of an idea was embraced and validated by a system that had overcome its history.

Sawtooth Wilderness, Idaho.

THE MOST FAMOUS FARM IN AMERICA

TEXT BY MARK HOY • PAINTING BY CHRISTOPHER MAGADINI

Malabar Farm always draws me back. When I first visited the farm in 1959 the spirit of Malabar's founder, the Pulitzer-Prize-winning novelist Louis Bromfield, remained a palpable presence. That was just three years after his death. I came away with a bushel full of strong memories: the rows of serious books and glossy photos of Hollywood celebrities that lined the walls of the Big House, a beat-up manure spreader depositing its odiferous load on the green fields.

Three decades have passed, and Malabar Farm is much changed. Now a part of the Ohio state park system, it is more tourist attraction than working farm. Still, each time I return to visit my family in Ohio, my homing instincts take me back to the farm. And after all my years of exploring Malabar, each time I make the pilgrimage I discover something new.

Louis Bromfield would have understood. His greatest joy came from wandering Malabar's more than nine hundred acres of fields and forests, escaping the hubbub of the thirty-two-room Big House he had built to house his family, staff, friends, and "freeloading celebrities." On long, solitary walks, Bromfield loved to muse over farming theories while he searched for elusive morel mushrooms or discovered an icy new spring bubbling up out of the ground he had returned to fertility. After his rambles he often sought sanctuary in his wood-paneled office, where he wrote the essays and books about conservation farming and sustainable agriculture that established Malabar as the most famous American farm during the 1940s and until his death in 1956.

When my wife and I last visited Malabar Farm, on a misty gray morning in June, we joined a small group of mostly older visitors who rode the bumpy gravel roads on a farm tour, escorted by a very young, very friendly state-park biologist. Our modified hay wagon bounced along behind a noisy little tractor that lumbered, huffing and whining, up a small hill to the family cemetery, where Louis Bromfield is buried.

There we all piled out onto solid ground, and the others stood listening politely while the young biologist recounted Bromfield family stories. They were good stories, but try as I might to listen, I found myself distracted by a fragrance that floated past me on the damp air; something subtle, floral, and somehow familiar. Giving in to the lure, I wandered down the hill behind the cemetery. There, in a long hedgerow along the lane, I found the source—and reintroduced myself to an old friend.

Multiflora rose. The lilting name and delicate white petals made me smile. It was as if a little piece of Louis Bromfield had lingered behind.

"And the fencerows along the roads and between the fields are not merely bare wire fences," he wrote in *Animals and Other People,* "they have been allowed to grow into hedgerows which check the moisture and provide shelter for the quail, the pheasants, the rabbits and wild game of every kind. And as I write, the hedges of multiflora rose which have gradually replaced the fences are in full bloom, filled with the nests of the great thrush family. Their perfume drifts through the open windows of the Big House into the room where I am working."

Born in 1896, Louis Bromfield grew up in nearby Mansfield, Ohio, where his father was a minor politician and unsuccessful restorer of abandoned farms; his mother was a descendant of some of the earliest settlers in the Western Reserve. He spent short stints at Cornell and Columbia universities before joining the French Army as an ambulance driver during World War I.

After the war, Bromfield returned to New York, where he worked as a journalist and served as music critic on the original staff of *Time* magazine. In 1921 he married Mary Appleton Wood, a socialite from an old New England family. He wrote four unpublished novels in his spare time before publishing his fifth effort, *The Green Bay Tree,* in 1924. His third published novel, *Early Autumn* (1926), won the Pulitzer Prize and marked him as a young writer to be watched. The 1928 year-end issue of *Vanity Fair* called Bromfield "the most prominent of our younger novelists" and displayed his photo in a

Tired of the footloose life of an international celebrity, Louis Bromfield used the millions earned by his novels to turn worn-out land in Ohio into a showplace of fertility.

"Nominated for the Hall of Fame" section alongside those of Thomas Mann, Pablo Picasso, Walter Gropius, Serge Diaghilev, S. M. Eisenstein, and Ernest Hemingway.

Bromfield's financial success had allowed him to move to France, where he and Mary restored an old monastery in Senlis, north of Paris. They socialized with many celebrities and writers, including F. Scott Fitzgerald and Gertrude Stein, who often visited Senlis to admire Bromfield's flourishing gardens. He traveled extensively, frequenting exotic locales such as India, which was the setting for two of his later novels, *The Rains Came* and *Night in Bombay*.

In late 1938, Bromfield was forced to move his family, which now included three daughters, to safer ground as war loomed in Europe. As if to prove that some expatriates *can* go home again, Bromfield decided to return to the United States.

But where exactly was home, after fourteen years in France? Bromfield remembered the rolling hills of his Ohio boyhood and set out to find a farm, a piece of ground where he could reestablish the life he had enjoyed in the French countryside. In his book *Pleasant Valley,* he described his feelings as he rediscovered a worn-out farm he had visited years before with his father during a long-ago political campaign:

"All these memories came flooding back during the short walk from the house to the great barn. Then I pushed open the door and walked into the smell of cattle and horses and hay and silage and I knew that I had come home and that never again would I be long separated from that smell because it meant security and stability and because in the end, after years of excitement and wandering and adventure, it had reclaimed me. It was in the blood and could not be denied."

Bromfield had come home, but he had not retired. He was in his forties, and the quick success of his early novels had faded. His later fiction was being disparaged by critics, many of whom complained of commercial motives. They noted with disdain that he also worked as a Hollywood screenwriter. Bromfield shrugged off the criticisms. The writing of fiction had become an increasingly unsatisfactory outlet for his restless creative energy. So, he began to turn his talents to The Plan.

The Plan called for combining three worn-out Ohio farms into a single demonstration farm where he could put into practice his personal theories on soil conservation. He would call his new farm Malabar, after a beautiful coastal region in India,

because much of the money for the farm had come from sale of the film rights to *The Rains Came.*

Tired of the footloose, fashionable life of an international celebrity, Bromfield was determined to return to the security of simpler times. With the help of an architect he planned his Big House, combining what he saw as the best elements of the old Western Reserve farmhouses of northern Ohio and the comfortable French country homes he admired. Beginning with an existing 19th Century farmhouse that overlooked the fields and woods of Malabar, he added a series of wings to make the house look as though it had evolved over a century of constant use. Then he proceeded to move in his boisterous family, sturdy French furniture, and pack of boxer dogs (as many as seven at one time had free run of the house) to put the final touches on the "well-worn" look.

Bromfield also planned out a farming operation that would combine the nostalgic self-sufficiency of family farms remembered from his boyhood and the latest soil-conservation techniques developed after the Dust Bowl disasters of the 1930s. Looking around the Ohio countryside at farms abandoned by men who had "mined" their productive soil until it no longer produced a decent living for their families, Bromfield set out to find a better way. Although Malabar was a millionaire's farm, he vowed to use only soil-restoration methods that could be adopted by the average dirt farmer.

In *Pleasant Valley* (1945), *Malabar Farm* (1948), *Out of the Earth* (1950), and *From My Experience* (1955), Bromfield turned from writing fiction to chronicling the progress of his work at Malabar, documenting his results as he went along. With the use of contour plowing, plantings of nitrogen-fixing cover crops and multiflora rose hedgerows, intensive woodlands management, and "trash farming" (disking lime and organic material back into his fields), he and his farm managers halted erosion and turned Malabar into a showplace of fertility.

Bromfield disdained the use of chemical fertilizers and weed-killers, arguing that not only were they too expensive for the average farmer's use, they also destroyed the living organisms in the soil that he sought to promote. Vegetables grown on the farm were so superior to anything found in local food markets that customers regularly drove miles out of their way to buy produce at Malabar's roadside stand.

The more Bromfield wrote, the more Malabar Farm gained an international reputation; it was at once a workers' collective, an

agricultural research plot, a celebrity retreat, and an old-fashioned family farm. In addition to frequent visits from his famous Hollywood, New York, and Paris acquaintances, Bromfield began to attract a steady stream of soil scientists, gardeners, politicians, and just plain dirt farmers, who came to hear more about his bold new experiments.

A robust man of tremendous drive, Bromfield often put in a full day in the fields before adjourning to his office for a night of serious writing. "The Boss" (as his family called him) expected everyone else on the farm, guests included, to labor at a similar pace. Sunday, normally a day of rest, was reserved for farm tours, as Bromfield's new devotees flocked in by the dozens—and eventually by the hundreds.

E. B. White visited Malabar and later wrote a poem as his "review" of Malabar for *The New Yorker*. It captured the atmosphere admirably:

Malabar Farm is the farm for me,
A place of unbridled activity.
A farm is always in some kind of tizzy,
But Bromfield's place is really busy:

Strangers arriving by every train,
Bromfield terracing against the rain,
Catamounts crying, mowers mowing,
Guest rooms full to overflowing,
Boxers in every room of the house,
Cows being milked to Brahms and
 Strauss,
Kids arriving by van or pung,
Bromfield up to his eyes in dung,
Sailors, trumpeters, mystics, actors,
All of them wanting to drive the tractors,
All of them eager to husk the corn,
Some of them sipping their drinks till morn.

One of the high points of celebrity chaos at Malabar was reached in May 1945, with the marriage of Humphrey Bogart and Lauren Bacall. Bogart and Bromfield had been close friends since the 1920s; it was Bromfield who insisted that Malabar would make the perfect setting, when the time came for Bogie to wed his young co-star (Bogart was then forty-five years old and three times divorced; Bacall, a tender twenty).

The reporters and gossip columnists who flocked to the farm agreed. But Bacall's nerves almost undid her (she was in the mid-

Louis Bromfield at Malabar with dogs. As many as seven boxers at a time had free run of the house.

127

dle of an unplanned bathroom stop when the Wedding March began). Bogart and his best man, Bromfield, reportedly succumbed to at least one pre-ceremony martini.

His pioneering work on the farming methods that would later become known as sustainable agriculture were not Bromfield's only contributions to conservation. His nonfiction books contain many passages of superb nature writing. He regarded Malabar Farm as a holistic enterprise, and its thriving wildlife populations became a source of endless fascination. On his long walks Bromfield not only observed the many species of birds that flocked to his hedgerows and woodlots, he counted them valuable allies in his efforts to control insect damage to his crops—a constant concern for any farmer. Bromfield even acknowledged the role of predators, such as foxes, in keeping rodent populations on the farm in check, although he still begrudged them their occasional foray into his chicken coops.

In addition to his literary output—Bromfield published more than thirty-five books and hundreds of articles—he was tireless in his conservation efforts. He served on the Ohio Wildlife Commission, was a founder of the Friends of the Land conservation group, and belonged to the National Audubon Society, the Association of French Working-Men Gardeners, the Agricultural Society of Brazil, and many other groups. Louis Bromfield was awarded the Audubon Medal in 1952, for "influencing the thinking of millions of people . . . through fluent and expressive command of language, with happy and pungent phrasing."

Today others remain less than thrilled by at least one aspect of Bromfield's conservation efforts. Scott Doty, current manager at Malabar Farm, admits that local landowners have come to rue Bromfield's multiflora rose plantings; the fast-growing canes spread rapidly across northern Ohio, deterring farmers' efforts to "clean up" their fencerows and eliminate what they regard as "wildlife pests." Never one to pass up an opportunity to jab a thorn in the side of conventional thinkers, Bromfield would doubtless have been pleased by the rose's tenacity.

More than thirty years after his death, Bromfield's true legacy remains a subject of debate. Despite his brilliant beginning as a writer of fiction, his novels have largely been ignored by modern readers and critics, who

regard them as overly romantic relics of a long-gone age. And Bromfield in his last years admitted that parts of his nonfiction—especially his ideas about small-farm self-sufficiency—were the product of wishful thinking, unattainable in modern times.

His dreams for Malabar Farm were also elusive. After years of financial struggle by a conservation group and a foundation to keep it functioning as an experimental farm and ecological preserve, Malabar is now run by the State of Ohio as a park. Only a few acres are still tilled as a demonstration plot using Bromfield's methods. More than half of the farm's annual 150,000 visitors see Malabar during Heritage Days, a fall festival of old-time farming and craft displays that have little, if anything, to do with Louis Bromfield and his iconoclastic ideas. Most visitors come only to tour the Big House and hear stories retold from the Bromfield legend.

But to a growing number of converts to sustainable agriculture and the fledgling industry producing organically grown foods, Bromfield has begun to look more and more like a prophet. His efforts to understand and encourage the fertility of living, organic soils and his oft-repeated contention that "poor land makes poor people" presaged modern concerns about chemical pollution of the nation's foodstuffs and the soil fertility losses caused by the overuse of herbicides and other farm chemicals.

Bromfield's reverence for the values embodied by the family farm also strikes a sympathetic chord with modern readers. In a recently published collection of the author's nonfiction, *Louis Bromfield at Malabar* (1988), editor Charles E. Little notes that Bromfield succeeded best at showing "that man belongs to the land as much as the other way around and that, when this fact is understood, a life of security, dignity, and happiness will ensue."

Bromfield summed up his feelings about the Malabar experience in an essay on how he had come to see the farm as an extended garden: "And so for fifteen years I have worked and suffered and sometimes spent money which I should not have spent, not merely upon restoring land and achieving rich crops, but in the creation of something more than that—a whole farm, a whole landscape, in which I could live in peace and with pride and which I could share with others to whom it would bring pleasure."

V

OF PLANTS AND MAN

INTIMATE MEADOWS

PHOTOGRAPHY BY MARY ELLEN SCHULTZ

Desert dandelion

California poppy and harvest brodiaea

Bluets

Filaree

Farewell to spring

Shooting star

TAMING THE WILD BLUEBERRY

TEXT BY FRANK GRAHAM JR. • PHOTOGRAPHY BY STEPHEN O. MUSKIE

The blueberry barrens of eastern Maine, where I am walking along a narrow dirt road that mimics the land's shallow humps and hollows, look as old as Africa. Though the dominant tone is a dark, shiny green, there are no soft shadows, there is no play of light, and a mean streak shows through. It is the kind of landscape that makes one think of black night and a grief-addled king wandering with his fool in a howling storm.

Black night, in fact, has just withdrawn from the barrens. The ground fog of late spring sits in abrupt depressions called "kettles." Norway pines with broad crowns grow singly here and there, like acacias on a tropical savanna. And along the horizon to the west and north, low, rounded shapes sort themselves out from the mist—the Norumbega Hills straggling up to the Canadian border some fifty miles away.

No, the land hereabouts doesn't put out a welcome mat. But a tolerant second look and increasing familiarity with this curious place make the word "barrens" seem a misnomer.

There is something stirring here after all, a way of life that for more than a century remained closer to that of hunter–gatherers than to that of modern agribusiness. This regimen, set against a unique mix of plants and animals conditioned to survive in a harsh landscape, is changing almost overnight. Wild blueberries, both a product of the barrens and a direct cause of their considerable expansion over the last hundred years, are entering the mainstream of American life. The harvesters, the landscape, even the berries, may never be the same again.

In 1980 growers in Maine harvested about 21 million pounds of wild blueberries. The total doubled within three years, and recently more than 52.3 million pounds were taken, in the largest harvest ever. A crop once perceived to be a glut on the market finds ready buyers today in Europe and Japan, as well as among big American firms such as Duncan Hines, Pillsbury, and Betty Crocker, which promote wild berries in muffin mixes and pie fillings.

With the new rush for big bucks, the wild-

ness threatens to disappear from the barrens as well as the berries. Machines, often heavily armored against omnipresent rocks, roll over the land. Insecticides and herbicides pour from the skies; fertilizers and irrigation water supplement nature's uncertain bounty. Changing social conditions, both on and off the barrens, turn Maine residents away from their traditional blueberry-picking role in the late summer harvest.

The barrens of eastern Maine can yield over 50 million pounds of sweet lowbush blueberries in a summer. George Curtis of Harrington was among the rakers for the sixty-fifth summer, filling ash baskets bought long ago for 75 cents.

Even so, the barrens remain a mirror of a time that was, of a country life as specialized as that of the furze-cutters on Hardy's Egdon Heath.

"The lowbush blueberry is *still* a wild plant, in spite of all the help we give it," Fred Olday said as we stepped off the road onto a marked blueberry plot in the heart of Washington County's barrens. "Most of our familiar fruit and vegetable plants have been so altered by selection that they couldn't survive in the wild anymore. Domesticated corn, for instance—the leaves form an envelope around the inflorescence, or flowering part, and it couldn't even disperse its seeds without our help."

Here he stooped and ran a hand over the shrubby plants at his feet. Each stem, though only six or eight inches tall, was ablaze in pink or white bell-shaped blossoms.

"If these fields were abandoned tomorrow," he said, "the shrubs and trees would come in and take over part of the land, yet some of the blueberry stems would go on producing berries indefinitely as wild plants."

Olday is research horticulturist for Jasper Wyman & Son, one of the oldest and most successful processors in the blueberry industry. The firm owns and leases about 6,000 acres of productive fields (and several times that in uncleared, bordering lands) in the

small towns of Cherryfield, Deblois, Beddington, and Columbia. Here lie eastern Maine's quintessential blueberry barrens, the well-mauled boonies that generations of Down Easters have been trying, by fits and starts, to wrestle from nature's clutches.

"These are poor, sandy soils on the barrens, not much more than powdered rock, and the nutrients tend to leach out quickly," Olday said. "They need a lot of help to grow anything besides heath plants and other tough vegetation."

To the unpracticed eye these haggard barrens appear unimaginably old, but according to University of Maine geologist Harold W. Borns Jr., they are the product of a glacier that retreated about 12,700 years ago. It left behind a jumble of gravel, pebbles, sand, and (in Borns' words) "very large boulders which apparently rolled directly off the edge of the ice."

The local terrain is known as an emerged glaciomarine delta, which is comparatively rare, restricted in the United States to coastal New England and found mostly in Maine. Such deltas resulted from the glacier's encounter with the sea. As the glacier retreated, according to Borns, the sand, gravel, and rocks washing out of the ice formed a series of deltas on the ocean floor, and then as the land rose after the glacier's great weight was removed from it, the delta emerged high and dry. Just up the road from the barrens where Olday and I stood, a kettle hole about seven feet deep and about one hundred feet across marked the spot where an iceberg had grounded out in the delta.

If the icebergs have left only their print in the gravel, the big boulders dropped here and there by the glacier in its retreat (called "erratics" by geologists) stand as symbols of the barrens' stony substance. The blueberry plants take root in the inhospitable soil around the rocks. The attempt to produce a profitable harvest on this land has been, in the words of a blueberry extension specialist, "more a matter of range management than crop production." Fred Olday is very much aware of the distinction.

"This is a very different fruit from the highbush blueberry grown commercially in New Jersey, Michigan, and other states," he explained. "The highbush berries are cultivated like strawberries or corn. They're large and, as any Maine native will tell you, not nearly as tasty as the small species of lowbush berries. There are several lowbush species. The one that makes up most of the wild crop in Maine and Canada's Maritime Provinces is called the sweet lowbush blueberry, *Vaccinium angustifolium.*"

"I've had friends who insist that these lowbush berries are really huckleberries," I said.

Olday shook his head. "The huckleberry is an entirely different beast. It has about ten big, hard seeds that crack between your teeth when you eat them. The lowbush berry has about three dozen small, soft seeds that disperse in cooking."

As it happens, a "new" berry has entered the barrens scene. Some years ago I visited a neighbor who is an enthusiastic and knowledgeable amateur botanist. She was sitting at her kitchen table, four or five bo-

Wyman research horticulturist Fred Olday applies liquid fertilizer to an experimental plot to determine the wild blueberry's nutritional needs.

139

Working rows 400 feet long and defined by twine, blueberry rakers— many of them Micmac Indians from Canada's Maritime Provinces— earn $2.75 a box and can fill twenty boxes a day from a good field, but the labor demands a good back.

tanical books around her. Some sort of research project?

"I'm stumped," she said. "I just saw a story in the paper about the blueberry harvest, and the writer mentioned a plant called barrenberry. I never heard of it, and my books don't say a word about it."

Assuming a self-satisfied expression, I told my friend I was just the man to clear up her confusion. Only the other week I had attended a meeting of growers at which someone had explained that "they" (the growers? the extension service? the feds?) were changing the vernacular name of an abundant plant on the barrens, the chokeberry (*Pyrus melanocarpa*).

It seemed that federal regulations required canners to list on their labels the names of all substances that exceed certain fractional proportions of the contents. Chokeberries, which superficially resemble blueberries, were occasionally finding their way into the cans. Although harmless themselves, their name was by no means a selling point on a label. So, some bright fellow decided, if we can't keep the chokeberries out of the cans, we can at least make their presence on the labels a little more exotic—and palatable. The name barrenberry is now part of the vernacular checklist of local plants.

It is the unenviable job of Fred Olday and other horticulturists in the industry to keep the wild taste in lowbush blueberries while increasing the yield and conditioning the berries to the rigors they face in both field

and processing plant. Olday has established experimental plots—long, narrow, and marked off by string—near Wyman's field headquarters in Deblois.

"The reason the research plots are so long is that blueberries grow in clones," he said. "It looks like there are hundreds of individual plants in this plot, but there are really only a half-dozen or so that are connected by a network of rhizomes and send up all these stems. By making each plot a hundred feet long, I'm able to study several clones at the same time."

A glance at the barrens during almost any season discloses the pattern of clones. Foliage and blossoms vary in color from one clone to another. (The mosaic is particularly striking in fall as the foliage in each clone turns color at its own pace.) Olday insists that he can distinguish the berries from different clones by taste.

"The plants bloom and the berries ripen at different times," he said, "and the flowers in one clone must be pollinated by insects coming from those in a different clone. This variability is a kind of insurance. Some clones, for instance, are more resistant than others to disease, so a whole area is not likely to be hit hard at one time."

When I visited, in mid-May, many of the clones were already in bloom, while others would begin to bear flowers several weeks later. Once the plant is fertilized, tiny, dark green, immature fruits appear. As the berries grow, the green pales and shows traces of light pink. The area of the fruit near the calyx leads the way, the pink there darkening to red earlier than elsewhere; then a deepening blue spreads over the skin. A waxy coating, or "bloom," gives the berry its frosty blue color. (A berry that is handled roughly loses its bloom and takes on a darker hue.) Here and there on the barrens one comes across clones with blackberries, a result of genetic variation.

The diameter of a full-grown wild blueberry varies from about an eighth of an inch in dry seasons to a quarter of an inch when there has been ample moisture. Industry people like to point out that their product is low in calories yet high in vitamins A and C and trace minerals.

Olday and his colleagues, for their part, are trying to figure out what nutrition the blueberry requires. They have switched to liquid fertilizers, which do not clog in wet weather as the granular varieties do and yet infiltrate coarse soils in light rain. Plant nutrition is related to pruning techniques, fire being the time-honored tool on the barrens. There is evidence that Indians burned over the land to get rid of competing plants long before white settlers arrived.

"The barrens have been burned deliberately for generations," Olday said. "First it was haphazard, and recently it's been more sophisticated. The lowbush blueberry is ex-ceptionally resistant to fire, and the traditional wisdom has been that burning not only removes competing plants and insect pests but also leaves ashes that help fertilize the regenerating stems. The other side of the coin is that repeated burning destroys the organic pad, where all the biological activity takes place, right down to the mineral soil."

As a rule the barrens are burned in two-year cycles. Driving through, a visitor sees fields green and blossoming on one side of the road, charred and lifeless on the other. A field burned early in spring will not bear fruit that year. Thus only about half of the barrens is in production during any one season. A plant's highest yield occurs in the second summer after burning. There is a slight drop in yield if you don't burn before the third summer, and a dramatic decline after that.

In recent years Wyman and some of the other large landowners have turned increasingly to pruning by mowing. Big tractors rumble across the terrain, towing a set of flail-mowers that work independently to rise and fall over the mounds and pits and cut the stems to within an inch of the ground. Wyman keeps a crew of mechanics on hand at its Deblois field headquarters to armor-plate its mowing vehicles. The more a tractor resembles a tank, the more efficient it proves on wild blueberries.

Some growers also use mechanical harvesters, but the machines leave many berries in the fields and, therefore, may never completely supplant rakers.

Burning and mowing are designed to prepare the plants to bear as many berries as possible. But for this, the humans who manipulate the crop need the intervention of some fellow creatures—imported honeybees.

The insecticides that have drenched the barrens for decades make no distinctions, felling insect friends and foes alike. Bees and other pollinating insects native to the area have long since been sharply reduced by poisoning, so growers are obliged to import honeybees from distant apiaries to make sure their fruit is set. Today, over the blossoming fields, there is a haze of honeybees, their presence likely to be noticed by even the most distracted traveler because of abundant signs tacked to posts and reading, "Beware of Bees." Walking or driving on the barrens, one is also likely to encounter pickup trucks with full gun racks.

Rifles and bees are more closely connected than one might suppose. Beekeepers stack their hives in the fields, where inevitably they are raided for grubs or honey by bears from the nearby thickets.

So, mimicking the logic of some ancient fairy tale, pickup trucks patrol the roads to kill the bears that raid the hives of rented

bees that replace the native insects that have been clobbered by insecticides. Ah, Lewis Carroll, thou shoulds't be living at this hour!

To compound the irony, honeybees are not ideally suited to the pollination of lowbush blueberries. The complex of smaller insects native to the barrens supplied a more efficient pollinating force than the larger bees, which apparently don't find the tiny blossoms terribly attractive. But the decline of the original complex and the drive toward higher yields have prodded the growers into this added expense. Wyman alone rents over 7,500 hives with perhaps 60 to 70 million bees at a cost of about a quarter-of-a-million dollars a season.

Talk of bees and bears is constant at "the Strawberry Patch," an old name for the Wyman field headquarters in Deblois. (The firm once had an experimental strawberry plot on the site.) Flatbed trailers, neatly stacked with hives waiting to be distributed in the fields, stood in the parking lot one June afternoon. Beekeepers Eli Mendes and Matty Robinson were pulling on their heavy "bee suits" preparatory to repairing a stack of hives smashed by a bear the night before in a remote part of the barrens.

"I brought more than 8,000 hives to Wyman and other Maine growers this spring," said Mendes, who operates an apiary in South Dartmouth, Massachusetts. "My brother David and I started beekeeping as a hobby about ten years ago and then decided to go into business. You work your bees either for honey or pollination. Pollinating crops is more stable because I can get a fixed fee, about thirty dollars a hive, and I'm on the road a lot moving the bees to different crops as they come into bloom. In the winter I take my bees to Florida for the citrus crop."

"You've got a nasty job this morning," a man standing near the truck told the two men. "The tops of the hives are smashed,

and the frames are all scattered around. The bees are *some* irritated."

Other men contributed stories, tall or otherwise, to the gathering. Everett Ramsdell, Wyman's general manager, topped them all.

"Years ago we put out a small trailer with some hives on it," he said. "When we came back in the morning the trailer was gone. But there were some bear tracks, so we followed them into the woods and after a while we found the trailer. That bear had pulled it in there so he could get at the hives when he wanted them!"

The stories were a reminder that, despite the chemical buffeting the barrens have taken, a flourishing ecosytem remains more

or less intact. In spring birdsong grows intense even before sunrise. Vesper sparrows, savannah sparrows, and yellowthroats lead the chorus, though there are rarer delights. Bobolinks rise from the shrubby cover and flutter over the berries, uttering what the ornithologist Arthur C. Bent called "a bubbling delirium of ecstatic music that flows from the gifted throat of the bird like sparkling champagne."

An upland sandpiper erupts in its high, trilled, drawn-out whistle. Ravens croak overhead, and a meadowlark sings its brief sweet song. At the end of summer, large flocks of robins and smaller troops of whimbrels (locally known as "blueberry curlews") arrive to

clean up the crop left after harvest. During the autumn migration, harriers quarter the fields in search of mice or small birds as diligently as humans combed them for berries a month or so earlier.

But already there is another sort of hunt going on across the barrens. On the horizon one sees a team of sweepers—three or four young women wielding sweep nets—moving through the fields. Their job is to collect samples of insects, particularly spanworms, living in the vegetation. The blueberry spanworm, the larva of a small geometrid moth, was a little-known part of the Washington County insect complex until 1981, when its population exploded. Especially destructive on blueberry flower buds and new shoots, the spanworm is one of several indications that something is going seriously wrong on the barrens.

When the sweepers sort the insects from the plant debris caught in their nets, they return with them to the Strawberry Patch and hand them over to a state entomologist. A sudden upsurge in the numbers of spanworms sends spray helicopters into action. The weapon of choice is Dylox, a controversial insecticide because laboratory tests indicate that it is mutagenic in some bacteria. Recently, the growers applied to the state for a loosening of restrictions on the use of Dylox because, they argued, the insecticide is relatively harmless to bees and the hives do not have to be removed from the fields during its application. The state complied.

Later in the season, as berries begin to form, other printed signs appear on the barrens. The bees have been taken elsewhere by then, and the new signs warn of Guthion, an insecticide aimed at a far older pest locally, the maggot of the blueberry fruit fly.

Photographer Stephen Muskie, preparing to take pictures at dawn from a helicopter applying Guthion, asked the pilot if he needed to wear a respirator.

"No, I don't wear one," the pilot replied.

"Then I guess it's okay," Muskie said, "because I'll only be up for a few minutes."

After the copter had completed its mission and set down again at the Strawberry Patch, Muskie remarked that he could smell the Guthion.

"No, that's just something they mix it with," the pilot assured him.

"But it's *part* of the Guthion once they are mixed and put in the air," Muskie pointed out.

The pilot shrugged and walked away.

After the glacier, fire was the instrument that molded the blueberry barrens as we know them. Alexander Baring, an Englishman who traveled through what are now the towns of Cherryfield and Columbia at the end of the 18th Century, left the oldest written account of the area.

"There is a plain of two or three miles in diameter very poor and barren," wrote Baring, the future Lord Ashburton, who was to negotiate with Daniel Webster the treaty that established the boundary between Maine and Canada. "The soil is perfectly barren and covered with a short kind of heath and no wood. It has the appearance of having been burned, but the soil is so hard that it can never have been good. The nature of the whole is singular and different from anything I ever saw. When you get over the plain, which is a hill with a tabletop, you descend again on good lands."

The story was taken up in our own time by

arence Day of the Agricultural Experiment tion at the University of Maine. Day cluded that Maine Indians had burned r the barrens for centuries to encourage berries to spread. Natural fires may also ve helped them take root in formerly ested areas.

"Gathering blueberries on the barrens was ublic privilege for more than a hundred rs after the neighboring seacoast towns were settled," Clarence Day wrote. "Families came from far and near and even before the Civil War picked blueberries for their own use and for sale."

A Portland firm in the lobster business apparently canned blueberries for a short time right after the Civil War. In 1868 the A. L. Stewart Company opened in Cherryfield. It is the oldest surviving company in the blueberry industry. (It was sold to a Canadian businessman some years ago and now operates under the name Cherryfield Foods.) J. Burleigh Crane, who has been in the blueberry business since 1950, serves as a consultant.

"Stewart began by taking big tin cans to the barrens, filling them with berries, mixing in sugar and water, and cooking the mixture over open fires," Crane said. "The story goes that the first time they tried it something went wrong and the whole mess blew up!"

But Stewart persisted and found markets for its product. Wyman and several other firms began canning blueberries about 1875, establishing eastern Maine as the industry's center. Soon the blueberry had become a staple of the local economy. Farmers and other landowners converted much of their acreage to growing berries, while people from the coastal towns depended for a good part of their annual income on the few weeks in late summer when they harvested berries and sold them to the processors. More and more land was cleared as the companies invested in large tracts.

"It seemed that everybody had a burning iron, which was simply a bent piece of pipe with a wick inside," Burleigh Crane said. "You put in fuel oil and lit the wick. Even forty years ago, when I started with Wyman, people would set fires in the woods and fields and just let them burn. I can remember a couple of men working for Wyman who would walk alongside the fields on Route 193 in Deblois with their burning irons, and pretty soon you'd see fires burning all along the road. Of course, this made the paper companies very nervous. They owned woodlands all over this part of Maine, so they finally got the state to bring the burning under control."

Another man who recalls the blueberry business as it once existed is Arnold Davis, who lives near Centerville, on a dirt road a mile and a half from his nearest neighbor.

"I started raking berries when I was six years old," Davis recalled recently in his little, brown-shingled house. He is a small, agile man, nearing his eightieth birthday. "Whole families would walk over here from

JOE LeMONNIER

With a picnic table for an outdoor altar, Father George Coutlee says Mass at the Strawberry Patch, a transient "town" for Wyman rakers. Each summer Father Coutlee travels with his parishioners in their annual trek from New Brunswick's Big Cove Reservation to Maine's barrens.

147

Jonesboro, where we lived then, and we would bring our food in jars and live in tents. We raked berries from dawn until seven at night, and then we'd go back to the tents, where my mother would cook dinner and do the laundry. On rainy days when we couldn't rake my father walked back to Jonesboro to pick up more groceries."

The rakers winnowed the berries by hand, turning a crank on a little machine to blow out the leaves, twigs, and other debris. (A new age came to the barrens a little later with the development of a winnowing machine powered by a two-cycle engine.) At day's end the workers filled wooden boxes with their berries, nailed on covers, and strapped them to a buckboard. Drawn by horses and lighted by a lantern hanging between the rear wheels, the buckboard set off on the all-night trip to the "factories" in Cherryfield.

Like many other Maine children of the time, Arnold Davis earned money on the blueberry barrens to help pay for clothes and other necessities as the school year approached. He raked almost every summer until he was thirty years old. "When the harvest comes around," he said, "I still feel as if I should be out there with a rake."

The cabin of the Murphy family—Ann, Derick, and Bill—from Caribou, Maine, boasts many of the comforts of home, including television and refrigerator. Their two Dobermans travel with them to the barrens, where the elder Murphys have raked berries for twenty-five years.

The serpent in this Eden was the blueberry fruit fly, which has the nasty habit of slitting the berry with its ovipositor and leaving an egg inside. The egg hatches into a maggot, a tiny eating-machine that was soon found to inhabit a significant portion of the crop. Before freezing became the standard method of processing berries, they were shipped in cans of various sizes. On opening a can, the consumer often found an unpleasant surprise— the carcasses of innumerable maggots floating in the syrup on top of the berries. Business fell off, and at one point in the 1940s, Massachusetts threatened to ban Maine blueberries.

"The growers made attempts before World War II to fight the maggot with calcium arsenate and other substances," Burleigh Crane recalled. "And after the war they turned to DDT. But for a while it was a haphazard kind of solution. I can remember that one fellow in a small plane used to do all the spraying in this part of the state. It wasn't very systematic—he'd just spray anything he saw—and after a while the state put in some regulations and he quit."

The turning point for the industry (and the barrens) came in World War II. Jolted by

the maggot and declining markets, processors decided to tax their product and establish a blueberry commission and a research project affiliated with the University of Maine. The funds helped buy an old farm in Jonesboro, which became the state-supervised research station, Blueberry Hill Farm.

After the war the industry was blessed with strong leaders, including Hollis Wyman, a Harvard-educated, politically oriented heir to the company that bears his surname. Wyman strengthened the family's business in both blueberries and sardines while becoming a power in the state senate. By providing a major source of income for local people and dispensing largesse to the poor at Thanksgiving and Christmas, Wyman became chief among the "blueberry barons."

"There were great changes at the beginning of the 1960s," said Burleigh Crane, whom Wyman brought into the business. "Advances in technology improved the quick-freezing process, which meant we could provide a much better berry to the consumer. Before freezing, for instance, the berries remained too soft in processing to remove the stems, and the consumer had to eat them or pick them out one by one from her muffins. Freezing the berries right away allows us to snap off the stems as they roll along the production belts."

Growers began to import both bees and harvest workers to keep up with the increased yields made possible by fertilizers, pesticides, and irrigation.

"We learned how to handle the bees," Crane recalled. "The trucks carrying the hives used to break down in front of somebody's house, and the bees would escape and get in the attic or kill a dog and there would be an awful uproar. One of our men took a trailerload up to the barrens to replace the hives smashed by a bear, and there was the bear standing in the field.

"'Jesus,' the driver groaned, 'there he is, waiting for his bees!'

"In the 1960s we used to pay bounties on the bears and even bring in hunters with dogs from the Carolinas. Now bear hunting has become a more popular sport in Maine and we don't have as much pressure on the bees."

The old guard was changing fast by the 1980s. Hollis Wyman retired, and the Stewarts sold their company. There was a general feeling in the industry that the bubble might have burst. The Maine crop soared to 45 million pounds, flooding the market at a time when a rise in the value of the dollar crippled sales efforts abroad.

About seven years ago the Maine Wild Blueberry Company barged onto this unstable scene with a challenge for the older firms. Seizing on the romance of the wild berry, it adopted an imaginative management style to create the largest processing firm in the business.

"A textile firm had pulled out of the town of Machias, leaving an abandoned mill and a lot of unemployed people," recalled company president Frederick "Bud" Kneeland, a former state police sergeant and later an employee of Wyman's. "So a Machias businessman named Robert Foster and I bought the building and renovated it as a modern blueberry processing plant. We also brought in a key man in our plans—Amr Ismail, an agronomist who had come to this country from Egypt and become Maine's blueberry extension specialist."

Ismail, born into a wealthy family, was slated to manage its two farms along the Nile until a college romance wrenched his life off course and pointed him toward Maine's barrens. Now he is known locally as "Mr. Blueberry."

"In the early sixties the political situation in Egypt was unstable," Ismail said. "My father advised me to get the best education possible so that I could work anywhere in the world. One of my professors at the University of Cairo had been at the University of Massachusetts, so I went on to get my master's degree in horticulture there. The big fruit crop in New England was apples, but I chose to work on tomatoes, which was more appropriate if I was going home."

But he met and married a Smith College student named Mary Louise Flanigan, and suddenly he had to revise his plans to go to Florida or Texas for a doctorate.

"There was no money now," he recalled. "The Ismails were madder than hell at me for marrying a foreigner, and the Flanigans weren't very happy with their daughter for marrying an Amr Ismail."

The best solution Amr Ismail could find on short notice was an assistantship with free tuition toward a doctorate at the University of Maine.

"The research money came from a blueberry project," he said. "I had never seen a blueberry plant, but I went to a greenhouse there to look at one, and I assured myself it was a true berry just like the tomato. My project dealt with the physiology and biochemistry of the blueberry plant."

The adaptable Ismail moved his wife and new daughter to Maine. Over the next decade, serving as extension blueberry specialist and superintendent of Blueberry Hill Farm, he became the leading authority on the Maine blueberry. He worked with growers and processors during the years when the wild crop doubled its yield. More than anyone else, Ismail became the spokesman for change in blueberry production.

"The important thing is to help the growers find ways to produce the best berry possible," Ismail said. "Once we get the berry in the processing plant, we can only screw it up."

Since joining Maine Wild, Ismail has done his best to see that nobody screws it up. At the company's state-of-the-art plant, berries are brought in from the fields and processed at once. (The new firm, which does not have the land holdings of the older ones, buys from independent growers, including Maine Indians.) Workers seated along running belts pick out any debris not removed in winnowing or washing. A further process puts the berries through a metal detector, which kicks out hard objects that may have passed through other screening stages. The berries are frozen in a tunnel at temperatures of 50 degrees below zero while wind jets hold them airborne to prevent their freezing in clusters.

After further cleaning and testing, the berries are distributed into cans of various sizes, packed with syrup, and sealed with metal lids that fold neatly over the cans' rims. Other machines cook the berries in the cans, then wash and cool the containers and send them to the world's kitchens.

Amid all the changes on the barrens, the blueberry rake remains constant. It is a steel instrument composed of a short, inverted handle and a flat, high-sided scoop tipped with thin tines. The raker, bending, pushes the rake forward into the plants and then pulls it up in a sweeping motion. As the tines strip the berries from the stems, they roll into a reservoir at the back of the scoop.

Most of the men and women engaged in the harvest began to wield a rake as children, and a powerful impetus toward change on the barrens today is the strict interpretation of child labor laws. Once upon a time, children not much beyond the toddler stage would contribute their dribble of berries to the family haul. But raking is no longer spliced into the nervous system of Washington County kids.

August has come to the barrens. The bees have long since been trundled off, the last aircraft has strafed the fields with Guthion, and rakers have signed on. The berries are best preserved right on the plants, and the idea is to delay raking until the crop is more than 90 percent ripe. Once the rakers move in, there is a certain urgency to complete the harvest before the first frost comes and softens the berries. With any luck, the workers will stay on the job for four or five weeks.

The 500 or so rakers taken on by Wyman's field crews mill about, eager to begin. A time clock, looking absurdly out of place, is fixed to a post in a field. The workers, many from out of state, will punch in and then try to make the best of the plots assigned them. Three or four Micmacs, recently in from Nova Scotia, pile out of their old car near a time clock. As a photographer begins to snap pictures, one of the men, with a black goatee and long, black, curly hair, scowls at him.

"Well, okay, I guess you can take my picture," he says with a shrug, and in a moment is chatting amiably.

"I call myself Albert King Fan," he says rapid-fire, stringing together the name of a blues musician and his own enthusiastic relation to him almost as one word. "I'm a sweeping man. They know me here in the fields by my singing rake. I run my hand across the teeth—zing!—and they know Albert King Fan is here!"

It is dawn, and the rough clink of rakes hitting woody stems sounds everywhere as the rakers try to get in a profitable morning before the sun warms the air up uncomfortably. The crew chiefs have already used twine to mark their fields into rows up to 400 feet long and ten or twelve feet wide. Each raker is supposed to remain within a designated strip, bending low and moving steadily through it, filling the pail he or she carries. The careful marking of strips ensures that the fields will be raked uniformly. Otherwise, the workers would be rushing to the likeliest spots, leaving the less densely fruited areas untouched.

"But you'll find cheaters up here," says a crew chief, nodding wisely. "They'll pull up the string between two good rows and appropriate both of them for themselves. Or, when they see a bad row is going to be assigned, they'll take a break and wait for a good one to be available."

The rakers take their full pails to the winnowing machine. Having cleaned the berries, they pour them into big plastic boxes (taking care that they are credited with the boxful). The boxes are then stacked on trucks and rushed to the plant.

Are blueberry rakers a dying breed? Many old-timers in the business think they are. To earn a good day's pay, a raker must be both fast and durable, a long-distance performer with good legs and a strong back.

Growers say that clam-diggers generally make the best rakers because they are already accustomed to maintaining a steady pace, bending and unbending over difficult terrain. A few years ago Down Easters regularly took time off from the mudflats in August to pick up some comparatively easy change on the barrens. Now, with the price of clams going through the roof, those wizards of ooze can't be lured from the shore.

Some of the rakers, however, return almost by force of habit. Eighty-four-year-old George Curtis, a regular on the barrens, has worked in the blueberry harvest for sixty-five years, the last fifteen for Wyman.

"Not long ago, I'd rake here in August and then go up to Aroostook County and dig potatoes," he said as he straightened up in a plot assigned him. "You'd think a person would be hardened up by raking blueberries, but it's different muscles. I'd get awful sore right here on the inside of the thighs digging potatoes."

Indians from the Maritime Provinces are increasingly important to the growers in making up for the shortage of local rakers. A month or so on Maine's barrens has become a tradition for many Indian families, some of whom look on their trip as a vacation as well as an opportunity to shop in the state's larger malls. Mary Augustine, seventy-two, has been coming to Wyman's fields for almost forty years from her home in Big Cove, New Brunswick.

"We have about fifteen hundred people on the reservation," she pointed out, "and in summer twelve hundred of them are down here. That's my son over there—I've always brought my children, and now they bring theirs. I can do all right because the growers pay you more for raking a field where the berries aren't very thick. In a good field like this one I can rake about twenty boxes a day at $2.75 a box. Last week I raked on bad ground and got only six boxes, but they gave me four dollars per box."

But many Indian families are beginning to lose their enthusiasm for the harvest. Part of the adventure used to be the freedom to live in tents or shacks on the fringes of the barrens with a few relatives and friends. Now federal regulations stipulate that the growers provide minimum standards of housing, toilets and running water, and separate buildings for cooking.

The growers argue that it is impractical to bring such facilities to widely separated points and have concentrated the workers'

Three generations of Mary Augustine's family from Big Cove rake Wyman's fields. "We have about fifteen hundred people on the reservation," she says, "and in summer twelve hundred of them are down here. I've always brought my children, and now they bring theirs."

cabins so amenities can be conveniently supplied. But both white and Indian rakers often complain that they are being thrown together with strangers, increasing the chance of fights, and are being subjected to the loud music and late partying that many of them came to the barrens to escape. One Indian referred to his new living site as a ghetto.

Wyman has moved most of the cabins into a large field adjacent to the Strawberry Patch in Deblois. Rakers gather there in the evenings after work, forming an instant and transient township. But its citizens have little civic pride. For the visiting Indians, one of the few rituals that hold the community together is Sunday Mass.

Father George Coutlee makes the annual trek to Maine with his parishioners from St. Anne's Church on the Big Cove Reservation.

"The reservation just empties out at this time of year because the trip has become part of the people's tradition," he said as he set up an altar outside the community cookhouse. His every movement was impeded by half a dozen children who hugged him, hung on him, teased him. "Even though I come from Quebec, my parishioners have great respect for me because I am their priest. So I decided to come, too. This is my tenth summer on the barrens. I raked with everybody else until a couple of years ago when I had a heart attack. I also say Mass at a couple of other places out on the barrens. The advantage here is that when it rains I can move the altar into the cookhouse."

One worry for the blueberry harvesters is technology, nibbling at the edges of the barrens in the form of mechanical harvesters. Until recently, these machines seemed only a pipe dream to most people in the business because of the rock-strewn, pitted, mounded terrain. But several firms have solved at least some of the problems, and the machines have become a familiar sight. Burleigh Crane has an open mind about them, partly because Cherryfield Foods' parent company has developed a reasonably efficient harvester that sells for about $15,000.

"We harvested one-third of our crop, about 2 million pounds, with the machines," Crane said. "They are fast and relatively efficient, but they still leave a lot of berries in the field."

Maine Wild's Bud Kneeland takes a negative view of the machine harvest. "We want to have everything hand-raked because we get a better berry that way," he said. "The machines pick up dust and bacteria, and you have to put in a lot of chlorine at the plant. I know that mechanical harvesters have worked for the growers of highbush blueberries, but those are bigger berries with a tougher skin, and the fields where they grow aren't as rough."

Still, some of the larger growers look on the machines as a solution to future labor shortages. The rakers do not believe the machines will ever completely supplant them, just as planes and tanks have not made the foot soldier obsolete. The worry remains that the mechanical harvesters will be perfected sufficiently to handle the better blueberry plots while humans will be relegated to harsher, less opulent terrain. And that, for the rakers, means slim pickings.

Scientists and technicians are at work in Maine, not only bringing change to the barrens but also documenting that change and exploring ways to cope with it.

David Yarborough, of the Department of Plant and Soil Sciences at the University of Maine, has traced the effectiveness of herbicides in altering the face of the barrens.

"In the early seventies the growers began to apply the herbicide Terbicil," he said. "It removed most of the grass cover but had little effect on woody weeds or goldenrods. Then along came Velpar, which controls woody weeds and goldenrods. Blueberries survive chemicals like Velpar because they don't take them up through their roots into the leaves as most other plants do. There would be some damage from spraying the full-grown plants, but as long as the growers apply Velpar before the blueberries leaf out, the plants aren't damaged."

The destruction of the blueberry's competitors, however, has tended to thin the barrens' plant cover, already meager, increasing erosion while making the fields even less inviting to a wide variety of pollinating insects. And although science holds the upper hand over weeds at the moment, the battle against insects and disease is lagging.

"Insects in blueberry fields are becoming more and more of a problem each year," extension blueberry specialist Tom DeGomez wrote in a recent newsletter to growers. "We are beginning to see economic damage from insects that in the past were of little importance."

DeGomez views the increase in pest insects and plant diseases as one of the trade-offs made by growers turning away from burning to flail-mowing in the pruning process. Yet one of the obvious advantages of mowing, besides its economic benefits, is that it spares the insect predators and parasites on which integrated pest management programs depend. Maine, to its credit, has taken a new interest in biological control.

A. Randall Alford, an entomologist at the

University of Maine, is part of a group investigating the spanworm's biology to find out where it might be vulnerable. "This is one of those caterpillars that seldom come out in daylight," he said, "but during the mating season the female moth uses a powerful sex pheromone to attract males. We feel that eventually we can sample populations and perhaps even exert some control by using the pheromone to trap the insects. We're also trying to develop a more effective fruit fly maggot trap by determining the chemicals and key visual stimuli that attract the egg-laying adults to the berries."

Studies at the university and at Blueberry Hill Farm may help limit the use of chemicals. "We won't have to spray by the calendar," says Del Emerson of Blueberry Hill, "but let natural controls take their course unless a pest gets completely out of control. There is a great need to put off spraying until it's justified."

Very little work has been done on the barrens to demonstrate the effect of all those chemicals on wildlife. One has to look to southern Maine, where Peter Vickery, an ornithologist, carried out a long-term study of the plight of the grasshopper sparrow on an area of barrens called the Kennebunk Plains, home of the species' only large breeding population in Maine. Vickery found that the number of breeding pairs decreased in every one of the four years he studied them, from a high of twenty-five pairs in 1984 to eleven in 1987.

"The decline in grasshopper sparrows is attributed to the increased use of the herbicide Velpar," he reported. "Grasshopper sparrows depend on areas with natural clumping grasses for nesting habitat."

The grasshopper sparrow seemed doomed on the Kennebunk Plains. A last-minute rescue came about when, after the passage of a state bond issue to provide $35 million for the purchase of sensitive wild lands, money became available to buy the critical portions of the plains. The sparrow's habitat will be managed in the future by The Nature Conservancy.

Despite a keen interest in parts of Washington County's barrens by officials of Maine's Critical Areas Program, the commercial forces involved do not offer much hope that there is a similar *deus ex machina* in the wings for the state's largest stretch of blueberry lands.

"Change and decay in all around I see," go the words of the old hymn. This doesn't describe the total scene on the barrens, which are still biologically and geologically special. But change is coming fast there for both man and beast. As man dilutes the wild landscape, thinning its variety in his quest for a tamed monoculture, the system goes awry. The orthodox solution is to intervene ever more intensively—in this case, to step up the use of chemicals.

Blueberry Hill's Del Emerson, born in nearby Columbia Falls and a long-time hunter and fisherman, is dismayed by what he sees.

"A couple of applications of Guthion and the animals move out," he says. "I don't find the ducks and grouse I used to in ponds and forests on the barrens. Still, blueberries give a lot of local people the means to stay here and make a living."

It's the old trade-off again.

OF BUCKEYES
AND BUCKEYES

TEXT BY JOHN FLEISCHMAN　•　PAINTING BY MANABU SAITO

It was a poor season for buckeyes, perhaps because of the dry weather but more likely because the children lost interest in harvesting them. A bumper crop may have gone to seed out in the woods; all I saw of it were two measly nuts left on the back steps, collected reflexively by little hands and soon forgotten.

I did see the kickoff of the buckeye harvest the October before. On a sunny Sunday front-porch morning, I looked up from the paper to see the children trooping Indian file, empty plastic bags flapping against their legs, down into the creek beyond the house. "Creek" is a rather grand title for the on-again, off-again rivulet at the bottom of a steep ravine that defeated the developers sixty years ago, when this part of Cincinnati was platted. It's perfect buckeye land—steep, wet, and unwanted.

The children staggered out of the creek about an hour later, mud up to the knees, faces scratched and flushed, each clutching a bag bulging with buckeyes. They had gathered some from the ground but discovered the best method of harvesting was to chuck a stick into the branches and duck. A quick bash with another stick loosened the prickly husk, revealing the shiny brown nut with its lighter circle of scar tissue. The eye of the buck. There can't be many wild fruits as satisfying to the touch as a dehusked buckeye. A satiny, mahogany-dark rustic billiard ball, it calls you to roll it around in your hand.

If one buckeye is a tactile treat, a bag of buckeyes is a feast. The children spilled their loot on the living room carpet. They lined them up in rows, then by fives, then by heaps, and then, after quarreling over whose buckeyes were whose, ran out of things to do with them beyond throwing a few back into the woods. By late afternoon, the remaining buckeyes were abandoned behind the front door. A grown-up rebagged them, and, a few days later, when no youngsters were watching, released them to the wild.

There is something human that hates to see nature's bounty go unexploited, but in roughly two hundred years of civilized Amer-

ican contact with the fruit of the Ohio buckeye, there still isn't much that can be done with them besides counting. This outrages us. Like the European horse chestnut (*Aesculus hippocastanum*), to which it is related botanically, the Ohio buckeye (*Aesculus glabra*) looks good enough to eat yet is unpalatable. Indeed, the whole tree is virtually useless. But the buckeye has one sovereign purpose—it provides cultural identity.

Almost from the beginning, the settlers of the Ohio territory were called "Buckeyes," a usage compounded by stump oratory, poetry, and football rah-rah until it became part of the geopolitical junk stashed in every American's mental attic: Boston is Beantown; Florida is the Sunshine State; Ohioans are Buckeyes.

Arboreal allegiance is a curious business. Nearly every state legislature has adopted a "state tree," but only Ohio and four others have serious tree identities. Maine is the Pine Tree State, Georgia the Peach, Mississippi the Magnolia and South Carolina the Palmetto. (I am excluding Washington's claim to be Evergreen as entirely too sweeping; Al-

Previous page: Flower, nut, and spiked husk of the Ohio buckeye. Above: In the late sixties and early seventies, Woody Hayes awarded buckeye-leaflet decals weekly to meritorious members of his Ohio State football team.

155

abama's camellias are, after all, shrubs.) Pine boards and peaches are valuable commodities, but have you ever heard someone from Maine hailed as a "stalwart Pine?" In Ohio, a Buckeye's good name is still valued. When the Ohio State University football coach was fired in 1987 on the eve of the annual grudge match against Michigan, OSU President Edward Jennings said Earle Bruce could still be trusted. "Coach Bruce has been a loyal Buckeye throughout his career," Jennings explained.

All this was only of passing interest to me until my youngest became the first in the family to be born in Ohio. I was born on Manhattan Island, but I have never been called a Gothamite or a Knickerbocker. Likely my son's arboreal birth sign will have no more effect on his life than being born a Gemini or a Tuesday's Child, yet the fact must be faced. The Ohio buckeye tree has taken my flesh and blood under its dominion. My son is a Buckeye.

It is an ancient term, at least by American standards. According to pioneer historian S. P. Hildreth, the first court of record in the Northwest Territory was convened in Marietta, Ohio, on September 2, 1788, by a procession of legal worthies headed by Colonel Ebenezer Sproat, a man of considerable height and bulk. Sproat carried a large, unsheathed sword and proclaimed "oyez, oyez, oyez" at suitable moments. Witnessing this novel display of white-skinned manners were a large number of Indians who greeted Sproat with shouts of "hetuck, hetuck, hetuck," supposedly the Indian word for "eye of the buck" or "buckeye," and supposedly in honor of Sproat's upright and manly appearance. The first human Buckeye, Colonel Sproat, proudly carried the nickname to his ample grave.

Etymology, like history, is written by the victors. The Indians had long known that ground-up buckeyes make a dandy fish stupefacient when broadcast on ponds. (The stunned fish could be scooped up easily.) On that historic occasion in Marietta, the Indian shouts of "hetuck" might have been an entirely different comment on the coming of litigation to the wild Middle West. But once in the air, the Buckeye nickname spread from Colonel Sproat to his compatriots. By the 1830s, writers were commonly calling the locals "Buckeyes." In any case, there were few Ohio Indians left to quibble about linguistics or botany by 1840, when the word leaped into the American vocabulary forever. It was botanical politics that made the Buckeye.

The candidate was William Henry Harrison, the Virginia-born aristocrat who had

extinguished local Indian quibbles forever at the battle of Tippecanoe. The conquering Harrison settled down just west of Cincinnati on the heights overlooking the Ohio River, where he quickly expanded a log house into a rambling but elegant clapboard mansion. With "Tyler Too" appended, the victor of Tippecanoe ("retrofitted with a rustic frontier background," as journalist Nicholas Von Hoffman would have it) became the rough-and-ready Whig candidate of what was then the robust trans-Appalachian West. An opposition newspaper just couldn't resist the gibe that Harrison "was better fitted to sit in a log cabin and drink hard cider than rule in the White House."

It was a classic political fumble, and the Whigs picked up the ball, running it right up Pennsylvania Avenue. In the first media-managed presidential campaign, Harrison's handlers put out an engraving of a dour Harrison seated in a rustic cabin with a barrel of cider against the wall and rows of buckeyes hanging from pegs. The combination of hard cider and hardball politics was a sure winner. An enthusiastic delegation of Union County Whigs arrived in Columbus for the 1840 state convention rolling a buckeye log cabin on wheels. The fad for "cabin-raisings" spread all the way to New York City, where a fifty-by-one-hundred-foot rustic dwelling was erected on Broadway near Prince Street.

A call for authentic buckeye memorabilia went out. A Whig convention in western Pennsylvania voted buckeye canes the official badge of authority for Harrison parade marshals. "Thereupon committees were sent to Ohio to procure a supply of canes for the occasion," William M. Farrar recalled in 1888, "with what success can be judged from the fact that while a procession extending over two miles in length and numbering more than 1,500 people halted on one of the Chartiers Creek hills until the one in front moved out of its way, an inventory taken showed the number of buckeye canes carried in the delegation to be 1,432, and in addition over a hundred strings of buckeye beads were worn by a crew of young ladies dressed in white, who rode in an immense canoe, and carried banners representing the several States of the Union."

With the campaign button still to be invented, the buckeye was the perfect piece of electoral merchandise—free, plentiful, and ecologically renewable. What this botanical symbolism meant to Harrison's contemporaries was never clear. Back in his "cabin," the candidate of the West was under strict orders to keep his mouth shut and his pen dry.

President Harrison finally shared his innermost thoughts in a one-and-a-half-hour inaugural address that he delivered, hatless and coatless, in a driving March rainstorm. He recommended the virtues of the Roman republic to the American people. A month later, he was dead of pneumonia. The buckeye was never a major issue in national politics again.

But "buckeye" was forever embedded in the American tongue as a synonym for residents of Ohio, a designation made official in 1953 by the state legislature. Long before then Ohio phone books were laced with Buckeye motels, Buckeye hat companies, Buckeye saw sharpeners, Buckeye foundries, and Buckeye collection bureaus. Despite this cornucopia of useful goods and services, the Ohio buckeye tree itself has yielded precious little.

It was not for lack of effort. The pioneers tried to find applications. The tree and its problematic fruit quickly caught their attention once they had crossed the Appalachians into the Ohio River Valley. The wood, early chroniclers reported, was soft enough to be worked without peril to valuable hand tools. Trunks were easily hollowed out for troughs, platters, and even cradles. Until the advent of plastic, buckeye wood was used to make artificial limbs. Folk wisdom had it that a buckeye carried in a rear pocket was a sovereign cure for rheumatism (although sitting on a buckeye would certainly give the wearer another kind of pain).

Daniel Drake, a pioneer Cincinnati physician and botanist, gave a fanciful after-dinner oration in 1847 in which he sketched out a long list of useful products from the buckeye, including primitive soap, hats woven from splints, medicines, and a flour made by washing a nut meal. He found redeeming virtues in the buckeye's most troublesome shortcomings. The relative incombustibility, opined Drake, made buckeye the ideal "back log" for the frontier fireplace, reflecting heat into the room.

Drake was stretching it. In its published proceedings for 1920 the Ohio Archaeological and Historical Society (now the Ohio Historical Society, or OHS) conceded a few of Drake's buckeye points but noted that "it was never extensively used . . . for many of the other qualities that he enumerates in his entertaining and inspiring address." If truth be known, the pioneers called it the "stinking" or "fetid" buckeye because they thought the bark smelled disgusting. The lumber was considered "inferior" and the flowers not particularly pretty.

Worst of all, the nuts were poisonous (al-though they are so bitter that the literature fails to record any individual who choked down a fatal dose). Squirrels eat (or at least gnaw) them, and modern botanists say the toxicity of the Ohio buckeye is overrated; still, to this day, no conscientious Ohio Valley farmer will allow buckeyes to sprout on pastureland.

The origin of the word, though, is clear. The 1920 proceedings of the OHS explain, "When the shell cracks and exposes to view the rich brown nut with the pale brown scar, the resemblance to the half-opened eye of a deer is not fancied but real. From this resemblance came the name buckeye."

More narrowly, Buckeyes are the sports teams of Ohio State. The plant's distinctive five-lobed leaflets were emblazoned on the regalia of Woody Hayes' successful football teams of the late sixties and early seventies. Hayes awarded little buckeye stickers to deserving players, who plastered them on their helmets. At a rival Ohio institution during this period of campus unrest, a classmate (a non-Buckeye and non-botanist) asked me why Hayes, the archetypal advocate of counter-counterculture, allowed his players to paint marijuana leaves on their football helmets.

If sometimes mistaken, the buckeye is always distinctive. It is also disputed. For years Ohio history books credited the first scientific identification to François André Michaux, the son of the great French botanist André Michaux. Thomas Jefferson invited the father and son to explore the trans-Appalachian interior. In his 1819 *North American Sylva,* the younger Michaux called the buckeye *Pavia ohioensis.* "I have found it only beyond the mountains, and particularly on the banks of the Ohio for an interval of about one hundred miles, between Pittsburgh and Marietta, where it is extremely common. It is called 'buckeye' by the inhabitants, but as this name has been given to the *pavia lutea,* I have denominated it 'Ohio buckeye' because it is most abundant on the banks of this river, and have prefixed the synonym of 'American horse chestnut' because it proved to be a proper horse chestnut by its fruit, which is prickly like that of the Asiatic species instead of that of the *paviae.*"

Michaux, however, was too late with his published description. The German botanist Carl Ludwig Willdenow had already named the species in 1809, and without leaving Berlin. Indeed, the "holotype"—the original specimen against which all comparisons must be made—was grown in the Berlin Botanical Garden from seed sent to Willdenow by an unknown American collector. An Ohio buck-

THE BUCKEYE FAMILY TREE

The Ohio buckeye belongs to a contentious genus. *A. glabra* is one of thirteen recognized members of the genus *Aesculus,* seven native to North America, one to Europe, and five to Asia. There are also several disputed varieties and at least one total misnomer.

The clear outsider is the so-called Mexican buckeye (*Ungnadia speciosa*), which does grow in Mexico and Texas but is not a buckeye at all. Mexico has a true buckeye, *A. parryi,* found only in Baja California.

An undisputed American member of the genus is the bottlebrush buckeye (*A. parviflora*), a shrub native to Alabama and southwest Georgia. A popular ornamental, it is planted widely in the northern United States. The painted or dwarf buckeye (*A. sylvatica*), also shrub-size, is from the southeastern Piedmont and coastal plains. California has its own native *Aesculus,* the California buckeye (*A. californica*), which has five-fingered leaflets but a smooth, pear-shaped fruit.

That brings us to the red buckeye (*A. pavia*), a native of the southern coastal plains, the central Texas plains, and the middle Mississippi Valley. The red is sometimes called the firecracker plant after its distinctive tall, bright-red flowers. The particolored buckeye used to be considered a separate species, *A. discolor,* but it has been reclassified as a variety of *pavia.*

Then comes the yellow or sweet buckeye of the southern Appalachian Mountains. Until 1988 it was known as *A. octandra.* It is *octandra* no longer. Recent research into the earliest published description of the species found a 1778 reference to *A. flava.* The yellow *flava* is not to be confused with the yellow woolly buckeye, which Texans sometimes call the red *pavia.*

Texans are also behind the thorniest dispute in the *Aesculus* realm, the so-called Texas buckeye, or *A. arguta.* The late Robert A. Vines, author of *Trees of Central Texas,* said that the *arguta* was mistakenly "listed as a variety under the name of *A. glabra* var. *arguta.*" However, James Hardin, a botanist at North Carolina State University in Raleigh, says this is no mistake. The acknowledged American authority on the genus, Hardin says the Texas buckeye is, at heart, an Ohio buckeye. At first glance the *arguta*'s seven to nine narrow leaves make it appear radically different from the five-fingered *glabra.* The appearance is deceptive. Hardin says the *arguta* variety "grades into the Ohio buckeye" as it moves from its primary western range through Missouri and Arkansas into western Kentucky. A Kentucky *arguta* specimen might be hard for a novice to identify, says Hardin, but to the trained eye its fruit and buds clearly reveal it to be *A. glabra.*

The final common "American" buckeye is our old friend *A. hippocastanum,* the European horse chestnut, originally native only to the Balkans. Its seed was first imported to the American colonies in the 1730s by the Philadelphia botanist John Bartram. Planted as a shade tree, the horse chestnut now thrives across a wide range in the United States. Experts differ on whether it "occasionally" or "rarely" escapes into the wild.

The human Buckeye, *Homo sapiens ohioensis,* is native only to Ohio.—*J. F.*

Curiously for this species of North American origin, the "holotype"—the original buckeye specimen against which all comparisons must be made—was grown from seed in the Berlin Botanical Garden.

JOE Le MONNIER

eye was flowering in Berlin even as Michaux was hacking his way into the new western territory over the mountains. Meantime Willdenow, noting the Ohio buckeye's connection to the European horse chestnut, put it in the genus *Aesculus* and from its distinctive hairless (*glabra*) buds, formally dubbed it *Aesculus glabra*.

The survival of Willdenow's Ohio buckeye holotype is a fascinating tale, according to Tod F. Stuessy, director of the Ohio State University Herbarium. During World War II, Willdenow's core collection, including the mounted Ohio buckeye leaflets and flowers, was moved to safety. Allied bombers destroyed 4 million other specimens in the Berlin collection, but the buckeye holotype survived. Stuessy is at a loss to explain how the seed came into Willdenow's possession so early or why, as late as 1920, the OHS was still saying Michaux had named it. As for Daniel Drake's calling it the *Pavia ohioensis* in 1847, Stuessy can only say, "Well, communication wasn't the greatest in those days."

Even with modern communications, it took two years of gentle persuasion for Stuessy to convince the Germans to lend a specimen from the Willdenow collection. Explaining the buckeye's celebrity to the Germans was relatively easy, he recalls: "I went through the whole buckeye thing—its use on the university seal, the sports teams, and how everyone in Ohio regards themselves as Buckeyes. They didn't have any problem with that. But they had never lent anything from the Willdenow before. Like most of the big historic botanical collections, the Willdenow is photographed so people can work from it anywhere—they couldn't understand why I wanted the specimen. 'What's the big deal?' they said. They offered to arrange for a special picture. I had to explain that for us it was not quite the same thing."

In 1987 Stuessy hand-carried the original Ohio buckeye specimen to Columbus for a two-year public display. The president of OSU authorized a grant to enshrine it in a special frame and a shockproof carrying case that required two men to lift it. Stuessy needed a portable museum because he took the holotype on the road to local OSU alumni chapters during the football season. Game films and pep talks are the usual programs for these booster gatherings, but Stuessy was amazed at how often his buckeye program was requested.

He remains a trifle puzzled by the nonbotanical attractions of the buckeye today. "It's such a tame symbol. I suppose maybe the settlers felt close to it, and Daniel Drake's speech generated a lot of general interest in the buckeye, but it's still rare for an institution to have a plant for a symbol. The only other one I know of is Indiana State University and the sycamore.

Whatever it represents, the original buckeye offered Stuessy a novel use—as a fund-raiser for the OSU Herbarium. He closed each presentation with the offer to give anyone who donated $100 a "plaque containing a color photo of the buckeye specimen ready for hanging in den or game room."

For those without a photo, the crudest way to tell an Ohio buckeye from a horse chestnut is to count the number of leaflets on several stems. Ohio buckeyes *usually* have five "fingers"; horse chestnuts *usually* have seven. Or, as Jan Catherwood told her seventh-grade Ohio history students at Shelby Junior High, "You are a Buckeye; you have five fingers. This is a buckeye twig; it has five fingers." Foresters look at the end buds; the Ohio buckeye's are ridged and definitely not fuzzy; the horse chestnut's are larger and very sticky. The fruit distinguishes the Ohio buckeye from the sweet buckeye (*Aesculus flava*). The Ohio buckeye husk is weakly thorny in young specimens and warty in old ones. The sweet buckeye is smooth.

(The fourth tree in the horse chestnut confusion is the American chestnut, *Castanea dentata,* once a plentiful native species that has been all but wiped out by an Asian bark fungus. The leaves and husks look nothing like those of buckeyes or horse chestnuts. The American chestnut was the traditional one to eat, as in Mel Torme's musical Christmas chestnut that begins, "Chestnuts roasting on an open fire." Almost all our eating chestnuts today are grown commercially in California on a fungus-resistant Chinese chestnut, *Castanea mollissima.*)

Botanizing aside, what appealed to the pioneering Buckeyes about the Ohio buckeye was not its similarity to the European horse chestnut but its singularity. They had crossed the Alleghenies hoping to find a new world, and here was the very proof of that newness. "It is not merely a native of the West," said Drake in his encomium to the *ohioensis,* "but peculiar to it . . . and is the only tree of our whole forest that does not grow elsewhere. What other tree could be so fit an emblem of our native population?"

The Ohio buckeye does grow elsewhere today, thanks to horticultural evangelizing. Planted and gone-wild specimens are now found all over the eastern United States and in Europe. It is hardy enough to survive as far north as Michigan and as far south as Texas. The Ohio Valley, though, remains its heartland. The heart of the heartland is the state of Ohio, which, after all, has a vested interest in the tree—even if the American Forestry Association's national champion Ohio buckeye is in Liberty, Kentucky. (The champ, standing 144 feet tall, is a singular specimen; despite its stupendous height, it is only thirty-two feet across at the crown. For comparison, the AFA's runner-up Ohio buckeye, in Eastlake, Ohio, is sixty-two feet tall and sixty-two feet across at the crown. The average height of a mature Ohio buckeye is around forty feet. The buckeye's "characteristic" shape is determined by how much room it can take from its neighbors.)

Living north of the Ohio River, Daniel Drake found the Ohio buckeye an admirable model for young Buckeyes, even beyond its myriad (although exaggerated) uses: "Who has not looked with admiration on the foliage of the buckeye in early spring, while the more sluggish tenants of the forest remain torpid in their winter quarters? . . . Its early putting forth, and the beauty of its leaves and blossoms, are appropriate types of our native population, whose rapid and beautiful development will not be denied... while the remarkable fact that almost every attempt to transplant it into our streets has been a failure shows that it will die in captivity, a guaranty that those who bear its name can never be enslaved."

Here too, Drake was only partially correct. Ohio buckeyes can be grown in town. Cincinnati's urban forester, Steve Sandfort, can rattle off a half-dozen prize specimens in his bailiwick, but he admits the Ohio buckeye is not a good "street tree." It can't tolerate a lot of soil disturbance and the other ills of city sidewalk life.

Early last April I went to the Ohio countryside to see the buckeye in its element. A friend who has a place just beyond the skirts of the city's sprawl agreed to let me walk in her woods, thirty acres of third-growth timber that she has been letting go wild for years. Did she have a big buckeye? She wasn't sure. We would have to see.

It was still early days in the woods, although the wildflowers were out in force. Struggling down a steep hillside in search of a big Ohio buckeye, we were hopelessly distracted by the shows of squirrel corn, Dutchman's-breeches, bloodroot, trout lilies, wild poppies, and windflowers. We came upon some buckeyes, the only trees to have leafed out so early, with their tall spikes of yellowish-green blossoms, but they were all scrawny saplings, twisted into no discernible common shape. Only at the very bottom of the slope did we find evidence of a major specimen—the stub of its trunk hollowed by

rot. From the base grew two hardy sprouts, showing the five-fingered leaflet and crowned with flowers.

Then it came to us that we had already seen the most characteristic form of Ohio buckeye in the modern wild. Accounts of the "primeval" Ohio Valley forest say buckeyes dominated in some climax stands, but here, in this much battered regrowth woods, the buckeye is a hardy citizen of the understory, an early blossomer that can tolerate the dominating summer shade of the oak, beech, and maple canopy. Looking uphill we realized that many of the spindly saplings we had passed were well over thirty feet tall, shoving a few branches into the sunshine begrudged them by their more substantial neighbors. Underfoot, young buckeyes sprouted in the underbrush. The Ohio buckeye is no king of trees but a smiling courtier, bending to the will of sylvan lords yet always keeping a wily eye open for modest opportunities. It survives.

To study such a fighter, my friend said, I had to have one of my own. She had little buckeyes to spare. And while I protested that my sliver of a city lot had no room for a buckeye, she marched back to the house for a shovel. We dug gingerly around a small tree and slowly eased it out of the earth. There was the seminal nut itself, husk fallen open, roots pushing down, stem up. It was a touching moment, a confirmation of something simple, yet still a revelation: From little buckeyes, mighty ones spring.

I took my root-bundled buckeye back to town, chopped out a place for it in the grassy strip between sidewalk and curb that the city grandly calls the "tree lawn," and planted it with a chicken-wire anti-dog fence. It seemed to prosper for a while, but in late summer the urban forester's official words came back to me. Heat, compacted soil, not-to-be-discouraged dogs, who knows? My buckeye wilted, the leaves drooping and then browning. The last one dropped off long before the maple down the street turned a leaf. Yet I left the stem to winter over in its cage. I dipped into Daniel Drake again. "In all our woods there is not a tree so hard to kill as the buckeye. The deepest 'girdling' does not 'deaden' it, and even after it is cut down and worked up into the side of a cabin it will send out young branches, denoting to all the world that Buckeyes are not easily conquered, and could with difficulty be destroyed."

It's spring again. Ohio climbs blinking out of winter into a mild light. And my buckeye has sprouted five incredibly fat, reddish, hairless buds—*Aesculus glabra,* the Ohio buckeye, the tree of native resilience.

SPECIAL PLACES

VI

THE MEANING OF CREEKS

TEXT BY PETER STEINHART • PHOTOGRAPH BY PAT O'HARA

Creeks don't get named for Civil War generals or Indian chiefs. They take their names from whatever's handy and are introduced without fanfare as Rock Creek, Mill Creek, or Mud Creek. They don't get celebrated in travel literature or national anthems. Tourists make no pilgrimages to them. They have to be renamed "brook" to get into a poem or a map of New England. Creeks are the trivial parts of our landscape, what scoundrels and rusting shopping carts are thrown into. Mark Twain heard a miner at Angels Camp declare that an abusive lady should "be bundled neck and crop into the creek."

But nearly everybody has a creek gurgling through their memories, a confiding waterway that rose in the spring of youth. A national park ranger's voice softens as he talks of a boyhood creek in Louisiana where he swam and fished. Conservationist David Brower's eyes sparkle as he recalls building dams on Strawberry Creek in the Berkeley of his youth. An Ohio woman feels suddenly at home again as she remembers catching crayfish in the creek behind her house.

A creek wound between my grandfather's apricot orchard and a neighbor's hillside pasture. Its banks were shaded with cottonwoods and redwood trees and a thick tangle of blackberry and wild grape vine. A path was cleared along the streambank, and on hot summer days its sun-dappled glades were cool and filled with the song of thrush and quail. The quiet creekwater flowed clear and cold over gravel bars I fished for brook trout.

Nothing historic ever happens in these recollected creeks. But their persistence in memory suggests that creeks are bigger than they seem, more a part of our hearts and minds than lofty mountains or mighty rivers.

Creektime is measured in strange lives, in sand-flecked caddisworms under the rocks, sudden gossamer clouds of mayflies in the afternoon, a salamander wriggling back to winter water, or minnows darting like slivers of inspiration into the dimness of creek fate. Mysteries float in creeks' riffles, crawl over their pebbled bottoms, and slink under the roots of trees. Thoreau declared, "The shallowest water is unfathomed; wherever a boat can float there is more than Atlantic depth and no danger of fancy or imagination running aground."

While big rivers are heavy with sophistication and sediment, creeks are clear, innocent, boisterous, full of dream and promise. Their mysteries are modest enough to tempt youth. A child can wade across or push aside the trail-side branches without a parent's moral imperatives and hygienic cautions. You can go it alone, jig for crayfish, swing from ropes into jubilant air. Creeks belong to childhood. In Greek art, they are sometimes represented as youths bearing plants.

To spend childhood days along creekbanks is to be drawn into the wider world. A creek reaches upward into the hills and mountains, where clouds brood and gods bluster. It reaches down to the lowlands and the bays, to fat old rivers, sad and murky with the silt of experience. A creek teaches one the curve of the Earth, the youthful swell of mountains, the age of the seas. Above all, a creek offers the mind a chance to penetrate the alien world of water and think like a tadpole or a trout. That is one of the great experiences of otherness, one of the leaps of perception that make us human and allow us to live with dream and obscurity. What drifts in creekwater is the possibility of other worlds inside and above our own. Poet Robert Frost wrote, "It flows between us, over us, and with us. And it is time, strength, tone, light, life, and love."

A creek may pluck one's imagination and bear it away like a drifting leaf. And helpless, we may trundle along after it, delighted by its liquid babble, dazzled by the leap and sparkle of sunlight on water. Creeks lead one on, like perfume on the wind. In fact, the word "creek" may derive from the word "crack," a cleft in the surface of things. Poets of the 17th Century talked of fate appearing "in every creek and turning of your lives." A creek is something that disappears around a bend, into the ground, into the next dimension. To follow a creek is to seek new acquaintance with life.

"A creek is something that disappears around a bend, into the ground, into the next dimension. To follow a creek is to seek new acquaintance with life."

163

I still find myself following creeks. In high mountain meadows I'll trace the course of brooks that gnaw into the lime-green grass and deep glacial duff, marveling at the sparkle of quartz and mica and the silvery quickness of fingerling trout. The pursuit liquefies my citified haste and cynicism. It lifts weight from my shoulders. Once, in the California desert, as hummingbirds darted from cactus blossoms, a storm cloud brooded on top of a distant ridge. In the sun-dried silence I heard the babble of rushing water. I followed my ears a half-mile over dusty hillsides and down scabrous ravines to an unexpected ribbon of clear, cold, rushing water, leaping from rock to rock, filling little pools. The discovery seemed Biblical, a benediction. It filled me with joy.

At such times I think creeks may be a part of our human consciousness. Perhaps we see in them reflections of our own dreams of liquid ease and silvery coursings. Perhaps it's the other way around—that creeks are the way Earth sees itself in us, recognizes in the branching of capillary and vein, neuron and thought, the dendritic pattern of rill and river. The gurgle of a brook may be the sound of confided ancestry. Perhaps that is why we universally find the sound of creeks reassuring. Perhaps that is why we carry creeksongs in our memories.

But as often as not the original creek is lost. Brower saw Strawberry Creek wedged into culverts. My ranger friend returned to his boyhood creek and found "it just didn't live up to the memories." Perhaps the adult eye sees outline but can no longer penetrate the meaning. Perhaps city life hardens our senses so that we no longer recognize the kinship of leaping water.

Or perhaps the destruction is real. In Pennsylvania, coal mining acidifies creeks: A map of Clarion County shows the blue veinwork of Allegheny mountain creeks, but virtually all of them have small skulls and crossbones beside them. In the Midwest, silt eroding off cultivated fields suffocates creeks. In the Southeast, second homes belly up to them, and as homeowners worry about fifty-year floods, they channelize and riprap and culvert the creeks. In the Northwest, logging waste and erosion chokes creeks. In California, housing tracts and industrial parks crowd right up to a creekbank, and as soon as a flood threatens, the channel is straightened, deepened, enclosed in concrete, and then fenced off so that children and lawsuits will not stray into its bone-white inhospitality.

Where laws are written to protect them, creeks may be so low on the list of priorities that the law dries up. There may be no staff at the state level to inspect creeks or follow permits. In California, water-quality officials are often forbidden to inspect lands about to be harvested by loggers. Pennsylvania's Division of Rivers and Wetlands Conservation has no field staff. Says Roger Fickes, of the Pennsylvania Department of Environmental Resources, "If we issue a permit with mitigation requirements, we almost never get out to see if permit conditions are met."

Creeks today seldom fall under the terms of wild and scenic rivers acts. In Ohio, for example, a waterway must be at least ten miles long to qualify for protection. Where creeks are not yet altered, landowners tend to think things will never change, and they are reluctant to get involved in efforts to protect them. Of 3,500,000 river miles in the United States, less than 30,000 are protected by scenic river laws. Federal laws protect a few short waterways, but they invariably have special qualities. Four-and-a-half miles of Pennsylvania's Bear Run is protected, for example, but largely because it hosts two unique invertebrates and Frank Lloyd Wright's famous house "Falling Water."

Creeks have not fared well in a culture which defines itself by sweep, size, and noise. We grew up a nation of mighty rivers and mountains—rivers to turn the wheels of commerce and mountains to echo the names of explorers. We belittled other countries for failing to come up to the brag of our scenery. "The wildest things in England are more than half tame," sneered Nathaniel Hawthorne. "We've got steamboats enough at St. Louis to tow Great Britain out into the Atlantic and stick her fast," crowed an American in 1857.

We would never boast that we were a nation of creeks. But might British character—its inwardness of thought and outwardness of purpose—have as much to do with the creeks in its salad landscape as with the sea thundering at its back? Might our own fragile sense of care and community be nurtured by the simplicity and summery song of childhood creeks? And what may be lost when a creek vanishes? Robert Frost lamented a brook he once knew gone under city concrete, "thrown deep in a sewer dungeon under stone," and wondered if the interment kept thoughts from rising and work and sleep from inspiriting the citizens who droned over the culvert.

There is an increasing interest in keeping creeks. People have begun to worry about what goes into water and to see that rivers and wells alike begin in creeks. The Izaak Walton League has, for twenty years, offered monitoring kits to anyone who wants to look after a stream, and there are now more than two hundred streams watched by the league, and an untold number of others watched by people who have written in for the kits. Several states have "adopt a stream" programs, under which citizens go out to clean up trash, construct trails, conduct research, or monitor the political fate of a creek. In Ohio nearly 4,000 citizens are stream-watchers. In North Carolina, 150 stream-watch groups watch about seven hundred miles of waterways. In California, local creek councils try to stop Corps of Engineers flood-control projects from destroying their neighborhood creeks.

But more is needed. A University of California at Davis study warns that 60 percent of California's surviving creeks are in trouble. In the Rocky Mountain states, there is little or no protection for streams. In cities, people dump chemicals into storm drains, killing everything in their creeks. Expanding suburbs push creeks underground and cut the bond of sunlight and water. "Mostly they are taken for granted," says John Kopec of Ohio's Scenic Rivers Program. "Many times they are abused."

My boyhood creek long ago fell victim to groundwater pumping, which lowered the water table; subdivision, which fenced it off; and channelization and culverting for flood control. It followed the fate of nearly all the creeks that flow into San Francisco Bay. Not a single one is left without at least some stretch straightened and enclosed in concrete. With the creeks went the intimacies of the valley, the song of thrushes, the cool shade of cottonwoods, the inspiration of youth. In their place came freeways, smog, and the buzzing haste of placelessness.

But I keep yet another vision of creeks, a small consolation for the loss of boyhood haunts. In it, a confiding creek gurgles through a small alpine meadow in the Sierra Nevada. It is a summer day, and the late-afternoon sun lines the golden haze with long blue forest shadows. My six-year-old son's blond hair catches the light as he stretches a fishing rod over the creek, dabbling at the water with a dry fly. The creek-water fairly boils with leaping rainbow trout. They are five- and six-inch fry, and their mouths are too small to close over the hook. But they dart impulsively, trying to draw him into their world just as he tries to lure them to his. And when one finally becomes snagged, he dances, shuffling triumphantly from foot to foot, the golden light of endless days in his eye, the silvery fish wriggling on his upheld leader. In the vision it is clear that it is he who has been caught.

RESEARCHING THE SLOUGH

TEXT BY MARK HOY • PHOTOGRAPHY BY GARY BRAASCH

The early morning light silhouettes the spruces on the green hillsides and outlines the commercial fishing boats as they pass on their way to the trolling grounds off the southern coast of Oregon. Photographer Gary Braasch and I paddle our light canoe in the opposite direction, up a shallow channel of Coos Bay, one of Oregon's largest estuaries. A gentle breeze at our backs brings with it the unmistakable scent of the sea; its crashing breakers are only a mile or two away.

Gliding near algae-matted mudflats littered with shell fragments, we pass clam-diggers who were up before dawn to take advantage of this morning's low tide. They wave us along with muddy hands and broad smiles.

Keeping to the deepest part of the channel, we slip over beds of eelgrass, the thin, green strands swaying with the hypnotic movement of the incoming tide. Another flick of the paddle and we cross an imaginary boundary. By our reckoning we have just become visitors in the South Slough National Estuarine Research Reserve.

Established in 1974, South Slough Reserve was the first estuarine area designated under a unique national program designed to allow scientists to study intensively the resources of a few coastal estuaries. Using the scientists' findings, the founders of the program hoped to give policymakers an opportunity to better manage the shrinking acres of tidal wetlands along our nation's coasts. South Slough Reserve's history—almost fifteen years of experiments, successes, and frustrations— parallels that of the entire National Estuarine Reserve Research System. Now, after years of struggle, the shape of what may be our best hope for managing coastal wetlands is beginning to emerge.

Like all estuaries, South Slough marks a zone of constant change and exchange: Saltwater mixes with freshwater, tidal forces stir the mixture, and the sun's radiant energy heats the brew to a temperature suitable for a virtual explosion of aquatic and water-dependent organisms. The estuary teems with life-forms. On an impulse, I dunk my

Conifers line a tidal creek at South Slough National Estuarine Research Reserve on the southern Oregon coast.

167

As we push on along the narrowing arm of tidal slough, our canoe proves its value in this tidewater exploration. Its smooth bottom slips easily over mudflats covered by just inches of incoming tidal flow. Its silent passage allows us to approach the wild residents of the slough with relative ease and photograph them from close range. A great blue heron abandons its frozen fishing posture to flap awkwardly past—but not before giving us an earful of avian displeasure. Tiny juvenile Dungeness crabs scuttle across the flats, little mushroom clouds of silty water erupting behind them before they settle into new hiding places. A pair of common mergansers dive for small fish and idly watch our approach. Abruptly, the mergansers take flight as well, sculling low across the surface of the slough, their wing tips painting a pattern of tandem touches on the still water.

We are outrunning the incoming tide, and our canoe begins to scrape bottom on every sandy bar. Finally, we run aground and are forced to drag our light craft up over the flats and wait for the tide to rescue us. The foul smell of rotten eggs rises as our rubber boots break open the smooth surface of the mudflats.

We manage to reach the tree line and discover a grassy point that is perfectly situated for a picnic. A sampling of Oregon's bounty of fresh foods emerges from our knapsacks— smoked salmon, Chardonnay wine, Tillamook cheddar cheese, Bartlett pears—and

Low tide at South Slough exposes mudflats where a researcher plots bird predation on mud-dwellers. Modest grants fund such studies.

hand into the murky water. To my surprise, it is the temperature of a baby's bath— much warmer than either the bone-chilling seawater flowing in on the tide or the cool rainwater gurgling down from the green hillsides.

Divided into two long, watery arms by a forested peninsula, the South Slough Estuarine Research Reserve covers about 5,000 acres of land, 600 of which are underwater during high tide. Today we are heading for an exploration of the more-secluded eastern tidal arm. We float past a commercial oysterman as he sloshes from one wooden stake culture to the next, breaking the oysters loose from the stakes and loading them onto his flat-bottomed boat. We hail him and pull alongside his muddy craft. He talks of the weather and the tides. We look greedily at his boat full of oysters and think of lunch.

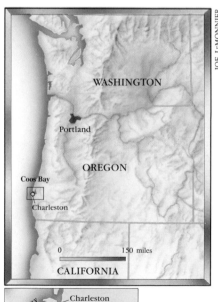

JOE LeMONNIER

lunch is at hand. The sun feels so warm and the sea breeze so refreshing that lunch becomes siesta, and we nearly doze into trouble: The canoe, with paddles stowed neatly inside, has been lifted off the mudflats by the incoming tide and is trying to float up the slough without us.

The Coastal Zone Management Act, passed by Congress in 1972, established what was originally called the National Estuarine Sanctuary Program to provide money for coastal states to acquire, develop, and operate estuarine areas as natural field laboratories. The need was obvious: As coastal property increased in value, estuarine areas along America's coastlines were being modified (and still are) at an alarming rate. Studies showed that more than half the nation's coastal wetlands had already been lost to development in the previous fifty years, and the pace was accelerating. Wetlands once considered worthless were being dredged and filled for development with little thought given to the potential damage to both coastal and marine life-forms.

Just as disturbing to scientists was the scarcity of controlled studies in the estuarine environment. The most basic processes at work in the estuary—including the primary productivity of plants, which thrive there in the womblike waters—were still largely a mystery.

Unlike the programs that established the national park or wildlife refuge systems, the estuarine sanctuary program never aimed to preserve "crown jewels"—all the outstanding, undisturbed estuaries around the nation's coastlines. That was impractical, because human endeavors on every coastline around the world have traditionally focused on the natural bays and estuaries that buffer the land from the sea. Instead, the founders of the program looked for *representative* areas—estuaries similar to other coastal wetlands in their area but still largely undisturbed by man's influence. It was hoped that these representative estuaries could be intensively studied by scientists, whose findings might provide valuable information to guide decision-makers as they pondered

future development in remaining estuarine areas.

A scheme was devised that split up the nation's coastlines into biogeographical regions. Each region was to have one representative estuarine sanctuary. In 1986, during congressional reauthorization of the Coastal Zone Management Act, the estuarine program's name was changed to the National Estuarine Reserve Research System, signaling an even greater emphasis on research efforts throughout the system. Today the national program includes twenty-seven biogeographical regions and seventeen established research reserves. Four additional reserves have been proposed.

At the base of the Estuary Study Trail at South Slough the late-afternoon sun dapples the landscape, highlighting the salt-marsh grasses as they sway softly in the breeze. The incoming tide floods through a breach in an old dredge-spoil dike. As water filters over the mudflats, inch by inch, it reclaims its hold on the intertidal zone—as it does twice a day, every day of the year.

This intertidal marsh and mudflat, where salt- and freshwater mingle in the estuary, is one of the most productive life zones on Earth. Its ability to produce raw tonnage of plant material—its primary productivity—is on a par with that of a tropical rainforest. By most estimates this brackish bay can produce five times as much plant life as an equivalent area of heavily cultivated midwestern cornfield—and without the aid of fertilizers, pesticides, or human labor. While scientists struggle in the laboratory to harness solar energy for man's use, the power of the sun has long been harnessed in the estuary and directed into food chains so interlocked that they are better envisioned as food webs.

To find out more about the food webs in the estuary, a visitor to the South Slough Reserve can hike back up the hill to the new, half-million-dollar interpretive center, which perches near the reserve's main access road. Visitors who come to the center for its dazzling view of the estuary often find themselves engrossed in the eye-catching displays on estuarine ecology. Most stay on to see a film or slide program about estuaries. Some even hike down the hill to get a closer look at the productive tidelands they may be discovering for the first time.

So what's an estuarine research reserve doing in the visitor-center business? It's all part of a larger plan, notes Mike Graybill, South Slough's lanky, energetic manager. Graybill's office is in the visitor-center building and shares the same sweeping view of the reserve, but he rarely gets the time to enjoy it. When he's not off serving on a local planning committee, meeting with officials of another state agency, or attending a local civic group's meeting to drum up support for South Slough, he's usually huddling with members of his staff to hatch new ideas for research projects on the reserve.

"South Slough wasn't preserved," notes Graybill, "so much as this reserve was created to be used. Our highest priority is to preserve its integrity, but in my mind the reserve is a special zoning district, dedicated to estuarine research and education."

The education side of the equation at South Slough—everything from educating policymakers on the value of well-managed estuaries to guiding grade-school children on nature walks in the estuary—dovetails with cooperative research projects. Each year the interpretive center serves as the jumping-off point for several thousand Oregon schoolchildren, whose teachers bring them on field trips to South Slough for a dose of estuarine education from the reserve staff.

The reserve's program for visiting schoolchildren, developed by former education specialist John Garner and a team of experts, has drawn wide acclaim and inquiries for more information from as far away as Australia. The program features a hands-on approach to estuarine education: Younger children help brew a mock "estuarine soup" from the varied plants and animals that inhabit the slough, while older schoolchildren hike the Estuary Study Trail on a "treasure hunt" to gather clues that eventually solve the "mystery" of the estuary.

Although education programs at South Slough have been popular and successful, estuarine research projects have been slow in coming to the reserve. The reasons are complicated. South Slough's remote location on the largely undeveloped southern Oregon coast has played a part. So has the problem of finding enough money for increasingly expensive research efforts.

To attract qualified scientists, the National Estuarine Reserve Research System now offers matching grants to researchers who show interest in estuarine areas. Although the funds are limited—total research-grant funding for the entire national program has stabilized at about $500,000 a year—the effort has begun to attract interest from the scientific community. The nearby Oregon Institute of Marine Biology, where Graybill worked and studied before taking over as manager at South Slough, is also providing an increasing number of scientists with research interests in the estuarine area.

Mike Graybill and other research reserve

managers say they're open to all types of estuarine research projects but are especially interested in work that will provide technical information about estuaries for use by state and local agencies. Graybill cites two current research projects at South Slough. One study will compare the environmental effects of two different types of commercial oyster-growing operations. A second is monitoring the waters of South Slough for the presence of tributyltin, or TBT, a marine-paint additive that is highly toxic to aquatic life. He also has proposed a comprehensive project to create a model of tidal flows throughout the Coos Bay estuary. Once completed, the model could provide information for dredging operations, sewage-treatment plants, and pollution-control monitoring efforts, and baseline data for future development plans in intertidal areas.

Oystermen and young anglers harvest the riches of South Slough's waters.

First of seventeen estuarine reserves in the federal–state network, Oregon's South Slough embraces 5,000 acres; 600 are submerged at high tide.

"Our goal," says Graybill, "is for South Slough to become a regional center of information on estuaries and to use that information to help form effective management policies in the intertidal zone."

Like most areas in the national estuarine program, South Slough Research Reserve is owned and operated by the state, not the federal government. The program calls for participating states to match all federal grants dollar for dollar, so Oregon taxpayers

now have a several-million-dollar investment in South Slough. One potential payoff for those taxpayers is the reserve's growing role as part of the state's land-use-planning system. Technical information from studies at South Slough will become an increasingly valuable tool for local planners faced with permit decisions in other coastal communities.

South Slough also fits nicely into the state's recent emphasis on innovative educational efforts. And while student visits

conserve its own resources. Although never zero-budgeted (bureaucratese for scheduled for elimination) by the Reagan Administration, the estuarine program has been severely restricted.

While small and continually underfunded, the National Estuarine Reserve Research System is a unique environmental program in the federal government:

✓ "This is the only national program that approaches estuarine issues in a systematic way," notes Art Jeffers, a project manager with the National Oceanic and Atmospheric Administration's Marine and Estuarine Management Division. "Other federal programs deal with coastal wetlands issues, but this is the only program that is ecosystem-oriented, interested in habitat for its ecosystem and ecological value. And this is the only program I am aware of that approaches the question of estuarine value and resources in a holistic fashion."

✓ It also brings coastal state governments and the federal bureaucracy together in an unusual power-sharing relationship. Since the states own most of the land and intertidal areas in estuarine reserves—and most reserve staff members are state employees—the federal government has little direct power to enforce regulations or goals for each area. This balance of power forces everyone involved to cooperate equally to keep the program going. Ironically, this interplay of federal and state governments is one reason the National Estuarine Reserve Research System probably will never become a victim of the federal budget ax. The state governments, with their considerable investments in land, equipment, and personnel at the estuarine reserve sites, have a strong, vested interest in continued federal funding for research and education grants. In addition, a national organization of the managers and staff members of the reserves, the National Estuarine Research Reserve Association, now promotes "programs of mutual concern" and coordination among the state reserves.

✓ Though it has taken more than fifteen years to get the program running smoothly, the estuarine reserve system may well be in the right place at the right time. Recent media reports have focused public attention on a range of coastal environmental issues, from nearshore ocean pollution to rising sea levels associated with global warming. Just in the nick of time, estuarine reserves are seen by many as logical research sites for the study of increasingly serious ocean-related problems.

"We're finally seeing a maturity of the reserve system around the country and a recognition of that maturity by the research com-

have become immensely popular as field trips for local school districts, they are just as rewarding for the reserve staff. "These kids are our hope for the future," John Garner once told me. "If we start them off on the right foot, perhaps their generation will do a better job of conserving estuarine resources than we've done."

At the federal level, the National Estuarine Reserve Research System has been struggling for the past few years simply to

munity," notes Joseph Uravitch, who took over as chief of the Marine and Estuarine Management Division in late 1987. Uravitch cites Old Woman Creek National Estuarine Research Reserve on Lake Erie—the only freshwater estuary in the system—where eight years of daily monitoring of water conditions and an impressive array of research projects are providing solid answers to management questions in the Great Lakes region. He also points to an ongoing study of diminished eelgrass beds at three East Coast research reserves—a cooperative study that may provide important information about pollution levels along the Atlantic seaboard.

To achieve the anticipated impact by the estuarine reserves on coastal-zone-management decisions, Uravitch plans a stronger focus. He wants to direct the system's research funds toward projects that could provide specific technical information on coastline-management issues.

"The public is getting good value for the money invested in estuarine research reserves," says Uravitch. "And since most of our reserve people are state-agency employees, in some ways they are a better vehicle to transfer that research information on to state and local governments—where most of the land-use decisions are going to be made—than we in the federal government would be."

Walking through a misty summer evening in the upland marsh at South Slough, I spot the resident herd of elk. They stand on the far side of the meadow, perhaps a dozen of them. Even though I freeze in my tracks, the big bull lifts his head from his evening browse and scents me. We stand staring at each other for a few moments until he reluctantly begins to nudge his charges toward an opening in the forest.

After the elk are gone, I stand in the meadow for a long time, the mist soaking me to the skin. If everyone could walk this trail, I think, the value of an estuary might simply seep in on them, like the incoming tide.

But the National Estuarine Reserve Research System's fifteen-year struggle for recognition provides ample proof that it's not that easy; not easy at all to focus attention on the drab mudflats and the hidden secrets of an area such as South Slough. Comparing the estuarine research reserves' efforts with popular campaigns to save the whales or the redwoods, project manager Art Jeffers concludes, "It's a good deal harder to sell an ecosystem than it is to sell an [individual] animal or a species, because people tend to relate to individuals rather than habitats. But it's the next major step in environmental awareness. An animal or a given species does not survive, let alone thrive, in the absence of its ecosystem and its habitat.

"So until we better understand the estuarine habitat—from a scientific point of view—and the public and the people who are making decisions about these resources understand it from an awareness point of view, it's going to be next to impossible to protect it. Or to use it in the best way possible for its value."

THE NATIONAL ESTUARINE RESERVE RESEARCH SYSTEM

- Wells National Estuarine Research Reserve, Maine
- Waquoit Bay, Massachusetts
- Narragansett Bay, Rhode Island
- Hudson River, New York (4 sites: Iona, Piermont, Stockport, Tivoli Bay)
- Chesapeake Bay, Maryland
- North Carolina NERR (4 sites: Currituck, Rachel Carson, Zeke's Island, Masonboro)
- Sapelo Island, Georgia
- Rookery Bay, Florida
- Apalachicola, Florida
- Jobos Bay, Puerto Rico
- Weeks Bay, Alabama
- Tijuana River, California
- Elkhorn Slough, California
- South Slough, Oregon
- Padilla Bay, Washington
- Old Woman Creek, Ohio
- Waimanu Valley, Hawaii

Proposed
- Great Bay, New Hampshire
- Delaware NERR
- Chesapeake Bay, Virginia
- South Carolina NERR

PORTRAIT OF A VANISHED SNAKE

TEXT BY DAVID QUAMMEN · PHOTOGRAPHY BY JIM BONES

It's a long river with a long history and a vast, confused inventory of contemporary problems, a river that winds out across centuries and cultures, draining one ecosystem through another into a third. Choked by dams and lakes, dividing neighbors in hatred, and forming a national boundary, the river is drawn in a wavering thin line from the depths of America's past into the present, and from the aspens of highland Colorado to the sabal palms of coastal Texas.

Despite such length and breadth, on an afternoon in December, at a place called The Tight Squeeze in a canyon called Mariscal, the Rio Grande has suddenly come into sharp focus. You are standing on a large flat-topped rock in midstream. Above you are canyon walls a thousand feet high. Below you, wrapped across the upstream face of the flat-topped rock, sunken and bent, is a canoe.

You know this canoe. You helped load it. Lashed firmly under the thwarts is half enough gear to support three men on a five-day trip through Big Bend National Park. The trip has only just begun; possibly it has also just ended.

Standing beside you on the rock, mildly disconsolate, are two river guides named Richard and Drew. Together the three of you stare down at a sleeping bag, several tents, a Coleman stove, and a coiled climbing rope, as those items jostle gently beneath the surface of surging, powerful, green water. It's like watching your shirts through the open lid of a Maytag. Picture yourself in the laundry room, late for work, and wondering recklessly whether you might be able to snatch one out, wring it, wear it. The canoe itself is another question. The canoe looks doomed. A large, rigid object alarmingly deformed by rushing water. Along with your shirts, the Maytag seems to have eaten a suitcase.

"How's your body temperature, little bro?" says Richard. Drew's body temperature is all right; he barely got wet, climbing nimbly out onto this midstream rock just before the canoe might have folded flat like a Coors can, pinning his legs gruesomely. Drew is frustrated, embarrassed, and bleeding from one shin, but hypothermia is not an immediate problem. Hypothermia will only become a problem when night arrives—sucking heat out of this cold stone canyon—and his sleeping bag is still underwater. Fortunately Richard has already run the Squeeze safely, in his own one-man canoe, carrying food and matches and some extra clothing. You and your kayak have also passed through, but that little boat holds barely more than one human and a canteen and a notebook. Lot of help you are. Then again,

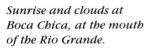

Sunrise and clouds at Boca Chica, at the mouth of the Rio Grande.

you're a journalist and not, anymore, a river guide.

"Okay," says Richard. "Okay." He makes gingerly up-and-down motions with his hand, as though patting the head of a Doberman. "Let's give this a little thought." Richard is senior guide and has automatically assumed captaincy of the crisis-management team. He is a fortyish man with the body of a jockey, the wardrobe of a vagrant, the wrinkled brown smile of a Yaqui medicine man, and the steady good sense of someone you'd like to have on the National Security Council. At this difficult moment Richard is calm and methodical. In fact you are all three calm and methodical, united in silent conviction that, no matter what happens next, the canoe is a hopeless wreck and the trip has gone flying off its rails. "Smoke a cigarette," Richard says to himself, and he does.

Late afternoon in Mariscal Canyon, beneath those high walls of Cretaceous limestone, three men stand on a rock. Around them the Rio Grande purrs like a cougar. Here, despite everything, it's still a proud and untamed river.

"Okay," says Richard again. "First thing, we need that other rope."

The wilderness canyons of Big Bend lie along the southwestern nub of Texas, a thousand miles downstream. But the river begins back in Colorado, and so does its human history.

Around the year 1200 A.D., something went wrong at the cliff dwellings of Mesa Verde. Some of the experts guess it was drought. Some guess resource depletion, harassment by other tribes, or maybe social strife that arose within the community and made those elaborate cliff cities unsustainable. No one knows for sure. There is an eloquently cryptic absence of clues. Whatever the cause, Mesa Verde and the other sites were abandoned. The Anasazi civilization disappeared, and their descendants seem to have followed the winter sun down into northern New Mexico, founding a Pueblo culture along the Upper Rio Grande. By the time the first Spanish explorers arrived there around 1540, the Pueblos were a settled people, living close to the riverside in an arid land, with centuries of experience at irrigated farming. Using a simple system of diversions and canals, they were growing corn, cotton, beans, melons, and a few other crops: not on some broad, fertile plain that might have seemed hospitable to agriculture, but on small, irregular patches of field plowed into the foothills and bottomland along that river. Their ditches were modest, economical, and therefore clever. One Spaniard, Castaño

Adobe church and pueblo walls, Pecos National Monument.

de Sosa, got a glimpse of Pueblo irrigation works as early as 1591 and called them "incredible to anyone who had not seen them with his own eyes."

Why had these people moved from the cliffs to the river? Besides the possible explanations mentioned above, there is one other. This one is spiritual and mythic; it is also sacredly private, so that Pueblos today seem reluctant to speak of it and an outsider can only catch hints. If the gods had abandoned a place, wouldn't a god-fearing people be forced to move also? If an important deity deserted the cliffs, if the spiritual climate had gone cold, could humans continue living there? According to one source—Paul Horgan, in his magisterial book, *Great River*—this missing deity was *A-wan-yu*, also known as the plumed serpent. Why the upland sites might have fallen out of favor with *A-wan-yu* is another mystery. But when the snake left, the people followed. They found their spiritual reunification along the river.

In a restaurant in Santa Fe, just before heading downriver toward your rendezvous with that midstream rock, you have asked a Pueblo man about the plumed-serpent myth and the Rio Grande. This man holds a doctorate in history; he works in the field of cultural research and preservation; he serves on an advisory board of the Smithsonian Institution. Furthermore you have heard that his aged mother is renowned as a keeper of oral tradition. Already he has told you something about the Pueblo relationship with nature. He has expressed a sense of custodianship over this fragile environment, a sense of the river's identity that contrasts starkly with the prevalent view, which sees Rio Grande water (all western water) as a valuable commodity no more sacral than boxcars of soybean. So you ask: How does the serpent myth fit into that?

A mistake. The Pueblo man shakes his head. He smiles uncomfortably, embarrassed

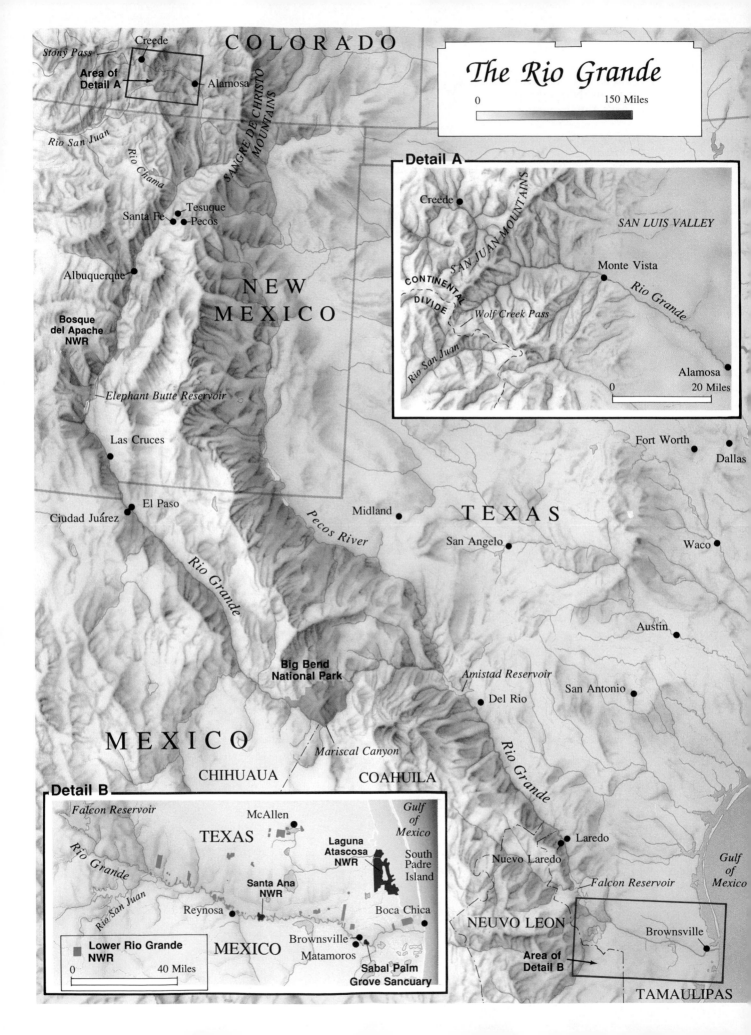

The Rio Grande

0   150 Miles

COLORADO

Stony Pass
Creede
Area of Detail A
Alamosa

Rio San Juan

Rio Chama

SANGRE DE CHRISTO MOUNTAINS

Santa Fe
Tesuque
Pecos

Albuquerque

NEW MEXICO

Bosque del Apache NWR

Elephant Butte Reservoir

Las Cruces

El Paso

Ciudad Juárez

Rio Grande

Pecos River

Midland

San Angelo

TEXAS

Fort Worth
Dallas

Waco

Austin

Amistad Reservoir

Del Rio

San Antonio

MEXICO

Big Bend National Park

Mariscal Canyon

CHIHUAUA

COAHUILA

Rio Grande

Laredo

Nuevo Laredo

Falcon Reservoir

NEUVO LEON

Area of Detail B

Brownsville

Gulf of Mexico

TAMAULIPAS

Detail A

Creede

SAN LUIS VALLEY

SAN JUAN MOUNTAINS

CONTINENTAL DIVIDE

Wolf Creek Pass

Monte Vista

Rio Grande

Rio San Juan

Alamosa

0   20 Miles

Detail B

Falcon Reservoir

Rio Grande

Rio San Juan

TEXAS

McAllen

Laguna Atascosa NWR

Santa Ana NWR

Gulf of Mexico

South Padre Island

Reynosa

Boca Chica

Brownsville
Matamoros

MEXICO

Sabal Palm Grove Sanctuary

■ Lower Rio Grande NWR

0   40 Miles

that his refusal to answer will be absolute. No, he says without words. No, we will not talk of the snake. That's a mystery too holy for lunchtime chat.

But he does say: "This Rio Grande system flows through a very specific universe. It's defined by shrines on the mountains along the drainage. That's a cosmological reality that's been upset by some of these interests." The interests to which he refers—thirsty cities like Albuquerque, private developers, agribusiness corporations, earth-moving and paper-waving entities like the Bureau of Reclamation—are pressing the Pueblos to exchange their water, and their water-bound traditions, for a commodity value in mere dollars. Around the Santa Fe area these days, an acre-foot worth of water rights can be sold for as much as $10,000, or leased away even more lucratively. The captains of progress imagine that such incentive should be irresistible to folk who still live in five-century-old adobe pueblos, deprived of air conditioners, deprived of money-market checking, raising their small patches of melon and corn. But the Pueblo historian in the business suit adds patiently: "It's very important what happens in the physical world, so that it doesn't upset the metaphysical world."

Drew is a victim of both crosscurrent and circumstance. The mangled and sunken canoe is not really his fault. Arguably it is yours. Drew's whitewater expertise has been earned as a raft oarsman, a very distinct skill, but you with your ambitious travel schedule and your kayak metabolism mandated fast, sleek boats. You wanted to see a long stretch of the river at Big Bend in a short stretch of time. The river itself took maybe 10 million years to carve Mariscal Canyon, however, and it was the river's prerogative to foil your goofy haste.

There were intimations. Just before Drew's mishap, for instance, you had the omen of the tarantula. It seemed like a good omen at the time.

"Pull off at this gravel bar on the right," Richard had said, "and we'll scout."

So you walked down to look at The Tight Squeeze. You saw the great, flat-topped slab of limestone, long since fallen from a cavernous gap in the canyon wall overhead and now clogging the channel, like a rabbit in the mouth of a snake, forcing almost the whole Rio Grande to gush through an eight-foot-wide notch along the Mexico side of the river. You saw the smaller rock, just upstream from that notch, obstructing the line of entrance. You saw the flow of water against the face of the midstream slab, and the subtle

Tight Squeeze, Mariscal Canyon, Big Bend National Park.

but threatening way that water slid off to the left, away from the runnable notch, toward a tiny slit on the other side choked with cottonwood limbs and menace. Together you and Drew stood and watched Richard do the run, angling his canoe around the obstruction, through the notch, then back sharp to the left and out of sight, making it look easy.

And then, turning toward your own boat, you saw the tarantula just an instant before setting your foot on its dark hairy bulk.

But you caught yourself in time. "Drew. Look here." While Richard waited downstream, somewhere, in an eddy behind the big rock, two men lingered to gawk at a spider. There is nothing more visually vivid than a tarantula in the wild—that prowling excess of legs and eyes, of fur and fangs, that ugliness so wildly eccentric it seems gorgeous. This tarantula barely acknowledged you. It paused, maybe self-conscious at your attention, maybe woozy from the stench of your breath as you knelt to admire it, then it set off again over the gravel. Possibly a male, getting an early start on its crepuscular ramble in search of mates.

You were glad to have found this animal with your eye and not your foot. "I'll take him for a good omen," you told Drew. A tarantula smashed dead under a neoprene bootie, eight legs writhing angrily from a smear of eight-eyed pulp, would have unsteadied you some.

So you threaded your way easily through The Tight Squeeze and set up in the blind eddy beside Richard, waiting for Drew.

Relative to the Pueblos, the Hispanic farmers are newcomers along the Upper Rio Grande. They have only been there four hundred years.

Relative to anyone else, they are an indigenous culture graced and guided by their own long-standing intimacy with the river. Santa Fe itself was founded in 1609 (a decade be-

179

fore the Pilgrims reached Plymouth), and very soon afterward two irrigation canals were carved out in gentle traverse above what would become cropfields for the settlement. Each of those canals led to smaller channels, branching down finally into crop rows, and each was known as an *acequia madre,* a mother ditch, suggesting among other things a certain filial affection felt by the farmers who watered and fed beneath them. Likewise when Albuquerque was founded, in 1706, an official report to the King of Spain announced proudly that the church had been built, the houses were in progress, and the *acequias* were *"sacadas y corrientes"*—they were dug and running. This was the pattern. It reflected not just a sense of priority but a necessity of survival. It had come to the Hispanic Rio Grande from arid Spain herself, earlier influenced by Moorish irrigation practices adapted from North Africa. In this pinched, arid valley between steep mountains it developed by gentle syncretism with the Pueblo techniques and traditions. No bit of folk knowledge, no bit of water, could afford to be wasted. And with passing centuries the same pattern—small plots of corn and beans and a few other crops, scratched into irregular fields below the *acequia madre* of each village—became more again than a necessity of survival. It became part of the weave of a culture.

For a long time these two irrigating societies, Pueblo and rural Hispanic, were compatible, even neighborly. There had been some ferocious strife (during the Spanish conquest, the Pueblo rebellion of 1680, and then the reconquest), but that was far in the past and not directly related to water. As little volume of water as the Rio Grande carries, back in those years it was enough for everyone. Then during just the last century came a new wave of immigration to the valley—call this one the Anglo conquest. Those late-

Irrigation canal, San Luis Valley, Colorado.

arriving but sometimes affluent Anglo settlers began buying land and water rights. Cities burgeoned along the river, especially Albuquerque and El Paso. The Bureau of Reclamation, the U.S. Army Corps of Engineers, and the New Mexico State Engineer got very interested in this modest trickle known by the misnomer Rio Grande. Dams were built in the upper valley, piling riverwater into reservoirs with deceptively picturesque names: Abiquiu, Cochiti, Elephant Butte, Caballo. Water was now precious. Therefore it was also expensive, and from this pair of truths followed one other: If a person or a community happened to have more water than money, they ought to be willing (even eager) to sell. Correct?

Well, maybe not. Anyway, that came to be the commanding syllogism in modern, and ever-more-urban, New Mexico.

In this context, today, the two oldest irrigation-based cultures in America seem to be matched against manifest destiny. Sadly, they are also matched against each other. Their most conspicuous point of conflict is a water-rights adjudication suit, an infamous tangle of legal procedures known familiarly as *Aamodt.* (To the lawyers: *New Mexico* ex. rel. *Reynolds* v. *Aamodt.*) More than twenty years in the arguing and still unsettled, *Aamodt* is not just a complicated case. It is also a crucial one, since it will eventually define the water rights of four pueblos on the Upper Rio Grande (Nambe, Tesuque, Pojoaque, and San Ildefonso) and, in the process, set a precedent that will be applicable to all other pueblos.

On the opposite scale of the balance, in *Aamodt,* are the rights of a thousand non-Indian water users. Many of those thousand are poor, rural, and Hispanic, dependent on the *acequia madre* for water and cultural identity.

Out here in the Southwest, people like quoting a certain cynical adage: "Water flows uphill to money." If that's true, neither side can win a final victory by way of *Aamodt.* The court will only determine which of two ancient cultures must give away its soul, and which may be allowed to sell it. Richard nosed his canoe to the eddy line, peeking upstream around the blind wall of limestone. Then he nosed back into the eddy—carefully, because reverse currents and swells made this a precarious spot in which to be idling. "Okay so far," Richard said. Drew was on his way.

Sculling against the eddy's push, holding position, you stared expectantly at the notch. You continued to stare for what seemed like an oddly long time.

Then a clunk. Low, muted, it was a bass note of boat against rock, just loud enough to be heard echoing off the canyon walls.

"Contact," said Richard.

You gaped at the notch, still waiting for Drew and his boat to come thumping through. They did not. Then a flash of red lifejacket caught your eye, far to the right, through the impassable little slit on the U.S. side of the river.

"Uh-oh," you said. "Jesus. He's over on the right."

The red jacket vanished. The stern of a canoe appeared. It entered the intake end of the slit, like a Pontiac about to be backed through a narrow stone doorway.

"This river," says Clair Reiniger, "it's like the victim of a war."

If there is a war being waged over Rio Grande water, Reiniger stands in the midst of it, occupying roughly the uneasy position of the International Red Cross. She herself nei-

ther owns nor covets any water rights. She is not Hispanic or Pueblo; neither bureaucrat nor engineer. Nor would she describe herself as an environmentalist. She is an Anglo woman, trained at Harvard as a landscape architect. For most of the past decade she has run an organization called Designwrights Collaborative, based in a small suite of offices near the plaza in Santa Fe. Her self-defined role has been to assist the rural poor of two cultures, Hispanic and Pueblo, toward a realization that perhaps water need not, always, flow uphill to money.

"We're like catalytic agents," she says of the Designwrights group. "We like to go in where there's an opportunity. Where you just need a little shot of energy, technical assistance, to make something happen. That's where we like to work. And we're trying to do that throughout the river. In the rural communities."

Since 1980 Reiniger and her associates have held hundreds of meetings, dozens of

Dusk falls on El Paso, Texas, and Juárez, Mexico: The largest urban center near the Rio Grande.

181

Left: Rio Grande head-water lake at Stony Pass, Colorado. Below: Autumn tundra at Stony Pass, San Juan Mountains. Next page: Rio Grande below Burro Bluff, Lower Canyon.

workshops, and a handful of large conferences, offering information and political skills, coaxing the forgotten folk of the river (including some Anglos) to discover the latent power and the breadth of options that derive from their ancestral ownership of water; building toward a coalition of water-rich, culture-rich, "impoverished" (in only the most reductively fiscal sense) rural people. "If they could begin to work together a little bit," Reiniger tells you, "they'd have an amazing amount of power."

But the *Aamodt* case has created rancor and distrust. "It's pitted neighbors against each other in a terrible way," she says. "The Hispanics have their *acequias,* and the Pueblos have their own water system. But they've been sharing the water, and dealing with it. Then the lawyers got in..." Reiniger's voice trails discreetly away from the subject of lawyers. Finally she adds: "The trust factor takes a major amount of time." Besides time, this sort of coalition-building must demand an unimaginable degree of patience. Clair Reiniger has spent both the time and the patience, talking endlessly over the past ten years with farmers, *acequia* officials, and Pueblo elders, nurturing their trust not only for each other but for herself, an Anglo woman in a world dominated by Pueblo and Hispanic men.

"Rural people are not getting control over their resources and their future," she says rather fiercely. "At all. They're not going to *have* any future, at the rate they're going. That's really where it's at. The only way they're going to is if they wake up and find out what the issues are, get informed, and start working together. And then they can start to redirect funds, and people, and resources in these state agencies, and have some effect policy-wise."

She takes a breath and admits: "It's a dream." But that's not meant to say the dream can't be achieved. "And it's grounded in a sort of bio-regional thinking. I guess I think the West should have been like Powell proposed." A century ago John Wesley Powell looked at the Rio Grande, among other rivers, and suggested that the American West should be settled and governed according to "natural districts," taking full account of watershed and ecology, rather than along rectilinear abstractions of sovereignty. "I think it should have been organized according to water drainages, instead of state boundaries," says Clair Reiniger. "It makes more sense. Especially since water drives everything."

Very suddenly, things had gotten exciting. Drew was marooned on the midstream

Clair Reiniger of Designwrights Collaborative.

rock. His canoe was down and damaged, like a broke-leg horse that someone should put out of its misery. Richard had tossed Drew a bagged rescue rope—not because there was anything much Drew could do with it, but because tossing a rope is simply what happens first in these situations, during the brief giddy period between alarm and lucidity. Your own kayak had been beached. You took the stern seat in Richard's canoe, sculling to hold it steady amid those swells and eddy currents while Richard stood precariously in midships, on top of the pile of gear, and stretched for a handhold on the back face of that flat-topped rock. It was a sheer face, seven feet high; Drew pulled him up. Then together they pulled you up, and the healthy canoe was left tethered below in the eddy, drifting round and round.

And now after a few moments of dour silence, and a cigarette, Richard has said: "First thing, we need that other rope."

Since Drew is tallest, you both hold his legs. Dangling head-down, he wrestles the climbing rope out of the sunken canoe, which is now wedged at a weird angle halfway into the slit, its stern jammed against stone. Still dangling, Drew ties one end of that rope to the boat's thwart. He loops the other rope over the stern, lets it flush back to him in the current, and ties off that loop. Two ropes, two points of attachment. A canoe full of water weighs roughly as much as a Toyota. Certainly three men can move a Toyota? Of course this one at present has no wheels.

The three of you pull. You strain, you bounce. You try various rhythms and every conceivable angle. You huff and, yes, you puff. The stern of the boat eases free of its catch-point and you all grunt in triumph, and the boat swings around straight in the slit: Here we go, all right, thank God. And then it sinks. Flattens itself to the bottom like a limpet.

"Whoa," says Richard.

You stop pulling. You stare.

"That canoe is history," you say.

"C'mon over here," Richard says. "Let's take a break." Sometimes in these situations, Richard explains, the flow of water and adrenaline can be hypnotic. It can distort judgment and sap morale. Sometimes the best thing is to step away, relax, smoke another cigarette, then approach the problem again with fresh eyes.

You all step away. But you're on a slab in midstream, halfway between Texas and Mexico. There isn't far to go.

At the other end of the Rio Grande, meanwhile, the war of the river is different but no less desperate. Along the last two hundred miles of channel, between Falcon Dam and the Gulf of Mexico, something quite precious is being lost. Down here the concern is not over the disappearance of traditional cultures but the disappearance of habitat. Now, admittedly, "habitat" is a bland term, "loss of habitat" is a sadly common refrain, and "clearing of Tamaulipan thorn scrub," though more precise, is still not emotionally galvanic; but behind those words lies the reality that startling ecological treasures, unmatched anywhere in the United States, are being squandered along that stretch of river.

And unlike the *Aamodt* case, it's happening fast.

In the primordial state, before Spanish explorers ever sailed into the mouth of what they initially named Rio de las Palmas, this lower stretch of the Rio Grande Valley was a singular ecological crossroads, a place where accidents of geology and climate and the river's flow had converged in just such a way as to promote extraordinary biological diversity. Here, along a seam defined by the river, the Chihuahuan desert merged with the Tamaulipan scrub vegetation of the Mexican

A marina at Elephant Butte Dam near Truth or Consequences, New Mexico: The first dam on the river.

coastal plain, which merged in turn, farther downstream, with great palm jungles flourishing within salt-vapor distance of the Gulf. The upland chaparral of dry southern Texas graded into the thirstier riparian forest near the river itself, and along one short segment of that riparian zone appeared a forest dominated by *Helietta parvifolia*, commonly called baretta, the only native citrus tree found north of the Rio Grande. Two major migratory flyways also came together here, the Mississippi and the Central, leading millions of birds each spring and autumn to this hospitable stopover pinched between the bulge of the Gulf Coast and the desert mountains just westward. Because of all such ecological overlap, the Lower Rio Grande Valley (which, flat and open, is more accurately a delta than a valley) supported a spectacular abundance of plant and animal species.

Ecologists today recognize remnants of seven distinct communities of flora and fauna, bunched along that two hundred miles of river like multicolored beads on a necklace. And for each of those seven, the ecologists have a label: *Chihuahuan thorn forest, upper valley flood forest, barettal community, upland thorn scrub, mid-valley riparian woodland, sabal palm forest, loma/tidal flats.* The Chihuahuan thorn forest is rich with black-brush acacia, sotol, Texas ebony, catclaw mimosa, and various other plants; it also supports the brown jay, three species of kingfisher, and the ferruginous pygmy owl. The barettal community includes, besides its unique species of citrus, the elf owl, the reticulate collared lizard, and the burrowing toad. The mid-valley riparian woodland, for just one other example, is a bottomland hardwood forest of cedar elm and ash and hackberry mixed with anaqua and retama, and it harbors the ocelot, the green jay, an abundance of chachalacas flapping noisy as turkeys through the understory, and that gorgeous lavender-bellied creature *Drymarchon corais erebennus,* the Texas indigo snake. Elsewhere in the lower valley are coati, reddish egret, Texas tortoise, northern cat-eyed snake, and a small population of jaguarundi. Of course any such group of labels, any such listing of species, can only hint at the full ecological mosaic. In reality this is a place that, like the Amazon, defies summary.

But the essence of the message is simple: variety, diversity, vast biological richness. That's how things stood, anyway, in the primordial state.

Then the primordial state was replaced, on the north side of the river, by the state of Texas. Tamaulipan thorn scrub was cleared, making way for huge fields of cane and cotton and vegetables. Industry came to the lower valley. Population boomed, and where once you found mid-valley riparian woodland, now you found the suburbs of McAllen; where once you found jungles of sabal palm, now you found Brownsville. Over 90 percent of the original habitat was destroyed. And on the Mexico side, the situation was equally dire.

So, at the urging of state wildlife officials and local conservationists, a decade ago the U.S. Fish and Wildlife Service launched a farsighted project called the Lower Rio Grande Valley National Wildlife Refuge. It represents much more than a purchase of land. It is an ambitious connect-the-dots scheme conceived to rescue the river ecosystem from fatal fragmentation. Its goal is to give federal protection to at least 107,500 acres, assembled from many small individual parcels, and to ally that acreage with other state-owned and private parcels into, eventually, an integrated ecological whole. It is seemingly hopeless, scientifically fascinating, and just maybe as profoundly premonitory as any conservation project in America. The battle to accomplish the refuge—and, by that means and others, to save a continuous corridor of ecosystem along the Lower Rio Grande—is crucial not just for the sake of the ocelot, or the Texas indigo snake, but because it's the same battle that will soon be fought everywhere.

By a miracle, with your next fit of tugging, the sunken canoe slides free.

Lo, it rises up off the rock, not quite like Lazarus but an inch or two anyway, and comes floating down through that impassable slit, still full of water and watery gear and riding low to the gunwales. Guiding with both ropes, the three of you ease it around into the eddy and there it holds, docile as an old Holstein. The river taketh, and the river giveth back.

"Amazing," you say.

Carefully, Richard climbs down the back face of the rock, groping with his toes for the top of the gear pile in the healthy canoe. Then he steadies the boat while you climb down too. Drew passes down one of the ropes, then feeds out slack on the other while Richard and you pull the Holstein toward shore. And now finally, after an hour and a half on that midstream rock, Drew drops into the water and swims for it.

There is a small sandy beach. Dusk is near. The last rays of daylight show themselves through a large hole in the stern of Drew's

AUDUBON ON THE RIO GRANDE: A WILDLIFE CORRIDOR TAKES SHAPE

Someone has said that the local chapters are the very soul of the National Audubon Society, and year after year these hotbeds of environmental activists demonstrate the effectiveness of grassroots power. As a case in point we submit the record of the Frontera Audubon Society, which keeps an eye on wildlife matters in a string of small communities in the Rio Grande Valley.

"Frontera led the way in changing the Lower Rio Grande Valley Wildlife Corridor from a concept to a reality," says Dede Armentrout, National Audubon's regional vice-president in the Southwest. "Before the chapter got involved, appropriations for the corridor amounted to about $100,000 to $300,000 a year. Now they're up to around $10 million. There were only a few thousand acres in the corridor about five years ago, but now there are over 40,000 acres, and more is being added all the time."

It began when Frontera appealed to the Audubon Council of Texas to set the wildlife corridor as its number-one state priority. That decision helped all of the state's conservation organizations to focus on the corridor. Then, rolling up its sleeves, the chapter spun off several projects, one of them the Valley Land Fund, a private charitable entity established to buy or receive plots of land too small or remote for the state or federal authorities to bother about but with high wildlife values.

Frontera also formed a coalition of leaders in business, agriculture, and tourism to work for the corridor, created a nature center in Weslaco, a river valley community, and won valuable support from the Texas congressional delegation. Now, among the corridor's biggest boosters are Representative Kika de la Garza, the powerful chairman of the House Agriculture Committee, and Senators Phil Gramm and Lloyd Bentsen. The latter is a fierce customer when it comes to federal spending, but has relatives in the valley.

Never underestimate the power of an Audubon chapter.

—*Frank Graham Jr.*

---

canoe. In the morning Richard will succeed in patching that hole with twenty feet of duct tape and a Ziploc bag, and against heavy odds the canyon trip will continue, placidly, to its full destination, but you don't know this at the moment. You wouldn't believe it at the moment. At the moment no one is going anywhere. While Richard unloads the soaked tents and the water-filled Coleman, while Drew tries to wring out his sleeping bag, you scrounge together a fire.

All that night the wind blows upstream, filling your face with sand.

"I've never worked in an area that's more unique than this, in terms of wildlife and habitat," says biologist Nita Fuller, a soft-spoken and precise woman not given to overstatement. "It's untouchable. As far as diversity."

Fuller, associate manager of national wildlife refuges for Arizona and New Mexico, until recently was project leader of the Lower Rio Grande Valley refuge and also manager of a smaller and older refuge known as the Santa Ana. The Santa Ana site comprises about three square miles of mid-valley riparian woodland in almost pristine condition, along the riverbank just east of McAllen.

Nita Fuller at Santa Ana National Wildlife Refuge.

*Above left: Upper Rio
Grande and volcanic tuff,
Colorado. Above: Rio
Chama badlands, New
Mexico. Next page: North
Clear Creek Falls, San
Juan Mountains. Left: Flood-
rippled sand, Rio Pecos,
New Mexico.*

"We classified more than 450 species of plants in Santa Ana alone. And it's only 2,000 acres," Fuller continues. "That's just irreplaceable. You can't replicate that in many areas of the country."

If such biological abundance were lost, Fuller knows, you probably couldn't replicate it in South Texas either. That's why the Lower Rio Grande Valley National Wildlife Refuge is important.

Established back in 1979, the refuge project had its real beginning in 1983, when its purpose and its means were formalized and approved in an official planning document of the Fish and Wildlife Service. The purpose of the project was to protect that extraordinary abundance of wildlife found in the various ecological communities of the lower river—in particular, to protect a list of 115 vertebrate species, each one either endangered or threatened or found here at only the northern periphery of its range. The means of the project were to be: 1) land acquisition by outright purchase, 2) preservation of habitat by easement agreements with other owners, and 3) revegetation efforts to restore habitat on land already cleared. The money for all this was to come from the Land and Water Conservation Fund, a federal repository of revenues from certain oil and gas taxes, which exists for exactly such projects. But the special significance of the Lower Rio Grande Valley National Wildlife Refuge is that it constitutes government recognition of a subtle but menacing scientific problem: maintaining species perpetuity in small, fragmented reserves. When any species is trapped within an island-like fragment of habitat, its population there will necessarily be small and its gene pool will therefore be impoverished. If either the population or the gene pool is *too* small, the species becomes vulnerable to extinction.

Over the past twenty years, theoretical ecologists working in a seemingly peripheral field known as "island biogeography" have turned up some worrisome implications about the prospect of species perpetuity—or lack of it—in all of our smaller and more insularized parks and refuges on the mainlands. Island species face a higher risk of extinction than mainland species, other things being equal; and species confined to island-like fragments of habitat face a higher risk also.

Some animals, even some plants, might disappear from the Lower Rio Grande for no other reason than that their islands of habitat were too tiny. "As a biologist," Nita Fuller says, "one of my great concerns is that we're at the break-point in terms of populations and species here in the valley. That if something is not done, in the short term, we're going to lose populations and species. And we already are."

She cites an example. Early narratives describe hundreds of rose-throated becards nesting in the area that is now Santa Ana. "There may be a number of reasons for their loss," Fuller acknowledges, "but they don't nest here anymore in the valley." Another example is the altamira oriole. Once there were hundreds of nests; now only about a dozen altamira orioles nest at Santa Ana each year. An even more vivid case is the ocelot, possibly the Santa Ana refuge's most famous and (by the tourists who come here to see wildlife) most valued species. A solitary predator, the ocelot requires large individual territories. If Santa Ana is a 2,000-acre island—with the river along one side and otherwise completely surrounded by highways and suburbs and fields of sugarcane—can it harbor in perpetuity a viable population of ocelots? Or will the ocelot be the next species to vanish?

You take a walk through the Santa Ana refuge with Nita Fuller. While the two of you stroll along trails overarched by cedar elm and hackberry, mesquite and Texas ebony, she talks about this desperately significant idea that she calls "the corridor concept." The corridor concept is a plan by which the U.S. Fish and Wildlife Service, the Texas Department of Parks and Wildlife, and a loose coalition of private conservation groups (including the admirably militant Frontera chapter of National Audubon Society) hope to answer the gloomy predictions of island biogeographical theory. It involves the projected enlargement of the Lower Rio Grande Valley National Wildlife Refuge to that eventual total (considered a bare minimum, not a magic sufficiency) of 107,500 acres, including stretches of all seven of the riparian communities between Falcon Dam and the Gulf, plus bits of three other habitat types slightly more distant from the river. It also involves some strategically placed state holdings (especially Bentsen State Park), some patches of private land left in uncleared scrub, the Santa Ana refuge itself, National Audubon's tiny but spectacular Sabal Palm Grove Sanctuary, and still another FWS refuge nearby, the Laguna Atascosa. If all these fragments of habitat, with their various ecological communities and their various ownerships, can just be linked together into a continuous corridor along the Lower Rio Grande, Fuller explains, the doom that otherwise awaits certain insularized species can perhaps be evaded.

She pauses to point out two kinds of epiphyte, ball moss and Spanish moss, festooned in the branches of the cedar elms. The altamira orioles use the Spanish moss, she says, for their hanging nests.

The corridor concept is the great dream behind much of Fuller's work. If the corridor can be achieved, the ocelot might survive in a viable population, traveling and interbreeding throughout a long ribbon of unbroken riparian habitat. If the corridor can be achieved, the reddish egret and the brown pelican and the reticulate collared lizard might survive also. Fuller calls your attention to the voice of a kiskadee somewhere overhead. The kiskadee might maintain its foothold here. Even the jaguarundi might begin to reappear in numbers. As she walks, Nita Fuller is conscious of the daunting challenge faced by her and her allies—rescuing a single precious noodle of wild land from the appetite of human development—and conscious also of the particularized realities of the woodland around her. This is Texas persimmon, she says. See how the green bark peels itself back in sheets, revealing that smooth purple skin. There's a small black fruit and the coyotes love it, she says.

Nita Fuller is an optimist. Despite the odds, despite the irregular flow of funding, despite the many riverside gaps where land has already been cleared, despite the woebegone economic condition of this part of Texas, and despite human nature itself, she seems genuinely to believe that a tenuous, thin, sufficient strip of wildness can be saved here, in perpetuity, along the river.

You stop walking. You gape toward a small rustle of motion that has caught your eye, twenty feet off the trail. You scan. Finally your eyes fix on a living shape, frozen in wariness, dark scales against the dark ground.

"Nita. Look here," you say. "An indigo snake."

"Ah yes. Very good."

And then, *sswwtt,* it disappears.

The Rio Grande stretches 1,885 miles, from the aspen-covered hillsides west of Creede, Colorado, to the remnant patches of sabal palm east of Brownsville, Texas. It is a long river with a long history and a great, sorry inventory of problems. A person could travel its full length armed with only a notebook and a map and a stomach for good chili and bad coffee, could stop every twenty miles,

Catclaw acacia and impenetrable brushland near Del Rio, Texas: Habitat for coatimundis and ring-tailed cats.

could speak there with a handful of local people, and could write a different dreary but important magazine article about the politico-ecological situation at each stop.

You have traveled its full length, thus armed. You have also traveled a bit of its history. You have driven many miles and read many pages and asked any number of people the seemingly stupid question: "What's the river like around here?" In Colorado, upstream from Creede, you have stood on the ice of something called Road Canyon Reservoir while four young men fished for brook trout through a chopped hole, using lunchmeat as bait, and that was the Rio Grande. Just east of Tres Piedras, New Mexico, you have walked out onto a highway bridge between the sheer walls of a five-hundred-foot gorge and watched high-school kids lobbing boulders over the rail, putting raccoons and kayakers at peril of sudden death, and that was the Rio Grande. Just west of Santa Fe you have hiked down a certain canyon and seen where Cochiti Reservoir has been allowed to back-flood into Bandelier National Monument, drowning important archeological sites of the early Pueblo people, and that too was the Rio Grande. At the Bosque del Apache National Wildlife Refuge, south of Socorro, you have gotten a glimpse of two whooping cranes standing among a flock of a thousand sandhills, and an eyeful of the problem of salt-cedar infestation along the river. In a town that calls itself Elephant Butte, you have seen the marina and the trailers, the bass boats and the bait stores, the fiberglass-repair shops and the water-jet-ski dealerships, and then you have glimpsed Elephant Butte Lake itself, New Mexico's largest and most boring body of water. And that was the Rio Grande.

Sixty miles below El Paso, near a plantation village inaptly named Esperanza, you have witnessed the river disappearing away into cottonfields. During irrigation seasons, you have been told, the main channel of the Rio Grande along here and for many miles on carries no water at all. A dry bed, growing fuzzy with desert brush. Then far down at Presidio the Rio Conchos pours in from Mexico, providing a renewal of flow just as the river enters its Big Bend. Much farther downstream, beyond the Santa Ana refuge, beyond Brownsville, you have stood on a spit of sand and seen a modest tongue of water (not much larger than what flows past Creede) emptying itself, tepid and humble and dirty, into the Gulf of Mexico. You have found it hard to believe that this little spew was the culmination of anything vast, noble, historic, let alone grand.

Your head and your notebooks and your clothes have become filled with the multiplicity of this river. Many of the images you have gathered, many of the facts, are sad and ugly. Along much of its length the Rio Grande is defeated. Along much, it is abused. In some places it is just gone. But by good fortune you have experienced also a place called The Tight Squeeze in a canyon called Mariscal, beneath thousand-foot walls of Cretaceous limestone, where in defiance of all other reality the Rio Grande is still a proud untamed river, muscled and dangerous, capable of flattening human hubris.

Richard is at the stove when you wake. Somehow he has drained it of water and gotten the thing lit. You rub sand out of your eyesockets. Drew has survived the night in his soggy bag. But it is a cold morning. You all three gather around the Coleman, where a large stew pot sits on a burner, already steaming. It is cowboy coffee, a gallon or so, a big hot bucket of black liquid and steeping grounds. With his face squinched to the Yaqui grin, Richard lifts the lid.

"Dip and smile, little brothers," he says.